The
Winter
House

BOOKS BY JOAN MacCRACKEN

The Sun, The Rain and The Insulin
Trisba and Sula
The Winter House

THE
WINTER
HOUSE

A Season of Sharing

JOAN MACCRACKEN

Tiffin Press of Maine

THE WINTER HOUSE
A Season of Sharing

Copyright © 2013

Published by
TIFFIN PRESS OF MAINE
110 Jones Point Road
Brooksville, Maine 04617
www.tiffinpressofmaine.com

Cover Art   Annie Poole
Interior Illustration   Molly Holmberg Brown
Design Consultant   Christine Harden

Permission granted by Penguin Group (USA), Inc to reprint brief excerpts from *The Help* by Kathryn Stockett   Copyright © 2009

This story is a figment of the author's imagination and thus a work of fiction. All characters are fictitious and should not be taken as a portrayal of any living person. Locations, names, businesses, organizations, and events are also used in a fictitious manner. Medical information is meant to be accurate but should not be used for any purpose of diagnosis or treatment.

ISBN 978-0-9646018-6-4

Library of Congress Control Number 2013132071
Library of Congress Cataloging-in-Publication Data
MacCracken, Joan, MD (1945-   )
The Winter House: A Season of Sharing
1. Women's issues 2. Maine-Aging in Place

To all my women friends who have played such a significant part in my life, and to Bob, my husband, who has stuck with me and supported my wild and crazy dreams.

A portion of the profits from the sale of this book will be donated to At Home Downeast, a program to support aging in place.

Prologue

ELIZABETH

The house was still. Elizabeth sat on the deck overlooking the bay and loneliness engulfed her. She could not hold back the tears. Why should she? Everyone was telling her to accept the grief, allow the waves of sadness to wash over her. In time it would get easier, they said. Damn, she thought, it wasn't easier coming downstairs in the morning. When Cliff was here, he always had the coffee on, soothing Maine Public Radio music playing, and on crisp, cool summer mornings, a cheery fire in the fireplace. He ate Raisin Bran and English muffins with lots of grape jelly, while Elizabeth ate poached eggs. They would sit and read the *New York Times* and sip their second cup of coffee. She wanted it all back.

The first several months after the accident were a blur. She couldn't remember who did what, where his clothes went, who closed out his office, or what happened to his fishing gear and golf clubs. She knew the kids had taken some of his clothes, but some went to Goodwill. Elizabeth had felt it would be easier to avoid looking at his things in every corner and closet. But maybe she had done that too soon. Who knew? His red-and-black-checked Woolrich jacket still hung on its hook in the mudroom. It was slowly losing his smell, his ever-present Old Spice smell — funny how that fragrance had come into her life. Elizabeth recalled the first time they had actually met. It was at college chapel one Thursday night of her sophomore year. All the fraternity boys slathered themselves with after-shave lotion before walking in for weekly chapel. She and her roommate, Sandy, whispered the brand names as the boys passed by. One evening Cliff, a senior, sat right in front of them, and simultaneously they giggled to each other, "Old Spice!" He turned around ever so smoothly and just caught Elizabeth's eye. Her chest pounded from embarrassment and excitement. She recognized him from her American Lit class, but they had never spoken. At the end of chapel he asked her for a Friday-night date, and she happily accepted. From then on, her sophomore year was one date after another. After spending a special summer together working in Boston, Cliff started at Harvard Business School, while she headed to Italy for her junior year abroad. Elizabeth saved all his love letters from that year of separation. Now their separation was permanent. One drunk driver, and Cliff was gone; her comfortable life had evaporated.

For several years Elizabeth had encouraged Cliff to retire completely and move full time to Maine. In anticipation of that occurring "someday," Cliff had agreed to winterize the house, adding thermal windows to the east to allow a stunning view of the water from the kitchen, a generator for possible power outages, and several other improvements and design changes for their aging years: stability bars in the showers, banisters on both sides of the stairs, and better lighting in the hallways. They had even added a solar tube that let natural light into the upstairs hallway; Elizabeth had seen it advertised in her *Maine Cottages* magazine. Cliff was delighted with the results, though he certainly wondered about the solar tube during the installation. A bedroom on the first floor would allow them to avoid the stairs in their later years, if need be. Cliff had a hard time imagining having to sleep downstairs ever. Now he would never have to.

Maine had become a spiritual refuge for Elizabeth over the years. Of course she loved Vermont, her birthplace, but Maine had the sea, the tides, the rocky coastline, and that unique light that she yearned to try to capture on canvas if she ever started to paint again. Maine was a world apart from southern New England, which was overpopulated and losing its authenticity. Living many years in Connecticut and New York City had kept Elizabeth away from her northern New England roots. Luckily their summers in Brooks Harbor replenished her soul.

Her college roommate had brought her to the Maine coast for the first time. Sandy's mother's family had come from Bass Harbor on Mount Desert Island, and Sandy had gone there every summer since she was a baby. Elizabeth first tasted lobster that summer, caught in Sandy's uncle's traps. To her surprise, lobsters weren't red until they were cooked. She received specific instructions on the method of eating lobster, always being sure to milk the tender meat out of every leg and to harvest the juicy tidbits located almost in the "armpits" of the tasty crustacean. For years Cliff bought lobsters from Billy Gray, a local fisherman in town, for the Fourth of July celebration with friends and neighbors. And the kids liked picking mussels off the rocks to add to the feast. The delighted crowd devoured the mussels, seasoned with wine and garlic.

Elizabeth's phone rang. She let it ring. She was in no mood to speak with anyone, not even her kids and especially not her older sister, Eve, who always assumed she knew what was right for her little sister. Eve was pushing Elizabeth to sell the house in Maine, keep the apartment in New York, travel more, and come visit her in North Carolina or at their condo in Florida. Eve, a retired realtor, claimed that the Maine house would be an easy sell to some couple from Texas or somewhere — and in any case who needed that huge house? "You'll just get lost wandering around in it," Eve remarked. "And besides, you'll freeze to death." One thing Elizabeth knew: she would figure it out herself, and no one, especially her older sister, would tell her how to live her life. Cliff was gone, her children and grandchildren had their own lives, and it was time for her to make a plan.

MARTY

Marty sat watching the sun drop over the Camden Hills. Her brother and his family would be well on their way to Boston, driving down Route 1 for the views and to avoid construction on Interstate 95. Their traditional stop at Moody's Diner for a final lobster roll would top off the annual two-week vacation. Missy, her Coon cat, returned from her hiding place and perched on the back of the couch, having avoided the busy hands and shrill squeals of her two grandnephews.

Thanks to the extra rooms in her small guest cottage, Marty could accommodate the entire Austin crew.

Her brother, Tom, and his wife, Susan, loved getting away from Cape Cod in the summer, even if just for two weeks in August. For many years when they lived in Boston, they had gone to the Cape on weekends, and when it came time to retire, they had moved there permanently. But now Tom and Susan hated all the summer tourists who crowded the towns and lined the beaches. So along with Steve, their son, his wife, Camilla, and their boys, Connor and Harrison, Tom and Susan drove the van to Maine to visit Marty.

This summer the two little boys climbed around on the rocks, exploring dark rocky crevices under the seaweed. Little crabs darted for cover as Connor lifted the slimy rockweed. Marty showed them how to squeeze the dried seaweed to make a distinctive pop. Their little fingers were not strong enough to snap the air sacs, but it wouldn't be long before they could. As the explorer scouts checked out the tide pools, Camilla searched for sea glass, sometimes coming back with handfuls. The remnants of old glass bottles, green and blue and clear, broken into pieces and ground smooth by sand crystals, provided treasures for seekers who would use them to decorate jars, candle holders, jewelry, or picture frames. Finding well-worn sea glass had become a bit more of a challenge since the creation of aluminum cans for beer and soda as well as returnable bottles. Still, Camilla was up to the hunt.

Steve and Tom had taken on the task of scraping and painting the window and door trim. This year Steve climbed up on a ladder to reach the second-floor windows as his father secured the ladder from below. They had agreed, though, that replacing the old shingles on the roof should be left to a professional roofer. Marty couldn't believe a new roof was necessary already, but supposedly salt air and seagulls aged shingles sooner. She hadn't yet noticed any leaks, though.

Dinnertime was fun for all. The children ate at their little table as the adults sat around and enjoyed a glass or two of wine and munched on black olives and Crispy Crackers. Politics led the topics this year, but Steve — the young banker — and his mother — a retired minister — could hold their own on finances and religion. Marty had her opinions too. Tom just listened mostly, missing some of the conversation because of a slight but progressive hearing loss.

The two weeks had flown by with only two mishaps: one short visit to the emergency room for a sprained ankle and a slightly scary sail when the wind picked up quickly from the southwest. But on the whole, it was another successful summer visit. Connor and Harrison built fairy houses in the backwoods that they hoped would still be there next summer. "We'll hope so," said Marty, knowing full well that the snows would flatten the little twigs.

Steve packed the van with the last duffel bag, the small tin of Camilla's sea glass, and Connor's cherished Mason jar filled with three small crabs, two mussels, and several periwinkles in a nest of seaweed. Marty gave the little ones a big bear hug and the traditional Eskimo kiss, rubbing noses together. Good-byes were getting harder, she thought, as she imagined the long winter. "We'll see you at Thanksgiving," Camilla said, hugging Marty. "Remember to bring that cranberry-orange relish we all love."

Marty had been going to Boston for Thanksgiving for

many years, while she was in medical school at Tufts and then for all those years of general practice in Vermont. She recalled that joyous year when Susan had finally completed her first pregnancy and brought their new baby Steve home on Thanksgiving Day. That year Marty had cooked the turkey. For the last several years since Tom and Susan's move to the Cape, Steve and Camilla had been hosting the event in Boston. They invited a few close friends from their neighborhood as well, making a large cheery gathering that Marty always looked forward to. She pitied folks who went out to dinner on Thanksgiving Day. Once Marty had done that and vowed never to repeat it. She much preferred being surrounded by family and old and new friends. She cherished the Austin tradition of gathering in a circle, holding hands, and taking the time to have each person give thanks for something. Last year little Connor had joined in with thanks for the apple pie. Camilla's grandmother, though wheelchair-bound at ninety-seven, was thankful to share the day with great-grandchildren, a pleasure never dreamt of in her youth.

One Thanksgiving celebration stood out in Marty's mind as if it were yesterday. For eighteen years after her divorce from Mitchell, she had been alone, pursuing a general practice after medical school and internship. Her days and nights were filled; she had little else to think about. But when she met Abigail, the new town nurse who had just ended her miserable marriage, Marty felt a closeness she could not immediately understand. They tried to be together as much as they could. They talked endlessly about everything — their divorces, their parents, their careers, their gardens, their pets, and their dreams. Almost simultaneously, Marty and Abigail concluded that they belonged together. That was New Year's Eve, and for almost eleven months afterward, they shared their homes and attempted to keep their relationship a secret. But when November came along, and the trip to Boston for the Thanksgiving holiday approached, Marty decided to take Abigail with her and see how her family reacted.

It was a snowy Wednesday as the two drove on icy roads to Beacon Hill. In the car Marty practiced her line of introduction: "Hi, Tom, this is Abigail, my friend," or "Hi, Tom, I want you to meet Abigail, my good friend," or "Abigail, I would like you to meet my brother, Tom."

"Oh, just let them figure it out, Marty," Abigail said gently. "It is what it is."

The snow was coming down heavily as the car skidded into the driveway. It had taken over five and a half hours, the usual trip being just about four. Tom opened the garage door, hugged Marty, and extended his hand to Abigail. "What a ride you must have had! Bet you two are glad to finally be here. I'm so glad to meet you, Abigail," Tom said, adding, "Any friend of Marty's is a friend of mine."

Otherwise, no notice was paid to the new bond until the Thanksgiving circle, when Susan said, "I am especially thankful for the companionship that Abigail has brought to Marty." Susan squeezed the hand of Marty, who was standing next to her. The following summer Steve bestowed the title of Aunt Abigail on Marty's special friend. Abigail loved being accepted into Marty's family. In fact, their partnership of love and respect remained honored until Abigail's death five years ago.

The clock chimed the hour, bringing her back to the present moment. The afterglow of the sunset painted the underbelly of the scattered clouds orange. As the living room darkened, Marty walked over to the refrigerator, opened it, and stared into its light. What should she have for supper?

JANET

Janet's heart raced as she grabbed frantically for the phone by the bed. The clock's face displayed 3:35 a.m. She waited to hear the news. "She's gone," the familiar voice said. Janet let out a huge sigh but could not speak. "She was in no pain and just slipped away," said Ruth, the hospice worker. As relief and grief simultaneously flooded her very being, Janet thanked Ruth for all she had done to help her ninety-three-year-old mother and said she would let the rest of the family know in the morning. Her mother had outlived most of her friends and many of her relatives. Janet and her brother had already written the obituary and settled on a gravesite and gravestone. Arrangements with the funeral home had been made. It would be a simple graveside burial.

The diagnosis of Alzheimer's had been made eight years ago, and Janet had watched her mother disintegrate slowly. She could picture her once-fashionable mother walking out of her apartment wearing two pairs of pants, a bra, and a pretty scarf. It was cruel that her ability to dress herself went so quickly, given that she had been a stylish matron. Her love of bracelets and necklaces continued, however, as she added more and more to her wrist and neck — tragic yet comical all at once! Her mother's generosity and social graciousness remained for a long time. She could talk on the phone and sound just fine, but her memory of the conversation was unreliable. She often forgot Janet's almost daily visits. "No," her mother would say to her son, who lived Baltimore, "I haven't seen Janet for quite awhile." Janet had found this upsetting.

Now Janet attempted to go back to sleep. After tossing and turning for at least an hour, she decided to get up and email the obituary to the Maine papers and her mother's home paper in Philadelphia. The lightness in her step surprised her. Relief was successfully overtaking grief, a mourning process that had begun at the time of diagnosis and continued for eight years as her mother became a mere shell of herself. Janet's mother had been completely lost to her for at least the last three years.

These past three years had also been extremely difficult without John, her second husband and closest friend. They had met at a hospice-training course in Ellsworth. As their friendship grew, so did the love between them. John, one of the ministers on the peninsula, had lost his wife to bacterial meningitis a few years before and was dedicating his life to his parishioners. But meeting Janet changed his bachelor life. They married and their eleven-year partnership had been one of Janet's happiest periods. She had become involved in local community organizations and felt at home on the coast. Hospice work, along with some church functions with John, had filled her life, and having John's children and grandchildren visit every summer was delightful. All were effective distractions from the challenges of dealing with her mother's progressive dementia. Then John's fatal heart attack at age sixty-eight threw Janet backward, backward into the foggy world of alcohol. She returned to drinking slowly, just one glass of wine a night, but her loneliness beckoned her to pour a second and then a third. Initially Janet could not bring herself to go back to an Alcoholic Anonymous meeting. Been there, done that, she had thought. She tried to hide her habit. But one night she backed her car into a telephone pole after an evening out with friends. Though the damage to the car was minor, it was just the wake-up call she needed. The next Wednesday night Janet attended an AA meeting in the next town.

AA felt supportive, just as it had the first time she had attended after her divorce. But then Janet was more than lonely; she was humiliated, furious, angry...well, downright outraged. Brent had left her after twenty years of marriage, running off with his legal assistant to Virginia, just as Peter, their only child, was leaving for the University of New Hampshire. The rage, the hurt, the alcohol drove her straight to a nervous breakdown. Fortunately, with excellent psychiatric support, the proper medication, AA meetings, and a few close friends, Janet had pulled herself up. She returned to her nursing job at Maine Medical Center in Portland. When her son fell in love with a Colorado girl and moved to Boulder for graduate school, Janet considered going out west. She realized, however, that she could never leave New England, and besides, her mother had by then relocated to Maine from Philadelphia. Later, she did move north with her mother and worked in Ellsworth at Maine Coast Memorial Hospital. It was there that she met John, and her life became whole.

Now she had been dry for about thirteen months, and she wanted to stay that way. She loved cold weather, but the darkness affected her. A twinge of depression had crept in last winter, and her seasonal affective disorder was barely ameliorated by a special lamp she used. This year

Janet wanted to be proactive and ensure that she would not regress to the bottle. Her physician had encouraged plenty of exercise and good amounts of vitamin D. She was faithfully taking vitamins, and every Thursday morning Janet attended yoga classes with six other women from ages thirty-five to seventy-six. Not only had Janet gained in flexibility, she also enjoyed the meditative moments at the end. Every New Year's Eve she made a resolution to do daily yoga at home, but somehow she lacked the discipline to do it alone. In class, the group dynamics were fun. Sometimes, after the yoga session, a small group went for lunch at the local market and talked about everything from pollution and politics to personal concerns. Janet enjoyed these friendships, particularly through the winter months.

CATHERINE

Quigley scampered to the kitchen window seat at the sound of Catherine's Buick pulling into the detached garage. As Catherine opened the kitchen door with one hand, balancing the mail, the newspaper, her purse, and a few groceries with the other, her special pal spun round and round, his tail wagging and little body shivering with joy. For the past eight years, Quigley had greeted her with the anticipation of a walk, a treat, and a loving scratch.

Laying the groceries on the table, Catherine noticed the blinking light on her answering machine — three messages, just since noon. Those messages could wait, she thought. She put away the milk and frozen TV dinners, and then the two headed for the door. Quigley ran ahead as she walked down the path to the cove, catching a final glimpse of the September sun, setting over Castine. She loved the orange afterglow and the grand finale of brilliant pink. "Red sky at night, sailor's delight!" her husband, Harold, used to say, and Catherine had always replied, "Red sky in the morning, sailors take warning!" They had laughed at themselves for being so predictable.

As she walked back up to the house, Catherine pondered asking Billy Gray to move the single bed downstairs into the nook off the living room in preparation for winter. The oil bill had soared last year to more than four dollars a gallon; she had to do something. Closing off the upstairs bedrooms would conserve fuel, and, besides, climbing those steep stairs was getting a bit harder. Catherine remembered her grandfather tucked into the nook after he had broken his hip getting off the tractor onto the ice. She sat on his bed while he read to her from Rudyard Kipling. Even better, he told stories about ice-skating out on the bay and sledding on their speedy Cape Racers, or about the special day in 1903 when they laid the final bricks for the chimney of the house. Her grandparents loved their home in Dendall Hollow; now, over a hundred years later, Catherine loved it too.

On Thursday nights Catherine usually ate a light snack for supper. The local community seniors' café provided plenty of calories at noon. Helping with clearing and rinsing the dishes there, she rarely sat down to eat the sweet desserts provided. Today's pecan pie, however, was too hard to resist.

As she finished a small bowl of Shredded Wheat, Catherine listened to her messages. "Hi, Catherine! This is Pat. Thanks so much for driving me to the doctor's office. I don't know what I would have done, with David so delayed and all. Can you come for supper next Monday after quilting club? Hope so. Let me know, and don't feel you need to bring anything. Call me tomorrow, 523-0961." Catherine laughed out loud. They had known each other for seventy years or more, and still Pat had to announce herself and leave the phone number. Some things never change, she thought.

Message number two: "Reverend Perry, here. Say, Catherine, so nice of you to volunteer to organize the church Christmas auction again this year. I'll try to get Dennis Packet to drive around and pick up the offerings. Sadie Caldwell has a brand new TV she wants to donate. Her kids gave it to her for her birthday, and she just can't get used to the damn — 'um, darn thing. Mabel Jones volunteered to be in charge of the food, says her mother is getting too old to do it. Let me know if I can be of any assistance. See you on Sunday, God willing." Catherine laughed at this message too. Mabel Jones's mother was at least ten years younger than Catherine. Guess I'm doing okay, she thought.

The third message came on: "This is Dr. Leonard's office calling to remind you of your checkup tomorrow at 2 p.m. Please have someone drive you, as your eyes will be dilated for a thorough exam. We look forward to seeing you." Catherine's daughter, Sarah, had volunteered to drive her to Ellsworth for the appointment with the ophthalmologist, and Catherine had accepted this time but really hated to impose on her daughter, who worked full time at a bank in Blue Hill. "It's no problem, Mom," Sarah had said, "that's what family is for." Catherine felt lucky to have close relatives nearby. It hadn't always been that way. Her three children left after high school. Sarah had gone to Bentley

College for an accounting degree and landed her first job in Boston. She had advanced quickly, gaining a branch-manager position, even while raising a child with diabetes. Her oldest, Harold Jr., worked in the construction business in Portland, and her other son, Will, had established an ophthalmology practice in New Jersey, just outside New York City. Catherine and Harold enjoyed visiting Will's family, going into Manhattan to see the Christmas lights and extravagant decorations. They loved watching their grandchildren ice-skate round and round at Rockefeller Center. One year Catherine actually put on rented skates to join her grandchildren, gliding around to the organ music. In her youth, Catherine and her classmates had skated on Wallace Pond, which bordered Brooks Harbor.

Catherine tried hard to remain strong after losing Harold, but after a particularly gloomy November, the anniversary of his death, she admitted to her daughter that she was longing for more family time. The next spring Sarah and her family left Boston and moved back to Maine to be closer to Catherine.

A Blue Hill bank job had opened up, and Sarah jumped at the opportunity. It was not that Catherine and Sarah saw each other every day, but it was just comforting to know that family was nearby and could help when needed.

Quigley jumped up on Catherine's legs, his usual means of asking to lick her cereal bowl. Catherine fed him only dried dog food and an occasional doggy-bone treat, but licking the cereal bowl was allowed, morning or night. "Come on, Quig, want to go out once more before bed?" She always talked to him, knowing he understood every word. As the moon rose over the bay, the reflections danced to an ancient rhythm, and a distant coyote howled. After turning out the lights, Catherine climbed the stairs. Quigley followed. The night air still had the warmth of September. Cold nights would not be far away, and soon frost would cover the ground. She would call Billy Gray in the morning to move the bed downstairs.

THE GATHERING

*E*lizabeth found *M. Austin, Virgil's Point Road,* in the community telephone book. As she dialed the number, she hoped that an answering machine would come on because she hadn't exactly figured out what she would say to Marty. For three days and three nights, Elizabeth had been reviewing her new idea. She had even had a dream about the idea, and it hadn't been a nightmare, either. In fact, she awoke from the dream feeling more confident than ever that she should pursue it.

It all seemed to come together over the last few weeks. On the radio she had listened to a program about aging in place, a new movement developed, in one sense, in opposition to moving into retirement villages. Many folks wanted to stay in their homes as long as they could. Certainly Elizabeth and Cliff never considered moving to a retirement facility, though many of their friends were doing just that. She and her husband had traveled a few times to Florida and once to South Carolina to visit with friends and had come away with the general impression that these places were pleasant enough — surely they suited many folks — but both continued to want to live in their own place. Elizabeth, especially, wanted to live in Maine, her adopted state. Now, with Cliff gone, she was considering her options.

Elizabeth knew she didn't want to remain in New York City anymore, particularly alone in their apartment. The few remaining friends she had there seemed more and more to be moving south for the winter months or moving to states where their children and grandchildren lived. Elizabeth wouldn't consider moving to California where her son Frank lived or to Italy with her younger daughter, Nell. And Boston — well, if she was going to settle in New England, she might as well be in Maine. Massachusetts never appealed to her much. She could visit Michael or Libby in Boston with an easy bus ride. Cliff's death had forced her to reevaluate her long-range plan, but in fact it hadn't really changed her dream to live in Maine year round. She just wondered if she would be too lonely in the big house.

Several times in the past, she and Cliff had come up to Maine for Christmas. Some years it was picture perfect. They would cut a tree in their field and drag it home to decorate with white lights and special ornaments. Gentle, light snow would fall as they walked to the little white church in the town for an evening candlelight Christmas Eve service. Afterward they shared warmed cider and homemade Christmas goodies with the small local congregation. In years past, however, major blizzards kept them from attempting the trip north, or a lack of snow made it a brownish holiday. Some years Cliff and Elizabeth decided to stay in New York, joining in the urban merriment. Once their grandchildren were born, she and Cliff tried to be with them to share the thrill of Santa's arrival. One Christmas, about four years ago, everyone but Frank and his family came to Maine for a joyous holiday. Nell flew from Italy with her daughter, Alcee, to experience a Maine winter. The cousins had a wonderful time together. A touch of snow fell on Christmas Eve, and the ponds were perfect for ice-skating.

Elizabeth had been doing a lot of reading about climate change and the effect of fossil-fuel use on the atmosphere. Her cousin from Washington D.C. was a world-renowned expert on the topic, and she had recently attended one of his lectures at Bowdoin College in Brunswick. She had been impressed with Vice President Al Gore's plea for individuals to take climate change seriously and do their part. Elizabeth thought hard about heating her big house for just one person.

Marty's phone rang several times. Then her voice came on: "Hello, sorry I'm not available to take your call right now. Please leave a message, and I will get back to you as soon as possible. Have a good day." Elizabeth heard the beep and took a deep breath.

"Say Marty, this is Elizabeth, Elizabeth Sloan. I have an idea I would like to run by you sometime. It's in regard to the conversation you and I had a few weeks ago about the long winters up here. Hope you can give me a call when you get a chance — 523-1945, or try my cell phone: 212-606-1926. Thanks. Hope you are out enjoying this beautiful fall day." She placed the phone down slowly and hoped her idea would be enticing to Marty.

Elizabeth wrote out her grocery list. She tried to prepare herself a regular meal every night and did fairly well in that regard. Several recipes from this summer's cooking class with Vincent Montaine were easy and delicious, and usually the leftovers tasted even better the next day. Funny how certain herbs and spices lend themselves to reheating! Preparing dinner for Cliff had been a joy for Elizabeth, and he had been appreciative of her creative culinary art. His repertoire included only breakfast meals like scrambled eggs and bacon or some mean sourdough blueberry pancakes, and his dark-roast coffee perked up everyone.

The grocery-store clientele had thinned out a lot after Labor Day, and many more would depart after Columbus Day. The reputation of Maine winters discouraged many from staying on. Now that Elizabeth had no particular reason to leave, she wanted to stay, to give it a shot. Why not? she thought. Nell had emailed from Italy: "Go for it, Mom!"

Right, Elizabeth thought, she would go for it, but with a bit of a twist.

Later that afternoon she called Sonia Davis, a well-respected realtor in Manhattan, and arranged to rent out the apartment for a year. Sonia explained that there was quite a demand for furnished apartments on the East Side, especially one with a view from the thirtieth floor and within walking distance of Central Park. "Good!" Elizabeth said, "I'll hold on to it for a while, but renting should be perfect."

"Well, I hope you know what you are doing," said Sonia. "I hear it's awfully cold up there in the winters."

Marty came home from her afternoon tennis game, having played better than usual, though her serve could have been a bit stronger. Years ago she used to serve a few aces in a match. Now she was happy just to get the ball in the right box.

Her message machine was blinking. Two messages. Marty found a piece of paper and pen. She had learned to write everything down, and sometimes she would have to replay the message because the speaker rattled off the phone number more quickly than she could scribble it on paper.

She pushed the button: "Hi, Aunt Marty. It's Steve. Camilla and I wondered if we could come up for the Columbus Day weekend. The boys would love to play on the beach again, and we'd thoroughly enjoy a break from the city. I'd be delighted to help you with some prewinter chores, like chopping up some wood or raking some leaves. Hope it will be okay." Steve knew that his aunt loved company, and her spot provided a haven for the two little boys. "Harrison and Connor have been talking about building more fairy houses ever since the summer." This was pleasant news for Marty. Company was fairly infrequent in the off-season.

The second message played. The female voice was familiar, but Marty could not quite place it. "Say, Marty, this is Elizabeth, Elizabeth Sloan. I have an idea I would like to run by you sometime. It's in regard to the conversation you and I had a few weeks ago...." Marty wrote down Elizabeth's phone number. She remembered that conversation they had had after Vincent's cooking class. Marty was feeling somewhat down that day, as it would have been Abigail's seventy-fifth birthday. Even after five years, both the anniversary of Abigail's death and her birthday were tough days to get through. So, that might have been why, on that day a few weeks earlier, she was more open with Elizabeth about the loneliness of her single life and the long winters.

Last winter had been her first full year in Maine, excluding the two weeks she left to visit with her brother and sister-in-law in Arizona in February. Tom and Susan had tried to convince her to move to the Southwest for the winter. They much preferred it to the damp Cape Cod weather. Actually, Marty loved cold weather and her community of friends that she was making through tennis, yoga, and the hospital board. The winter community, though much smaller than the summer population, seemed to watch out for each other. But still, Tom and Susan worried about Marty in her house down the long driveway and far from any immediate neighbor. In a way, Marty understood their concern. She did wonder how many years she would opt to stay in her Maine home through the long dark months. Moving to a retirement community, however, was not an option she wanted to choose. After brewing some Earl Gray tea, Marty settled into her favorite stuffed chair and dialed Elizabeth's number.

Three rings and Elizabeth picked up: "Hello."

"Hi, Elizabeth, this is Marty. What's on your mind?" Marty was not one for small talk and traditionally got right to the point.

"Well, thanks for calling me back. You know that I have been thinking about staying here through the winter. I really have heard from several people that the community in the off-season is quite active and that the winter isn't all that bad. You know I have wanted to try it for some time, but I was never able to get Cliff to commit to full retirement. Now that he is gone, I guess the decision is up to me, and I have been thinking a lot about it. I know that you tried it last year and lived to tell of it."

"Yes, it was a good experience for me, but as I told you,

the nights are a little long, with it dark so early. But I have made more friends by staying here year round."

"Well, I have an idea and was wondering what you would think of it. I know you are a pretty direct person and will tell me exactly what you think."

"I guess I'm known for that. Try me."

"You and I love Maine, and I am sure we love our homes. Giving them up at this time does not seem to be something we want to do, at least in the summertime, when our friends and families love to join us. But for each of us to heat our houses and plow our driveways and eat alone through the winter months may not be the best thing for us or for the environment. What would you think of getting three or four single women to live together for the winter only? Each could return to her own house as the spring flowers arrive. It would be sort of like we experienced in college, like a dormitory or sorority house. Cliff and I recently remodeled this house, and there are five bedrooms; maybe one could be used for guests, if any of our family or friends wanted to come in the off-season. And each of the four bedrooms has its own bathroom."

"Sounds like you have really been thinking a lot about this," Marty said.

"Yes, I have, and I think it could work. Of course, we have to find the right women who would be up for such an adventure. It might not be an attractive idea to many gals who are wed to their routines. However, I figure maybe three other women in this town might consider the idea. I thought of you because, first, I figured we could have some fun cooking together, and, second, we could argue about politics...just kidding."

"Well, I am pleased that you thought of asking me. It's

a very intriguing idea." Marty didn't really know Elizabeth that well and wondered if she was ready to make such a commitment. "It certainly is a novel plan and might just work out. Do you have any other women you are considering?"

"Not really. I thought you might have a better idea of who lives alone here in town and who might consider such an idea."

"Well, I can think of one person who might be interested. Let me think about this concept a bit more, and maybe I can run it by a friend of mine whose husband died three years ago. She's in my yoga class."

"That would be great. I'm glad to hear that you are at least open to the idea. Of course, once we find three or four women, we'll have to figure out the specifics of the arrangement. Let's just take first things first."

"Elizabeth, I'll get back to you in a few days."

"Great, look forward to hearing from you then."

Marty mulled over this idea of sharing a house with other women for the winter. She came up with several reasons not to try it, but really they were small and probably surmountable obstacles compared with reasons in favor — like darkness before four in the afternoon, the heating bills, and her long icy driveway. She thought of laughter and cooperation, trying to cook some of Vincent's delicious, yet occasionally complicated recipes. She had found Elizabeth a very pleasant person. She pictured watching TV or movies with others, maybe even munching together on popcorn. Though she did have her nightly glass of red wine or an occasional Dark'N'Stormy alone, she knew it was safer to drink with others. As the health advisories claimed, older individuals should cut down on their quantity of alcohol or eliminate it altogether. Marty preferred to quote the literature claiming that a glass of red wine is good for your heart. Who knows? At her age she wasn't likely to change. And she wasn't so sure she wanted to replace the red wine with a resveratrol pill, a bunch of red grapes, or Concord grape juice, although they are good for the heart too. A funny image of four old ladies eating grapes for their health made her chuckle.

Marty slept on the idea and decided to present the winter-house concept to Janet after morning yoga. No harm in seeing what her thoughts were on the subject.

The next morning Marty walked down her long driveway to retrieve the morning paper and noticed the brilliant reds and yellows scattered among the green mantle of fir and spruce. The maples that provided sweet sap in late March now announced the coming of crisp, cool nights. She would call Steve and welcome him for the Columbus Day weekend. It would be great to see the little boys again. If the colored leaves stayed around until then, they could press the brightest reds between some book pages.

Thursday was Marty's busy day: morning yoga class from 9:30 to 11:30, then lunch with her yoga friends, then in the afternoon a meeting of the service committee of the Unitarian Universalist Church in Castine, and in the evening the monthly hospital board meeting. With healthcare dollars so tight now and state reimbursements delayed, the board would have to approve significant cuts in the budget, and some hospital staff would be losing their jobs. Though she still missed contact with her patients, Marty was glad to be away from the intensity of current healthcare delivery.

Last week's yoga class had been quite a workout for her seventy-six-year-old body, but she was pleased with her progress and looked forward to the next session. She had noticed improvement in her tennis game since starting weekly yoga class. She adored her instructor, Beth, who obviously loved having a wide range of ages and abilities in the class. At first Marty had been extremely self-conscious and found many of the positions hard to attain, but with persistence and proper guidance, she had made progress. In fact, her downward-facing-dog position felt better all the time, and her upper-arm strength was increasing so much she could almost go directly into the cobra position. Headstands remained a challenge, but Beth promised that with slow progress and taking baby steps, Marty would someday be comfortable upside down. Of this Marty wasn't too sure, but she had observed another older woman in the class doing a headstand after several months of work. Maybe it would be possible, she thought. "Never say never!" her father used to say.

Janet and Marty had become friends through the yoga class, and many similar interests surfaced during their lunchtime chats. Through a few conversations, she learned that Janet had once met Marty's partner, Abigail, at a nursing conference and then had discovered that they had attended the same nursing school in Boston. Strange, how life's paths intertwine. It was comforting to Marty to know that Janet had known Abigail.

Marty parked her Subaru, located her trusty umbrella, and walked briskly to the entrance of the yoga studio. The rain had started as a light drizzle as she pulled out of her driveway but was now pouring down. It would be good for the newly planted peach tree and the fresh grass seed she had just sown, if it didn't all wash away. October usually had some heavy downpours, and it looked as though this month would be no exception.

Beth greeted the class with her usual perky welcome. By now the seven women were familiar with the beginning routine. They took their preferred spots on the rubber mats. Marty enjoyed the place near the window where the morning sun entered, but today rain was splashing against the pane. Janet, usually on the pad next to her, hadn't arrived yet. Several younger women chose the first two rows, eager to pick up every yoga move.

After the initial three long oms, the flow of instruction varied from class to class, with Beth concentrating on certain strengthening positions as well as those that increase flexibility. With her hair dripping, Janet quietly took her place next to Marty. "I forgot my umbrella," she whispered.

Marty smiled back.

The rain blew against the window. As the women proceeded into the various positions, Beth pointed out individual corrections needed. She instructed, "Arms at shoulder height. Right foot pointed forward, left foot on an angle. Knee directly over the ankle." Marty could feel the tremor in her thigh as she held Warrior 2 position for the count, but she knew this helped her lunge for the tennis ball or climb the stairs. She held through the full count. Then they switched to the other side.

Janet followed along. She was late getting to class because of yet another phone call regarding her mother's estate. Janet thought everything had been fairly cut and dried with her mother's finances. They had had a joint bank account for the past four years. Janet had notified Social Security of her mother's death, and her accountant was ready to help with her mother's final tax return. But Maine inheritance taxes and the federal estate taxes had been changing, and because of the diagnosis of Alzheimer's, her mother's will needed to be reviewed. All this information in Janet's head made the thought of a meditative moment very appealing. She held the yoga position but really just wanted to lie down, breathe quietly, and clear her head.

Beth liked to finish the session with a headstand before the relaxing pose. Several of the young women stretched their legs to the ceiling, and, just like that, they were upside down. Both Janet and Marty needed assistance. Much of the exercise depended on the positioning of the fingers, wrists, and forearms. The top of the head was not supposed to absorb much weight. Of course, getting upside down with the legs parallel to the wall would take some doing. Both preferred to go more slowly at their age, feeling the strength needed in their arms. They were pleased with putting their butts up close to the wall and walking their legs in gradually. Baby steps, Beth insisted.

"Great job, everybody," Beth said. "Hope to see you next week."

The women placed the purple blocks, the rugs, the belts, and the pads back in their respective places. Beth liked the rugs piled with fringes facing out. Marty had most of these supplies at home and knew she should try to use them in between classes. Maybe some day she would.

Janet caught Marty's attention. "Can you do lunch today?" she asked.

"I'd love to. I was hoping you had time because I have something to talk to you about," Marty replied.

"Good, I could use a little debriefing myself," Janet added. They walked outside and noticed the warmth as the sun peeked through the clouds. The rain had brought a fresh fragrance and cleaned the cars. As they walked down the street to the local country store, each woman felt pleased to have someone to talk with.

Marty gathered a cup of chili, a few crackers, and a small carton of milk. Janet preferred the barley-bean soup with some Asiago cheese sprinkled on top. She took a Diet Coke out of the cooler. None of the other yoga women showed up, and that was just fine with Marty and Janet. The generation gap might have interfered with their pending conversations.

"You first," Marty said. She figured it would be better to get Janet to debrief herself, as she called it, before trying to put a new adventurous idea in her head.

"Well, it's all sort of stupid, really. I seem to be getting so mired down in the closing of my mother's estate. Laws are changing all the time. Maine and the feds differ on estate-tax rules. I can't locate the original copy of my mother's birth certificate and have to write to Harrisburg, the capital, to request a duplicate. Can you believe that? After all these years, I have to prove that my mother existed. And she left several modest donations to so many small organizations that I have to research whether they're still around. One organization folded twenty years ago, so that causes problems with the specifications of the will. But, bless her soul, she was kind and thoughtful. I'm sure they'll all appreciate the token donations. Mother even remembered the Philadelphia Garden Club." Janet took a deep breath and let out a sigh. "Oh, these really are just little hassles, I know. I've been told that closing out an estate can take at least a year, if not two." She took a gulp of her soda. "I just want to put all my mother's papers away and file them in a box in the attic for posterity. My mother lived a good life, except for the last eight years. I'm hoping for a different ending for myself, that's for sure." Janet stopped her banter and took a few spoonfuls of soup.

Marty paused. "Yeah, Alzheimer's is a tough disease, and we seem to be seeing more of it as folks live longer. Genetics plays only a part of it, though — more in the younger-onset type of Alzheimer's. It all remains quite a mystery, and I don't think I will live long enough to learn the answer. The best we can do is to enjoy our lives now, each precious day we have. Just think, maybe you and I will live long enough to do headstands." Marty laughed and Janet smiled.

"I know you're right. It was just such a long decline with my mother, and I can't exactly say I'm over the loss of John, either." Looking down, Janet stirred her soup slowly.

"I know you have had several rough years. But I just have a feeling things will start looking up." Marty tried to sound upbeat for her friend. She did wonder if Janet could pull herself "up by the bootstraps," as Marty's father used to say. "Let me run an idea by you."

"Sure, I'd love to change the topic." Janet sipped her Coke.

"Well, yesterday Elizabeth Sloan called me. She and I took cooking lessons together this summer. Do you know her?"

"I think she and her husband came to church once or twice on Christmas Eve, but besides that, I don't know her, no."

"You probably heard that her husband was killed by a

drunken driver last February in New York City."

"Oh, that's terrible. I must have missed the obituary," Janet said.

"It seems that Elizabeth loves Maine and has wanted to live here year round for some time, but Cliff wasn't quite ready to give up his work in New York. They came up for summers for many years and a few weekends in the off-season. Her kids are on their own, and she has been talking about giving Maine a try as a permanent residence. She owns a big house down on Spruce Point, right on the bay."

Janet interrupted, "I think I've seen it from the water. It's actually just across the cove from the church."

"Oh, I guess you're right. Well, anyway, we've had some conversations about Maine winters and the local year-round Brooks Harbor community. I've been pretty positive to her about my experience last winter. I really don't think it's as bad as most people imagine. But you'd know better than I do, having lived here for several years. She's concerned about a few things, like whether the long evenings might get to her. She hasn't lived alone much. She's trying to think 'green' and not heat such a big house for only one person. Elizabeth has this idea to invite three other women to move in and live with her for the winter months. She figures giving up one's own house permanently might be too big a change, but moving into one house for the winter might be an intriguing adventure. And if it didn't work out, you can just move back to your own home." Marty paused.

Janet replied, "First reaction: sounds like an interesting idea. I've been alone three years now without John, and I can't say it's been easy. Of course, a lot of my time I've been visiting my mother in Ellsworth, and that got harder and harder. John's kids and grandkids come up in the summer, but the rest of the time I'm alone. I've tried to keep involved in the community, like the library committee and hospice, but I have drifted away from the goings on at the church. This yoga class has been very important to me."

"Yeah, I must admit I look forward to every Thursday morning, too." Marty inhaled and continued. "Elizabeth has four bedrooms, each with a private bath. There's a small room that could be used as a guest room if we had any visitors. You know most folks prefer to visit in the summer."

"Yes, that is no joke," Janet quipped.

"According to Elizabeth, we would each get a water view of Eggemoggin Reach. She figures we'd have to heat only one house instead of four, plow only one driveway instead of four, and we'd have some folks to talk to during those long winter nights."

"I guess you could think of it sort of like a dormitory. I remember our nursing-school dorm. We had so much fun. I was worried about living in Boston, but the dorm provided instant friends, and I still keep up with some of those girls," Janet replied.

"My college roommates remain some of my closest friends. I can remember staying up late into the night, having some of the most amazing conversations. Today, with all those co-ed dormitories, girls miss out on something. But then, I'm just old-fashioned, I guess."

"Oh, you're not that old, Marty. It's all in your mind, you know. And look at you. You still play tennis. I gave that up ten years ago, when my knees got weak."

"Now that you're stronger with yoga, you might even be able to start tennis up again," Marty stated.

"That's doubtful, my dear." Janet laughed.

"So, what more do you want to know about this crazy winter-house idea?"

"Who else has Elizabeth asked?"

"She asked me to think of someone because she figured I might know the single women in town. I thought of you because you're the right age, you live alone, and anyone who is seventy-six..."

"I'm seventy-five!" Janet insisted.

"And anyone who is seventy-five and is willing to try a headstand would be willing to try an adventure like this," Marty said.

"You might just have pegged me right." Janet thought of the long, dark nights and the loss of her mother and her fight with the darkness and the bottle. This could be the change she needed. As they departed from the country store, Marty asked Janet if she had any ideas for a fourth woman, and she replied that she'd have to give that some thought. No immediate name came to mind, though she knew several women living alone. Janet commented, "It might take a little time to find the right fit."

Driving home, Janet thought about her connections in the community. She had recently started attending a Buddhist meditation group but didn't know many of the participants. Then she thought of her hospice connections. That organization had introduced her to many volunteers as well as several local families over the twenty-four years she had served in this region. Certainly the recent personal connection with hospice during her mother's final weeks had reinforced her complete appreciation of the organization. She thought of the library committee that she enjoyed so much. Though it was a very informal group of mostly women, they had accomplished a lot, including expanding the town library a few years ago. That had been a wonderful collaborative effort of the "natives" and those folks "from away."

Janet turned off the main road. The Gott house — John's house, now hers, at least temporarily — sat on top of Dendall Hill, overlooking the small town. The church steeple was in plain sight; something that had given John comfort, as he felt the light in the steeple gave a sense of security to the townspeople. A small solar panel now powered the steeple light, an energy-saving device that was installed just before John's retirement, and he had been quite proud of it. As Janet drove down past Dendall Hollow and headed up the hill, a light went on in her brain. "Catherine!" she said out loud. That might be a fit, she thought.

Janet collected her mail and proceeded inside with only one thing on her mind. Call Catherine. Or should she? They had certainly known each other for quite some time. It must have been ten years or more since they had first met. Janet had been the hospice volunteer for Catherine's husband, Harold, who had been a wonderful man — a hard-working electrician and plumber. When he could no longer work, he worried about Catherine's future. He died rather quickly of pancreatic cancer. Janet could picture the last day. The bay was almost still, with a mere shimmer of ripples, and the cool November sun cast its subtle reflection on the salt water. White dots danced and twinkled on the bedroom walls. Catherine sat holding her husband's pale, bluish hand. She stroked his unshaven face. Harold had not eaten in a week. The three adult children stood beside their mother, hands on her shoulder and around each other. Their minister had stopped in during the early hours that day. A calm look of peace had arrived on Harold's face sometime in the morning. His breathing had slowed. Then, in the late afternoon, he died.

A tear dripped down Janet's cheek. She couldn't help thinking of her own husband's death. He was alone in a cold car, having just stopped at the store for a few last-minute items for their eleventh anniversary celebration. They found him slumped over in the driver's seat with the ignition key in his hand. The groceries were by his side. The autopsy had shown a massive heart attack. He didn't suffer, they said. It was quick, and she had no time to say good-bye; neither had his kids. Their eleven years together had been so special, and he had brought her out of her shell of self-doubt. Once a single woman, then a married woman for twenty years, then a divorcée for eleven years, then married for eleven, now widowed for three. Should communal living with three other women fit into the scheme of things?

So what about Catherine Howard? She had lived here all her life, had many friends and family living in the area. Whenever Janet saw her, she was involved in something. They both served on the local library committee, which was how Janet kept in touch. But Catherine's life seemed quite full. All those students she had taught over the years used to look her up when they returned to town. Her reputation as a tough high-school English teacher was legendary. Whenever anyone wanted something done and done right, it was Catherine they would call upon. She still lived in the house where she was born. Now that's some history, Janet thought. Maybe Catherine would just laugh at the idea of leaving her house, even for five months.

But something encouraged Janet to go visit her neighbor Catherine. It had been a while since they had chatted about their lives. Janet felt there was no harm in exploring this option. Catherine would tell her exactly what she thought; of that there was little doubt.

After showering and getting out of her yoga clothes, Janet called Catherine. No answer. Janet left a message. As she hung up, she remembered that Catherine read to the little children in the afternoon at the library. Probably she would be home in time for tea. Janet thought a face-to-face presentation would be best.

Scanning the *Bangor Daily News* headlines — "*Queen Mary II* to Drop Anchor off Bar Harbor for Fall Tourist Crowd"..."Bangor International Airport Struggles for Passengers"..."Governor's Race Accelerates" — Janet penciled in on her calendar a drive over to Mt. Desert Island. She had missed the arrival of the *Queen Elizabeth II* a few years ago, and now that historic ship was sitting in Dubai, a place Janet knew she'd never get to. Her mother had sailed across the Atlantic on the original *Queen Elizabeth* about fifty years ago — a memory that lasted well into her dementia. Even before her dementia had set in, she had made her daughter promise to travel to Europe someday on an ocean liner. "Oh, the glory of it!" her mother would say. Janet might not make the crossing, but maybe she could have lunch or tea on the ship during her Bar Harbor port of call.

The phone rang. "Hi, Janet," Catherine said. "Just got back in from reading to the children; we had six today."

"That's great. Thanks for calling back. I have something I would like to talk with you about. Are you free now?"

"Sure, come on over. I'll put the teapot on." Catherine

replied, with her usual cheer. "I just need to walk Quigley briefly, so give me ten minutes or so.

"No rush. Take your time. I think I'll walk down, so it will be about fifteen minutes."

"Perfect, see you then, Janet." Catherine wondered what this could be about. She would never forget the tenderness that Janet showed Harold in his final days. Since Janet's husband's death a few years ago, it seemed to Catherine that her neighbor had become a bit of a loner.

Janet put her jacket back on and walked out the door. A walk downhill would be easy, and returning would give her a good cardiovascular workout. The leaves were changing. A few large, bright red, maple leaves lay on the roadside. She watched a fish hawk circling overhead and tried to compose her conversation with Catherine.

As Janet neared the porch entrance, Quigley ran to the window seat, barking at the visitor. The handcrafted pine woodpecker on Catherine's door was a perfect knocker. "Come on in," Catherine called. Janet entered. "Tea's just about ready. Nice to see you, Janet."

"Good to see you, too. Seems like it's been a while since we have had tea together."

"Too long, I'd say." Catherine poured the tea. "What do you take in your tea?"

"Just a bit of milk would be fine," Janet replied.

They sat down at the kitchen table. There was just enough room for two place mats. Catherine shuffled a few piles around and apologized for the clutter, but she explained that she always had projects under way, like knitting or quilting, ordering new flowers from Breck's catalog, or writing a letter to an old student. Catherine placed a plateful of gingersnaps on the table. Janet noticed on the kitchen walls little painted signs with encouraging words, an embroidered Scottish blessing, a photo of Barack and Michelle Obama, and a shelf of trinkets from several foreign countries. Janet recalled their previous conversation about her travels; Catherine loved the Elderhostel trips that she started after Harold's death. "Every once in a while it's good to leave home," she had said.

"So what's on your mind?" Catherine asked.

"Well, I have been presented with an idea by Marty Austin and thought I would run it by you. I can't imagine what you might think of this, but I am wondering how it strikes you."

"Now, you've really got me curious!"

"Well, the concept is bringing three or four single women under one roof in the winter months...in order to save money, share conversation, and provide safety and comfort in numbers." Janet paused.

"Go on."

"Elizabeth Sloan proposes having three women move into her large home for five months or so. Do you know her?"

"I know who she is but don't think she knows me," Catherine said.

"Elizabeth is from away, as is Marty — and me as well, I guess. I..."

Catherine interrupted. "Oh, I hate that phrase 'from away.' Over the years I have known many people from away, and frankly many of them are more real than those natives who use the term so often. I'm just quite sick of the label. It is a term that divides us, and that will not make a community whole. Quite honestly, some of my friends from here are just a bit small in my opinion, though I usually just keep my thoughts to myself. I am fairly quiet, but that doesn't imply I don't have my opinions. I guess I have just learned to keep them to myself in certain circumstances." Catherine took a breath. "Sorry, but you hit a sensitive nerve, obviously. Some of my best friends have summered in Maine for years and love it as much as I do. Defining folks as native or from away seems to be a strong local tradition, and I, for one, would like to see that distinction slip away." She sat back, reached for the teapot, and topped off her teacup.

"Well, that's nice to hear because this winter-household proposal would have only you representing the portion with Brooks Harbor birthrights and a long multigenerational relationship here." Janet smiled, hesitating to even say the word native.

"Now, tell me more," Catherine said.

"Elizabeth, who lost her husband this past February, wants to try living in Maine year round. She has been coming here for many summers and has lived in New York in the winters. Now, without her husband, she realizes she has to make her own plans for a future. Elizabeth's been reading about sustainable practices and figures it would make sense to have others live in the house with her. Her house is big, five bedrooms, and she believes it would be rather ridiculous to heat the whole house in the winter for just one person. She also is not sure how she would handle the long, dark evenings. She's wondering if other women who live alone here might like to try this sort of dorm-like experience." Janet took a sip of tea. "Elizabeth thought of Marty; she knows her from their cooking class. Marty thought of me, and I thought of you." She paused. "Of course, I have no idea if you would even consider moving out of your home for the winter." Janet stopped and refilled her cup too.

"It's funny you bring this idea to me now. I have been thinking a lot about living alone. I've done it now for twelve years. And it's been okay — I mean, with Quigley I'm not exactly alone, but just the other day I was thinking I needed to do something about the expense of heating the house. Billy Gray said he'd come over and move my bed downstairs so I wouldn't have to heat the upstairs. And my hip has been acting up, and doing the stairs is getting hard too. Sarah thinks I should move in with her family, as she has an extra downstairs bedroom. But I just hate to be a burden on anyone and besides, I like my freedom. I'm so lucky to have family around, but I'm just not sure I'm ready to move in with them yet. Must just be that old Yankee independence," Catherine admitted.

"Or stubbornness," Janet added with a grin.

Catherine continued, "Seems like some of the younger crowd don't understand our wanting to remain self-reliant. My guess is that most of the folks up this way care a lot about their independence. Why, our country was created for independence, and we New Englanders have our share of pride in it."

"There may be a time when each of us will need a lot more attention than we require now, and I hope if it comes to that, I'll graciously accept it," Janet said.

"Yes," Catherine added. "If I'm not capable of reasoning, I hope I'll at least be manageable. Probably be best if I just popped off one night with my old ticker just calling it quits.... My, this conversation is getting a bit off track."

"I think it's good to chat about the future. Maybe more of us should be proactive and have a plan instead of just hoping the aging process will hold off."

"Let me think over this idea of yours. Obviously, I

would want to meet with Elizabeth and Marty and see if we'd be able to get along with each other for five months. Of course, if it didn't work out, we could always go back to our own houses. This old house hasn't been vacant since my grandfather went off to war in 1917. He was gone for just one year, I think — maybe two — and my grandmother moved in with her mother. I guess she was pregnant with my Uncle Cyrus. Anyway, for what that's worth, this little cape was built in 1903 and has served its occupants well. We've made some necessary renovations over the years, but Grandfather built a solid home." Catherine reached for a gingersnap, her third. "I'd want to pay my fair share, you know," she added.

"We haven't even begun to talk about those specifics. We're just trying to find four women who might consider it an adventure in living, a temporary winter quarters with a water view."

November's grayness was arriving on schedule. A Halloween rainstorm had brought down the last of the leaves. On a sunny afternoon in the first week of November, the four women gathered at Elizabeth's house. Marty picked up Janet and then Catherine, and they drove together to check out their possible winter quarters.

Elizabeth was excited to meet these women and see if her idea could become a reality. She had lived alone less than a year, but these other women had been alone for several years. No doubt it would be quite a big change for them. After a tour of the house, they all had tea in the living room and decided to give a small introduction to each other and answer the question as to why each might consider this move a positive step. Each had her specific reasons for considering the unusual adventure. Two things were consistent for all of them. They loved Maine — specifically, Brooks Harbor — and wanted to remain for the winter. Marty, Janet, and Catherine knew that the winters could be long and lonely. Elizabeth appreciated their honesty.

Catherine and Marty raised the issue of their pets, loyal companions for years. They felt that Quigley and Missy could adjust to the new environment and to each other. Elizabeth voiced a desire to have pets in the house, as she had had pets growing up. Janet had no objection to animals.

Catherine and Marty discovered that they were both early risers whereas Elizabeth and Janet tended to sleep in a bit longer, especially with the morning's darkness. The large house and private bedrooms could easily accommodate these differences. Each listed her usual activities during the day and evenings. Catherine topped the group on community commitments. Elizabeth was in awe of the involvement, but then again Catherine had lived here all her life and liked to be a doer. Elizabeth admitted that having been a summer resident for so many years, she had no idea what went on in the off-season; still she was looking forward to exploring her options. She dreamed of getting back to painting, a hobby she had neglected all her married years.

Elizabeth had suggested that the women could draw the room choices out of a hat and told them there was one small problem; though each bedroom had an attached bathroom, only one had a bathtub. It could have been a problem, but Marty said right up front that she always showered and wouldn't need a bathtub, and Catherine preferred a shower, as she found it hard to get out of a tub. Janet was delighted with their preferences because she loved a good long soak before bed. She, therefore, could have the upstairs front room with the bathtub, and Marty offered the first-floor bedroom to Catherine so she wouldn't have to climb the stairs. Catherine appreciated this thoughtfulness, and Marty was delighted to take the back room upstairs with pine paneling reminiscent of her bedroom at Virgil's Point. Luckily no one would miss out on a water view; Elizabeth's husband, Cliff, had made sure of that.

Catherine wanted to know about the financial arrangement. She thought they might as well talk about it right up front. Elizabeth had been thinking hard about this, as she figured it would come up. Cliff had left her with a substantial estate, and the life-insurance policy was doubled due to his accidental death. She had no mortgage on this house, and none on the New York apartment either, so her expenses were quite low except for property taxes and insurance. She suggested that the four of them could split the utilities for the winter. Since everyone except Catherine had a cell phone, Catherine insisted on paying for the landline.

When they came to the discussion about cooking, Catherine, with a smile, offered to do the dishes. Meal preparation was never one of her strong points, though she had dutifully cooked for her family for years. Marty and Elizabeth enjoyed cooking and trying out new recipes, and as long as Janet and Catherine didn't mind being guinea pigs, they were willing to prepare most of the suppers. The women decided to keep a shopping list and split the grocery bills. It seemed that it could work. They'd share the shopping or even make it a group outing.

Elizabeth admitted to being a bit nervous. It was

uncharted territory, but they all agreed to try it. Each knew that if it didn't work out for some reason, any one of them could return to her home. All had had dormitory experiences in college and agreed that they enjoyed the company of other women. It appeared they were eager to get to know each other better.

So that was it. The last decision was when to move in. The group decided to wait until after Thanksgiving. Marty would head to Boston to be with her brother and all the family. Janet would invite her stepchildren and grandchildren for the long weekend, while Catherine planned to be in Blue Hill with her daughter, her two sons, and all the grandchildren. Elizabeth was off to Italy for two weeks to touch base with her daughter Nell and her granddaughter, Alcee. And after the holidays, the four women would gather at what they now called the Winter House.

DECEMBER

*D*ecember 1 was move-in day. The two inches of snow that fell on Thanksgiving Day had melted, and the walkways were dry. Janet, Marty, and Catherine decided to settle in all at once, like arriving at a college dorm the first day of school, only this time they wouldn't have their parents with them, just two strong local boys to carry in the special items that each woman wanted and a suitcase or two of winter clothes.

First to arrive was Catherine. "Welcome, Catherine," said Elizabeth, "and Quigley, of course." The dog ran to her side. Elizabeth had made friends with Quigley a few weeks before. Growing up, Elizabeth had had dogs but not since high school in Vermont. Unfortunately, Cliff had been allergic to dogs and cats, and besides, a New York City apartment wasn't the ideal spot for a dog. She was delighted to have a pet around again. Her childhood dog, Copper, a spaniel-terrier mix, always slept on her bed and waited for her to come home from evenings out. One time Elizabeth was very late getting back, and Copper had awakened her parents. It was a good thing too, because Elizabeth and her two friends, stuck in the snow with a flat tire, had begun the long walk home with only sneakers, no boots. Copper lived for sixteen years, several years after Elizabeth had left her parents' house, but he always remembered her when she came home from college. When he finally died of kidney failure, she felt she'd lost a big part of her childhood.

"Her room is back here on your right." Elizabeth guided Jerry Blakey, a husky young man, down the hall as he carried three large boxes. His brother, Jimmy, followed along with two suitcases and a small sewing kit under his arm. Then Jerry and Jimmy brought in a red recliner chair, a portable Singer sewing machine, and a miniature TV. The final load included three plants: a ficus tree, a spider plant, and a scented geranium. Catherine always had to have something to water. She felt it gave a bit of routine or discipline to her life.

"Thank you," Catherine said. "I guess that's about it." She dug into her purse for some cash and handed it to Jimmy and Jerry, whose grandfather used to teach with her. Fine young men, she thought.

"Thanks, Miz Catherine, we'll go over to Virgil's Point now," Jerry said.

"That will be fine. I'm sure Dr. Austin will be ready. It's the house on the right, after the lighthouse." Catherine had met Marty and her partner, Abigail, many years ago, when they first bought the old Blaisdell place. They had stayed fairly isolated out there in the summer, just enjoying one another. Catherine figured they liked it that way. She never did get to know Abigail. She saw Marty on and off after Abigail's death, but they had never become close friends. Actually, she was looking forward to the opportunity to spend a significant amount of time together.

"I'll have some hot cider ready for you two when you get back," Elizabeth added. The brothers smiled and continue on with their moving job.

"Catherine, would you care for some tea?"

"Thanks, but I think I'll just unpack a little before the next arrival."

While Catherine unpacked, Elizabeth busied herself in the kitchen. She thought it would be fun to have a big welcoming supper and had prepared a new recipe that she had learned this past summer at her cooking class. Cooking relaxed Elizabeth, and her teacher, Vincent, brought such gusto to his recipes. This was an easy one, but so flavorful: Vinny's rigatoni with broccoli. She hoped that her three new housemates liked anchovies. The class had chosen this as one of the best dishes they had prepared, and Marty, who also took the class, had especially loved it. As Elizabeth cut the anchovies and broccoli into small pieces, she took some deep breaths to increase the relaxation. Three women were entering her life, occupying her house today. The next five months could either drag on or fly by, all depending on the atmosphere they created. Each one plunged into the opportunity knowing that there was risk involved, but she imagined that anybody could stand even the toughest circumstances for five months.

Elizabeth grinned as she recalled Lucy, her freshman roommate, at Middlebury College. Now that had been a rough year, a catastrophe, really. They had little in common, despite the college's attempt to select compatible roommates. Lucy came from the Midwest with a very provincial upbringing — at least that was Elizabeth's take — and had been under strict rules in her home on the outskirts of Chicago. When she entered Middlebury, she went wild, breaking all curfews and drinking in local motels. One night she came back to their dorm room so inebriated she could barely get her clothes off and climb into bed. What Elizabeth found most offensive was Lucy's smoking in the room, which irritated her asthma. On the questionnaire for roommate selection, Elizabeth had strongly indicated her preference for a nonsmoker. Lucy was placed on social probation for the second semester and had to struggle to stay on the dean's list. She was bright but had no common sense at all. After a direct confrontation, the two agreed that Lucy must not smoke in their room. Somehow, they just avoided each other, hanging out with other friends. Her freshman year could not have ended soon enough.

Now Elizabeth wanted so much for the Winter House to work out. Many people had told her that the winter wasn't that bad in Maine. Taking a bit of a risk felt right. Her parents had been pleased when she went off to Italy for her junior year, and it had widened her horizons greatly. She was hoping for the same with this leap. She knew her sister, Eve, didn't understand the decision and even had the gall to call it a "charity act." Elizabeth's kids, though they each voiced their opinions in different ways, just wanted her to be happy. Nell, her younger daughter, had emailed from Italy, saying she approved and looked forward to meeting all the "ladies," as she called them. In his usual distant manner, her oldest, Frank, had sent a message wishing her well. The other two, Michael and Libby, who both loved coming to Maine on vacation, were happy to hear that the house would still be available for their visits in the summer months. Besides watching out for their own interests, they seemed pleased that their mother was moving forward now. Libby had been not so subtle, in her psychologist's voice, when she mentioned gently that grief beyond a year would be considered abnormal and perhaps require therapy. A year? That seemed a statistic of the naïve.

Actually, Elizabeth was craving close companionship. Maybe the last few years with Cliff hadn't been all that exciting. How many weekends and evenings had she spent with her husband, who was more absorbed with his iPhone and his next business move? And that was in his "partial-retirement mode." Full retirement for Cliff, even at seventy-two, really wasn't an option. His work had defined his life. He loved the pace of New York City and his new initiatives. Cliff could relax with his chain saw out in the woods; however, his heart was in making deals. They'd put on a good front for family and friends, but life without the kids had become a bit stale; still, a stale marriage was better than being alone, she had thought.

Quigley came down the hall from Catherine's room, barking at the sound of the brothers returning with the next housemate to move in. It was an easy greeting, as Marty and Elizabeth had started the planning of this adventure well over two months ago and had enjoyed each other's company while chopping ingredients for the weekly summer cooking class. Quigley sniffed the carrying cage that Missy arrived in but backed off abruptly as the cat let out a hiss. The four women had decided that these two pets would just have to learn to get along. Missy was quite good at keeping a low profile, and she'd probably live mostly in the upper back bedroom that Marty had selected.

"This time you'll have to climb some stairs," Elizabeth said to the boys. "I'll get your cider ready." With a few trips, Jimmy and Jerry managed with ease to carry the computer table, a three-shelved bookcase, and several heavy boxes of books up the front stairs and then around to the back. Marty's prize possession, which she carried upstairs herself, was a dark mahogany dragon lamp that her grandfather had brought back from his medical-missionary work in China. It had always been in her parents' living room next to the piano, and though the shade had been somewhat damaged over the years, it still looked stately next to her reading chair. This bedroom already had a beautiful stuffed easy chair, so Marty just decided to bring the lamp along. The family history it possessed made her feel at home. Her file cabinets, mostly filled with old medical information, were too heavy to bring over, and besides, she had nearly everything she needed on her computer now. As corresponding secretary of her college class, she tried to keep those files up to date. The class was getting smaller, but those still living loved their Middlebury days. The coincidence that Elizabeth had also attended Middlebury, though she arrived just after Marty had left, strengthened their connection.

Jerry and Jimmy dropped off a final load of luggage, a yoga mat, and sports equipment. "That's all of it," said Jerry, who waited by the doorway. Marty thanked and paid the two boys for their time. After she put the two suitcases, mat, tennis racquet, and cross-country ski boots in her roomy closet, she released Missy from her traveling cage. The cat silently crept under the bed. It would take her a while to get accustomed to the new surroundings, but that was true for everyone.

"Good cider, Miz Sloan," said Jerry. Jimmy nodded in agreement. Though he was a hard worker, he wasn't much of a talker. Their father had died in a boating accident a few years before, and their mother was wheelchair-bound with arthritis. The summer yard work that Jimmy and Jerry did for Elizabeth helped to put food on the table for the Blakey family.

"Guess I'll be needing you to plow the driveway this winter and maybe shovel the walks. Do you own a plow?" Elizabeth asked.

"Pa's plow truck is broke right now, but we hope to have it fixed before too long."

"Good, then I'll count on you two as our snow-removal men. I understand last winter the storms dumped a lot of snow."

"Yep, more snow than we'd seen in years. I'd be surprised if we got dumped on like that again," Jerry said. Jimmy nodded.

"Well, I expect Mrs. Gott will be looking for you soon. I'll call her and tell her you are on your way over. We don't have much more daylight, but she doesn't live too far away. Actually, as the crow flies, she lives just across the cove, but the cove juts into the land, and you have to drive up and around to reach her house." Elizabeth quickly realized that she was describing an environment completely familiar to these boys.

Catherine, Marty, and Elizabeth gathered in the kitchen as Jimmy and Jerry left. "Anyone for tea?" Elizabeth asked. All three thought that might be just fine. Here they were, three out of the four. It felt a bit strange to all of them, having been alone in their own houses for varying times. Elizabeth noticed sweat in her armpit, and it wasn't hot inside. She was nervous. Probably they all were. Catherine broke the silence and asked about Elizabeth's children. A large portrait of four kids from years ago hung on the wall.

She pointed to each one, "That's Frank, the oldest. He lives in California now. Then Michael, he's in Boston. Libby lives just outside of Boston, and Nell, our youngest, has been in Italy for several years." Elizabeth picked up a photograph on the piano and pointed out her grandchildren. For their fiftieth wedding anniversary, most of the family had gathered, and the grandchildren had gotten along famously.

"Grandchildren are such fun," Catherine said, "and I cannot believe that I even have two little four-year-old great-granddaughters, Ella and Emma. They're identical twins, and really I can hardly tell them apart. They'll have to come over sometime. They just love to play with Quigley."

"I'd love to meet them," Elizabeth responded. "I used to work in a preschool in Connecticut, quite some time ago. I found the little ones fascinating, and a four-year-old's imagination is tremendous."

Marty piped in, "My grandnephews were with me this summer. We explored along the coast, investigated the tide pools, and caught little crabs. It's a paradise for the young."

"And old," added Catherine with a smile. She'd get no disagreement from this group. Maine may not have been their birthplace, but Marty and Elizabeth had adopted the state with utter enthusiasm.

Catherine and Marty offered to help set the table for supper. Elizabeth gave them a quick tour of the kitchen and pantry. Silverware in the top drawer to the left of the dishwasher, dishes above the dishwasher, glasses to the right of the sink, napkins and matches in the sideboard in the dining room. Fresh red candles were already on the table. For this special occasion Elizabeth wanted her favorite purple tablecloth. She loved the combination of red and purple. In no time, as darkness descended, the table was set.

Janet knocked and walked in. "Sorry to take so long. My brother phoned about some business with my mother's estate, and I had been trying to reach him for several days. We'd been playing telephone tag, so I figured I'd better just deal with it," Janet explained. Jerry and Jimmy followed her up the stairs to the front bedroom. They each carried a load and made several trips. A rocking chair, a fluffy down quilt, a large triangle pillow, a blue yoga mat, and a box of assorted shoes and boots came up the stairs. A bag of plastic balls in various sizes, an old tennis racquet, and a guitar followed. Jimmy and Jerry struggled with the final item, a tan Amelia Earhart suitcase, which must have held all the clothes Janet needed and more because it took the two brothers to hoist it up the stairs.

"May I write you a check?" Janet asked, never having cash on hand.

"Yeah, sure, you can make it out to Jerome Blakey."

"Sorry, I meant to get to the bank this morning but didn't make it," Janet replied. She knew the custom of the local workers, who preferred cash for their labor. There was a large rural industry that Uncle Sam never saw. She filled out the check and tipped the young men generously. They had been extremely patient. "Hope that covers it."

Jerry shyly looked at the check and smiled. "Thanks a lot." He and Jimmy said good-bye to the four women and promised to be back when the snow arrived — or sooner, if there was anything else they needed help with.

Nice boys, the women thought as they watched the boys leave.

"Well," Elizabeth said, "It's good to have you all finally here. I'll get back to completing the cooking if you all want to do a little unpacking and organizing. Please make yourselves at home and let me know if I can help you in any way. Should we eat in about an hour?"

That sounded fine to everyone.

"I'm going to take Quigley out for a short walk down the driveway," Catherine said. "He needs to sniff around." At the mention of a walk, Quigley spun around and stood by the door. He'd apparently been waiting for his turn. Marty asked if she might come along. The three then made their way outside.

Upstairs Janet began to unpack her clothes. She'd enjoyed thinning down her wardrobe for this winter. Over the years she had collected many sweaters and scarves, some of her mother's. Moving out for the winter gave her the opportunity to leave many things behind, and it felt good. A new beginning, and who knew where this would take her. She was eager for the change.

After about an hour Elizabeth called out, "Dinner's ready." The other three came to the kitchen and carried their plates to the table, already set with wine glasses. Janet and Catherine had each insisted privately to Elizabeth that it didn't bother them if others imbibed around them, but neither would be drinking. Catherine had never liked the taste of alcohol and had remained a lifelong teetotaler, with her uncle's drinking problem etched in her memory. Janet planned to stay away from any spirits; she had learned the hard way that she couldn't handle them. Both women gladly accepted a celebratory glass of nonalcoholic sparkling pear wine made in Maine and purchased for this occasion.

"Here's to our new adventure," Marty said. They clicked glasses all around.

Catherine slept well, with Quigley at the foot of her bed. She awoke at her usual time of 6 a.m., but instead of getting up right away, she investigated her surroundings. In the darkness she turned on the light by her new bed. A peaceful Anne Kilham painting hung on the mint green wall to her left. She had actually met the artist in Rockland several years ago and frequently used Kilham stationery for writing to her students. The ceiling was higher and flatter than that of her own second-floor bedroom, which had a dormer window, creating many angles. The two windows here would provide her with quite a bit of light in the daytime, good for needlepoint and reading. Catherine welcomed the change to face east. The sun would rise in about an hour, as these early winter days were short now. An old woven Navajo rug covered a good part of the floor. Although it was beautiful and probably quite an antique, the frayed edge could trip her up, so she planned to suggest that they put it away until summer. Catherine didn't want to ask for many changes, as she appreciated Elizabeth's generosity in sharing her home and wanted to make it an easy transition for her. She also wanted to help Elizabeth join into the year-round community and meet some new folks.

Quigley snuggled up to Catherine's shoulder. He was no early riser and loved to snooze on and off, even as his mistress usually busied herself in the kitchen. Catherine remembered well the day eight years ago when Billy Gray brought this fluffy white puppy to her. "You need a dog," Billy said, "and I just happen to have one." Though she really wasn't sure she needed a puppy, she could not resist the little three-pound ball of fluff. Her husband had been dead four years, and Colonel, their old yellow lab, had died, probably of heartache and arthritis, two years later. So without much fuss, Catherine kept the puppy and named him Quigley, after Sir James Buchanan Quigley, her great-grandfather from Wales. They became instant companions.

By 6:30 a.m. Catherine was ready for her morning coffee. She tiptoed quietly down the hall into the kitchen, where Elizabeth had loaded the coffee machine the night before. A gentle push of the button produced the sound of brewing coffee. Marty came quietly down the stairs, following the coffee aroma, but Missy stayed put for the time being. Quigley stretched his rear legs, first one and then the other, and waited by the door. Marty and Catherine put on their coats, hats, and gloves, and the three went out for a little brisk morning air to retrieve the *Bangor Daily News*. A subtle yellow glow appeared to the east.

"How did you sleep?" Marty asked Catherine.

"Just fine, thanks," she replied. "I've never had much trouble sleeping at night, but I just can't take naps, so I tend to go to bed early."

"I had to learn how to do daytime power naps during my long days of practice and waiting for deliveries. So that's been a special skill I've kept even through retirement. I close my eyes and sleep seventeen minutes. Amazing, really. I heard that Walter Cronkite — or was it Jim Lehrer? — could do that too," Marty added.

"I envy you. My Harold could catch a wink or two right after lunch, and then be ready for a full afternoon of work. It's a good skill to have. I guess I just keep going till I drop," Catherine said with a smile. Most people envied her energy.

They picked up the paper and returned for their first cup of morning coffee. Quigley strayed into the woods just off the driveway to smell some new scents but returned to Catherine's side at the back door. He was ready for breakfast.

The December scene around Brooks Harbor was busy with seasonal concerts, town and school events, and, of course, the anticipation of significant snowfalls. Would the marshes freeze over before the snowfall to make ice-skating glorious? Or would the first heavy snow dump on the village and make for snowmen, snow forts, and cross-country skiing? Snowmobilers greased up their engines and prepared to venture out on the hidden trails deep in the woods. By December everyone awaited the cold, but for the last several years freezing temperatures well below zero, lasting weeks on end, had not arrived. Even the skeptics of global warming had to admit that the seasons were different from what they experienced in childhood. They just didn't believe the change was man-made.

The town-wide holiday winter fair and potluck had developed into quite a tradition on the second Saturday of December. Years before, the two churches had competed with each other for Christmas fairs and auctions, but now many groups came together to hold one big event at the community center. Catherine enjoyed the chance to take part in this more inclusive affair, and there was no telling what groups would join in. Many folks volunteered now, and the townspeople eagerly awaited its coming. The fair — as a fundraiser for the most needy of the town and a way to provide Christmas toys for the less fortunate children — was a uplifting event. And besides, the smorgasbord of potluck dishes and desserts was exceptional. Some said the feast could not be matched anywhere, though Hancock, a village a bit farther downeast, refuted that claim.

Catherine's week was full, as usual. She invited Elizabeth to come along to a planning meeting for the winter fair, but Elizabeth declined; she didn't feel ready for a committee. She did, however, agreed to attend the seasonal event. Janet was already committed to the birdhouse project with the fifth and six graders. Last year the little red and blue wooden birdhouses had sold out within the first half hour, so now the kids wanted to produce more — enough for the entire town. At seven dollars apiece, they were a bargain. Marty wanted to avoid any more meetings than her current commitments. Last winter she had made a special casserole for the potluck and had gotten rave reviews. For this fair she would double the recipe and take it as a donation from the Winter House women.

"It will be like a coming-out party," said Janet, smiling. At the market she had heard a few men talking about this group of women who were "shacking up together down there on Spruce Point." The men laughed at the cash register as Janet waited in line with her bananas and milk. "Guess they couldn't find any good men." They chortled again. Janet kept quiet. She didn't recognize any of them, and there was little use in explaining anything to them. Although loneliness doesn't discriminate, this move was not exactly something that men would do.

The day of the holiday fair arrived, and all seemed ready. The posters around town predicted that Santa Claus would arrive at 5 p.m. as the Christmas tree was being lit. Catherine's twin great-granddaughters, Ella and

Emma, had been chosen to turn on the lights this year. Two days before, a gentle snowstorm had covered the area with two to three inches of light snow, so the scene was set for Santa's arrival. For years, in what was now a tradition, Billy Gray's father, Russell, who had a long white beard and a rather round midriff, had ho-ho-hoed his way in an old red pickup truck to the town landing, where the tree was located. He would tell the children to be good little boys and girls and that soon Christmas Eve would arrive. Russell would drive away with the muffler rumbling, back toward Graytown, all the kids waving good-bye.

In the afternoon the community center started to fill up with all varieties of arts and crafts — fancy felt hats with stripes and colorful bands, periwinkle-shell earrings and bracelets, standing puppets made from bleached lobster claws and dressed in oilskins, all sizes of knitted mittens for small and large hands, and tiny Christmas-tree ornaments made from mussel shells and pine cones. The fifth and sixth graders displayed birdhouses in three different colors and two different sizes. The price had increased to eight dollars. The used-book table — hardcover, one dollar: paperbacks, fifty cents — attracted many customers who preferred to curl up with a good mystery or memoir instead of watching television.

As townsfolk entered, they paid a small entrance fee, took a door prize number, and then deposited their potluck contribution on the food tables. The Happy Helpers, a local volunteer group, organized the food dishes and laid out utensils and plates. The new community center had plenty of space for arts and crafts tables too. Many had learned to take some time to look around at the crafts before sitting down to eat. No one could predict what good culinary additions might arrive late. But some folks headed right for the food and filled their plates high with baked beans, coleslaw, tuna casserole, rice pilaf, creamed scallops, and green-gelatin fruit salad with tiny marshmallows. One kindergartner walked away with a plateful of macaroni and cheese, two red-skinned hot dogs, and a large cup of pink lemonade.

The Winter House women arrived after the tree lighting. Marty, Janet, and Elizabeth sat together along with Catherine's daughter, Sarah, and the twins, who were still surprised by Santa's visit to Brooks Harbor. They saved a seat for Catherine, who had been surrounded by friends as soon as she walked in. Several townspeople who usually drove by Catherine's house on their way to work must have noticed the lack of lights. Word travels fast in a small town, and many probably wanted to get firsthand information. Catherine smiled, greeted her friends, and spoke to each one. Finally, she came over with her oldest friend, Patricia Sullivan, and introduced her to her new friends.

"Nice to meet you," Pat said, nodding to each. "I know I have spoken to a few of you on the phone already when I'm looking for Catherine. She's always been a hard gal to track down, but I suppose you are learning that. How do you keep up with her?"

"We are trying," said Elizabeth with a smile. "She's a great role model for an active senior citizen."

"Yeah, you can say that, all right," said Pat. "Well, I best be getting back to my husband. He's itching to get into the food line. Have a good time." Pat scurried off to join David, who tipped his John Deere baseball cap to the ladies as Pat pointed out Catherine's new friends.

Janet visited the birdhouse table and noticed sales were good. She bought one to give to Elizabeth for Christmas. They had decided to exchange small gifts, setting a limit of under ten dollars. Each wanted the fun of putting presents under their Christmas tree. Because they had all spent Thanksgiving with their extended families, the women chose to stay in Brooks Harbor and enjoy a low-key holiday together.

Up on the stage, beneath the Star of Bethlehem, Reverend Perry used the new speaker system to give thanks for the meal and for the generosity of all the volunteers. The food line now stretched around the room. Billy Gray, assisted by Jimmy and Jerry, set up more tables.

After the main course, the desserts came out, and the line formed again. Chocolate cakes, carrot cakes, marble cakes, cupcakes with sprinkles, lemon bars, huge chocolate-chip cookies, and pies — apple, banana cream, pecan, peach, blueberry, strawberry-rhubarb, mince, and even tomato pie. Dessert plates were as big as the main-course plates. A fairly large man dressed in green pants and shirt, and sporting a Red Sox cap, took a small sliver of each pie, as did the very thin teenage boy who had been selling tickets. Elizabeth noticed Jerry and Jimmy filling their plates high too and wondered how things were really going for the brothers. Their house was leaning, the roof sagging more and more, and the clutter of old refrigerators and toilets on the front lawn would soon be covered by winter's cleansing blanket. She tried to employ them as much as she could, but it certainly wasn't enough for them to survive on. Secretly, she hoped for a big snow season so they could earn money plowing as long as the old plow truck held out. She watched Catherine's face beam at former students who came over to chat. Her great-grandchildren giggled as they ate their sprinkle-covered cupcakes.

When a large glass jar was passed around from table to table for cash donations, the local ukulele group, seven strong, started the entertainment with three holiday songs. A short sing-along piece was unsuccessful, as most continued to enjoy their desserts. Janet thought the group was having so much fun, she resolved to start ukulele lessons and give up on the guitar. Then Ronnie Anderson, a fifth grader, played Pachelbel's Canon in D on his cello as his mother, Valerie, the elementary-school music teacher, accompanied him on the flute. A few folks in the crowd stood to applaud their effort. Then Valerie led the audience in an old rendition of "I'm Dreaming of a White Christmas," and this time the audience was ready to sing. The town's fire chief came on stage with a few of his firefighters, and they belted out "Rudolph, the Red-Nosed Reindeer." Ella and Emma giggled because the fire chief actually had a pretty red nose.

Then came the door-prize drawing. To her complete surprise, Catherine won: a choice of ten pounds of lobster or one cord of cut and split wood. She had time to decide, as the prizes wouldn't be available until spring. What a hoot, she thought. Never in her entire life had she won a door prize, and her great-granddaughters were equally excited. "Nanny, you won, you won!" cried Emma and Ella.

The Winter House women offered to assist with the cleanup after the event, but the Happy Helpers said they had enough volunteers. Local firefighters, aided by seventh and eighth graders, took down the tables and put the chairs away. Most attendees picked up their potluck dishes and took them home along with bags of purchased goodies. The weather forecast for ten to twelve inches of snow overnight thrilled some folks and disturbed others. But it was December, so most people were prepared, and luckily Marty and the others had cut and dragged home a small balsam fir from Elizabeth's woods that morning for the household Christmas tree.

"We'll be by to plow you all out tomorrow if we get a good amount. We've got the plow truck working just fine," said Jerry to Elizabeth as he held the door for them. "Now watch your step, ladies," he added.

"Thanks a lot, Jerry," she replied. She noticed his brother nodding but saying nothing.

On the way home Catherine was still laughing about the door prize. Elizabeth had taken it all in. She'd never attended one of these local holiday events before and couldn't quite imagine her husband there. The down-home atmosphere was almost surreal, a throwback to the fifties, a far cry from the glitz and glitter of New York City in the twenty-first century. Yet an authenticity — a genuine air of community pride, generosity, and enjoyment — permeated the surroundings. The pace was slower here. For a fleeting moment Elizabeth pictured Cliff's old blue T-shirt: "Maine — Life in the Slow Lane," with a moose in a hammock. She only wished that he had had the time to climb into the hammock. In the darkness of the back seat of Marty's car, Elizabeth felt her throat tighten for a second, but the tears held off. Tonight she just wanted to enjoy the community spirit.

For the next two weeks, it snowed about every third day. The Blakey boys kept the driveway plowed and shoveled the entrance. One evening the elementary-school band performed a concert of holiday songs. Catherine knew almost every one of the children; she had been reading aloud to them after school for several years.

Elizabeth observed that the community life went on, some events were canceled but others, held as scheduled. Marty and Janet continued yoga class on Thursday mornings, and Marty started to encourage Janet to join her Monday tennis group and try the sport again.

"Come on, Janet. If I can do it, you can, too. I know that Sally and Polly would enjoy meeting you; we need subs, and really we just have social fun and move the old joints around a bit. It's not exactly Forest Hills!" Marty took an imaginary swing. Janet knew she had become almost a recluse since John's death. She was slowly coming out of it and joining the Winter House group seemed a positive move, potentially life-changing.

"Maybe that will be one of my New Year's resolutions," Janet replied. "Let me think on it."

While the schoolchildren had vacation, Catherine had two weeks off from her after-school reading program. She still had a few handmade gifts to finish. She'd already made mittens for Ella and Emma, a scarf for Sarah, table place mats for her son's family in New Jersey, and a quilt for Harold's wife. In addition, she had promised her granddaughter, Mary Ida, a yellow cable-knit cardigan sweater. My Lord, Catherine thought, what was I thinking? Her fingers were getting stiffer, and with her eyesight failing, she found working with the small needles quite a challenge. But given all the snow and with school out, she thought she'd have time to complete the sweater. If she had any extra time, she hoped to knit short scarves for her new housemates.

That would have to be a secret late-night work project, if she could stay awake.

The morning sea mist rose from the bay as the sun climbed up over the faraway hills of Mt. Desert. The thermometer read ten degrees Fahrenheit, and long spikes of icicles hung from the porch roof, reflecting sunbeams into small rainbows. A few brown woody stalks of the daylilies stood tall, poking through the blanket of snow, and the evergreen boughs drooped under the snow's weight. Elizabeth stared out the window. Could she create a scene like this on canvas? That was her dream: to start again, pick up a brush and capture beauty and peace. "You've got a lot of talent, young lady," Professor Stevens at Middlebury had assured her when she wondered about her future in the art world. But that was many years ago. Now she needed to gain back her confidence and learn newer techniques. Bob Chester might be just the instructor for her. She admired his work and had heard that he was now taking on new students. In January she would investigate the situation. Today she just wanted to be still.

"Brrr, that's cold," said Catherine, looking at the outdoor thermometer as she pulled on her boots, coat, hat, scarf, and mittens. She put two layers on Quigley — a red pullover knit sweater and an insulated denim jacket with a tie under his belly. Both would break the force of the wind and give him some insulation. His own coat had thickened up quite well, but Catherine liked to dress him with extra protection. Finally the green booties with Velcro ties went on. Quigley didn't mind them at all. She'd made them for him from a pattern she'd seen in *Yankee Magazine,* and they worked, shielding his paws. "There," she said, "we're ready for our walk. Come on, Quig. See you in a bit, Elizabeth." Out they went, down to the mailbox for the newspaper. Catherine walked carefully, carrying an old wood ski pole to give her stability, a trick she had learned from her father. As she returned to the kitchen with the paper, Marty and Janet were rushing off to yoga class. They were running a little late. The dark mornings challenged their morning routine.

Catherine poured a second cup of coffee and read the headlines. Only then did she notice Elizabeth sitting quietly in the living room, gazing out the window.

Elizabeth was lost in memories of Italy. "Good morning, Madame, will your husband be joining you this morning?" Francisco, the ever-gracious host at the Villa di Tiza, wanted so much to please these American honeymooners.

"Yes, he will be right down, thank you." Elizabeth replied. She had not yet grown accustomed to the label "husband." Exchanging their vows just three days before with a small group of family and friends in Vermont seemed almost a dream. Cliff had surprised her with the honeymoon destination, and she was thrilled to return to Italy. She had vivid memories of Rome during her junior year away from Middlebury. Elizabeth recalled her voyage over on the *Queen Frederica*, a Greek ocean liner, and her first sightings of the Roman ruins. She loved the nights in Naples and the countryside of Siena, but most of all she cherished the unexpected arrival of Cliff that glorious April.

That was when she fell hard for him. She hadn't really recognized how much she had missed him until they embraced at the airport. Their letters had been passionate, yet nothing was like that week in Venice: the little inn with three guest rooms, the gardens, the art museums, and the elegant dinners. They had slept in separate rooms, or at least they paid for two rooms when the innkeeper demanded their passports and noted they were not married. Cliff and Elizabeth respected these rules; in fact, Elizabeth had been raised to keep her virginity until marriage, but with the intense feelings she had for Cliff, this internalized restriction was not easy. She was convinced they would be together forever. And now, here they were, back in Italy and married, husband and wife, until death do us part.

A tear dropped from Elizabeth's cheek, and she slowly wiped it away. The scene of Cliff joining her for breakfast faded out, and as hard as she tried, she could no longer see his face. The living-room clock chimed, startling her. Then after a few more minutes of watching the bay, she rose and went into the kitchen. Her coffee had gotten cold.

"Any coffee left?" Elizabeth asked Catherine. "Maybe I'll make another pot. It seems like one of those mornings."

"That's not a bad idea. I imagine it isn't going to warm up outside too much today, and I have projects to accomplish," Catherine added.

"You're very industrious, Catherine."

"Well, I dove into many of these crafts after Harold died. I needed something to keep my mind off the loneliness, and it helped."

"You've lived alone for twelve years? Wow, that seems like a long time."

"Yes, it is. But it has gotten easier with time, I guess. At first it was really hard without him. I missed him terribly. Of course, I tried to stay busy in the community and said 'Yes,' to everything and everybody. But then I got so overextended that I didn't have any time for myself. I slowly learned to find a balance."

"I really miss Cliff, even though we were apart a lot," Elizabeth admitted.

"It is more the finality of it that hurts. You just can't talk with them anymore, though I connect with Harold on my beach walks, telling him what's going on with the family and all. He used to love to walk along the beach, so that's where I usually have my talks."

"I've been having flashbacks lately, and they seem so real. I see his face and sometimes even sense his body next to mine. It's strange …yet comforting …but then he's gone." Elizabeth sipped her coffee.

"That's very normal, Elizabeth. I remember once hearing Harold whispering in my ear, saying 'It's not what you think. Live your life fully now.' And then he vanished. I heard him loud and clear and have been trying to follow his advice," Catherine said. "I still miss him and always will. But I was determined to move on with my life and not just get stuck mourning his loss. Everyone handles the death of a loved one differently, and the stages of grief and acceptance don't come exactly in the order that Kübler-Ross, in *Death and Dying*, explained. I used to get angry at the most unusual times. When something special in the family happened, like a graduation award, a successful state championship, the birth of a great-grandchild, I'd get angry — well sad, well, both, I guess. It's just that Harold didn't get to share in the pride and joy. It is hard." Catherine let out a deep sigh.

"Yes, I can imagine. I guess I have that to look forward to …or not. I'm still pretty new at this widowhood thing, and I really appreciate having you around to talk to."

Elizabeth poured herself more coffee and offered to top off Catherine's cup.

"Save it for Marty and Janet. They ought to be back pretty soon and can reheat it." Catherine finished up her reading of the editorials and obituaries. Elizabeth took the travel section, noticing an article on Venice.

On Christmas Eve Catherine's family came over to wish everyone a merry Christmas. Emma and Ella were excited about Santa Claus coming to their house and told all the "ladies," as they called them, what was on their wish list.

"I want a kitty," said Emma, the taller twin.

"Me too," added Ella. "I want to call her 'Kitty'."

"What's your cat's name?" Emma asked Marty, who stroked the cat on her lap.

"Oh, this is Missy. She's lived with me a long time." Marty loved speaking with children.

"Oh," said Emma. "Nanny, does Quigley like it here?"

"He's getting used to the place and even leaves Missy alone," said Catherine.

"Oh, that's good. They should be friends," added Ella.

"That would be nice," said Marty. "It might take some time."

Then Catherine handed gifts to her family, so they could put them under the tree. They all insisted they would open them on Christmas Day when Catherine came over for turkey dinner at Sarah's. That was a tradition in the Howard family, and Catherine would be there, for sure.

Then the whole gang gathered around the piano, and Catherine played some favorite Christmas carols. Emma and Ella requested "Jingle Bells." Catherine was surprised that her fingers moved easily over the keys. Elizabeth was thrilled to hear the Steinway played again and recalled Cliff's mother playing in this living room. Everyone smiled as they sang "Santa Claus is Coming to Town." Marty remembered her father reciting " 'Twas the Night before Christmas" and wondered if visions of sugarplums danced in the twins' heads.

Elizabeth and Marty had made a special gingerbread house for the little girls, whose eyes twinkled as they noticed Old St. Nick's boots stuck in the chimney of the gingerbread house. The roof was made with green and red M & M candies, the shutters with delicate white frosting.

"What do you say?" Mary Ida asked her daughters.

"Thank you," the two girls chorused.

"You are so welcome. Come visit us again; we love seeing you all," Elizabeth added.

The moonlight on the snow lit their way to the cars and cast the shadows of the dark fir and spruce. A subtle ring around the moon predicted more snow.

Back in the house Marty and Elizabeth began preparations for the Christmas Eve dinner. A new fiddlehead-soup recipe with cream and a touch of lemon intrigued the two. Marty usually picked fresh fiddleheads in May and froze them, but this time they used the canned variety. Billy Gray had dropped off four pound-and-a-half lobsters, soft shell but still beefy, just as he promised. Whenever Cliff and Elizabeth had come up for the holidays, they had lobsters and champagne on Christmas Eve. Years ago lobsters were almost a staple for the lobstermen and their families. Still Catherine loved the rich, sweet shellfish, especially dipped in butter. Her family always had pickles and potato chips with lobster, but because of her hypertension, Catherine tried to watch excess salt intake. So, no pickles and no chips!

"I'm glad we decided to have our celebration tonight," said Marty.

"It will be good to help with the food kitchen tomorrow," Janet commented. "Each year the need seems to be growing. The city of Ellsworth has sponsored a holiday feast for the last several years, and many folks have come to count on a Christmas dinner at the auditorium."

"Well, I'm really looking forward to helping with it," said Elizabeth.

Before dinner the women exchanged little gifts. Janet presented to Elizabeth the birdhouse and to Catherine and Marty, antique brooches that had been her mother's. Catherine had made short, colorful scarves for each of them, while Marty offered some locally made bars of pine-scented soap. Elizabeth had thought hard about a gift for each housemate. In the end she decided to purchase a new game called Bananagrams — something like Scrabble, without the board. Elizabeth had learned about it from a friend whose family always exchanged puzzles, and she thought it would be a fun way to share some time together.

Elizabeth served the first course, the delightful and savory fiddlehead soup, and Marty dropped four hypnotized lobsters into a boiling pot. As dinner progressed, conversations ranged from old family customs and childhood memories to Maine's new energy plan of harnessing the tides. Offshore wind towers and tidal turbines were being considered for the state's energy needs. Since the disastrous Gulf oil spill, and with the continued dependence on Middle Eastern oil, many alternatives were being considered. Elizabeth's husband's consulting firm had just been getting into these new capital investments.

Before any of them realized, the evening had flown by. They had decided to attend the ten-o'clock candlelight ceremony — a joint service of the two town churches. It seemed a neighborly thing to do, and the congregations were happy to have a packed house, even if most of the attendees rarely placed a foot in the door at other times of the year. For the Winter House women, it was a time to be together and share their new friendships.

JANUARY

*E*lizabeth pulled into the garage and just sat in her car, mentally patting herself on the back for successfully completing her first watercolor class. She had actually been dreading the idea of appearing at the studio; it had been so long since she had attempted painting. But with Bob Chester's short review, the techniques had all started to come back to her. By the end of the class, she knew this was the right thing to do, and she would continue the instruction. Besides, Bob had been so complimentary; it was almost embarrassing, but it felt good.

The warmth of the house and a delicious aroma greeted Elizabeth in the kitchen. Marty had been preparing a special beef stew just as Elizabeth had left for her class. A single lamp was on in the living room, and her three housemates were lying on the rug with their feet up on the sofa. They had their arms crossed over their chests. Mozart's Fourth Horn Concerto played softly.

"Hello, Elizabeth," they all chimed. "Come join us."

"What are you doing?"

"We are practicing restorative relaxation. Janet and I learned it this week in yoga class," Marty said. "Beth, our instructor, encouraged us to take the time to relax our bodies and pamper ourselves."

"Well, I wish I had a camera," Elizabeth joked.

"Yeah, we could get our picture in the *Weekly Packet*," Marty quipped. "Activities at the Winter House."

"Maybe I will join you; let me first put my things down." Then she moved the small coffee table and lay with her feet on the red stuffed chair. Under her head she placed a small throw pillow. "Ah, this does feel good."

Marty began: "Lift your right leg and slowly circle your ankle, first one direction and then the other. Now point your toe and hold and then flex your ankle and hold. See if you can rotate your foot out and then in. Now concentrate and see if you can ignite your baby-toe border."

"That's an interesting instruction, but I'm not sure I follow," said Elizabeth.

Janet interjected, "See if you can concentrate on just your baby toe; first with your foot squared, try to flex and then extend just the baby toe, and you should feel the outer edge of your foot energized."

Catherine put her foot down on the sofa. It had been quite a bit of work to hold up her leg, but the relaxation part with her feet on the cushion felt fine. During her many years of teaching, she had stood on her feet all day and recalled nights when her legs ached. This maneuver might have helped or at least relaxed some of the tensions from the long day.

"Now let's do the left foot," requested Marty. Janet was

amazed at how much her friend sounded like Beth, their yoga teacher.

"How was art class?" Catherine inquired.

"Quite good," Elizabeth remarked. "I think I will continue. There were some very nice people there, and Bob Chester couldn't have been more encouraging."

"That's great," said Marty. "I've heard he is a wonderful teacher and a talented artist as well. Sometimes those two things don't go hand in hand."

"Yes, I'm lucky he is nearby and has space for me," Elizabeth said.

"You never know what you can find in a small Maine town," Janet added.

"Okay, now, with your legs resting comfortably on the sofa or chair, let your arms fall to your sides, palms up, and touch your thumbs to the floor. Now take in a breath through your nose and start filling from below and then all the way up to your high ribs. On the exhale, surrender to the gravity, front ribs to the back. Do this slowly three times, making your exhale twice as long as the inhale," Marty instructed.

Catherine and Elizabeth tried to follow the instructions, but it didn't come easily. Perhaps you had to attend yoga classes for a while to get the hang of the breathing. But they tried. For all four women to be on the floor in the living room was a first, and no one appeared uncomfortable.

Elizabeth recalled her teenage sleepovers in Vermont, when all the girls would lie on the floor in a circle and put their heads on someone's stomach. Then they were supposed to laugh, which would shake the head of the other, making her laugh, and soon the whole room was laughing. Elizabeth wondered if she would ever laugh again with such delight and glee. She knew it had been a while since she felt like laughing.

The kitchen timer chimed. "Dinner's ready," Marty said. "We can do more yoga another time. Now everyone roll over on your right side and slowly sit up, bringing your head up last." Everyone complied and then gradually stood. Catherine needed a hand getting off the floor and graciously accepted assistance. At almost eighty, she was learning that relying totally on herself was not always necessary, and a little help was sometimes a big plus. She went into her bedroom and retrieved her favorite brown sweater. Catherine loved sitting by the window in the dining room, but a bit of a draft came around the curtain when the wind picked up. Everyone had established her place at the table, and the routine was comfortable.

"This is delicious," Janet remarked.

"A lot tastier than Dinty Moore," Catherine added. They ate at different speeds.

"Anyone care for seconds?" asked Marty.

"I'll eat my seconds for lunch tomorrow," said Catherine, who tried hard to watch her calories but had a sweet tooth for dessert.

"Me too," said Janet.

"I'm fine too, but I think you nailed it, Marty," said Elizabeth. "The black pepper, bacon with rosemary, and a touch of red wine were just right. Vincent would be very proud of you."

"Thanks. It was so simple," Marty added.

Catherine chuckled to herself. She had heard it said, "There are people who live to eat, and there are people who eat to live." She figured she was one of the latter. It did make her laugh when cooks were complimented on their culinary creations, and they always replied without fail, "Oh, it really is so simple." She had never heard a skilled cook say in response to a compliment, "Oh, it took hours and was quite difficult." No seasoned cook would ever admit to that. But that was the way Catherine thought about preparing food. What a joy it was now that Marty and Elizabeth loved to cook, and Catherine and Janet just had to do the dishes. Although she thought this arrangement might not last, Catherine was certainly enjoying it for the time being.

With dinner over and the dishes done, Janet retreated upstairs for the long hot bath that she loved. She was reading a fabulous book that Marty had recommended — *Cutting for Stone* by Abraham Verghese — and couldn't wait to get back to it. It was well written, and the story of medical mission work intrigued her. Long ago she had considered using her nursing skills in a third-world country, but her life's path had not taken her there — at least, not yet.

Before bed Quigley needed a walk, and Marty offered to accompany Catherine down the snowy driveway. She threw on her spiked boots, which gave her good grip, and offered Catherine an arm. Snow on the ground made it harder for a dog to find a private spot to do his business. Jerry and Jimmy had cleared out an extra area for Quigley to use to avoid the shoveled walkways. In the eight-degree January darkness, Catherine and Marty walked down the driveway, their nostrils burning and their breath appearing like exhaled smoke. The snow crunched under their feet. Marty gazed at the North Star, and Catherine commented that it had been Harold's favorite, easily found after locating the Big Dipper.

Back in the house Elizabeth noticed that three letters had arrived for her. Getting personal letters these days was unusual, given the increasing use of email and the telephone. She still received junk mail addressed to Clifford H. Sloan, and that continued to upset her. She noticed an advertisement for Viking River cruises, reminding her of their last trip together to Russia. A newsletter from her supplemental insurance plan, a *Cooking Light* magazine, the Middlebury alumni magazine, the *New Yorker*, and a Talbot's catalog were in the basket too, but tonight the personal letters interested her.

Elizabeth recognized the handwriting of her sister, Eve. She knew it would be another invitation to visit them at their condo in Florida. Eve could not conceive that anyone would enjoy Maine in the winter. Elizabeth laid that one aside. The next letter, with a handwritten address, was from the Middlebury College alumni office. Middlebury had played a significant role in her young adult life. It turned out to be the right choice for her, though initially she had wondered whether she should leave Vermont and attend a larger school in a city. In time the size of its student body, its beauty, and the students themselves reinforced her decision. And meeting Cliff had taken her on an entirely unanticipated path.

Dear Elizabeth,

We were saddened to hear about Cliff's accidental death. The entire Middlebury family extends our regrets for your loss. You and Cliff have been extremely generous in donations to your alma mater. We would like to invite you to our graduation this year to accept an award for your having been such loyal and generous supporters of the college. We note that your fiftieth class reunion will take place this

*year. Please let us know if you will be able to attend
this June 3 event.*

> *Sincerely,*
> *Peter Crosby*
> *Director Alumni Affairs,*
> *Middlebury College*

Elizabeth had no initial reaction. She wasn't sure
whether this was a sly way of encouraging further donations or whether the college was genuine in recognizing
their contribution to the school. She wondered if they had
heard about the donation from Cliff's estate, which would
be made in due time. Surely the attorney dealing with the
details of his estate would not yet have notified them. Or
would he? Whatever, Elizabeth decided to think about this.
This year graduation did coincide with her class reunion,
and it would be fun to see her old friends again. Returning
as a widow would be quite a different experience, but it was
five months away, and maybe widowhood would be easier
then, though she wasn't too sure.

The Italian stamp on the third letter caught her eye.
The return address was Nell's, but the handwriting was
that of her granddaughter, Alcee. For many years Alcee
had written to her grandmother, practicing her English
and telling her about school activities. Elizabeth kept these
precious letters; it wasn't easy living far away from a grand-
child, but luckily, she and Cliff were able to fly to Italy for
an annual visit. Alcee's July holidays in Maine, when she
was twelve and thirteen, had created a special bond. Now
Alcee's life in Italy was crowded with studies, music, and a
boyfriend. During her visit to Siena last November, Elizabeth had noticed that Alcee's boyfriend took precedence.

She and Alcee talked on Skype every few months, but it wasn't the same as being with each other in person.

Dear Nonna,

It has been a long time since I have spoken to you and I am sorry for that. Mamma and I keep very busy and she works very hard to prepare for her new exhibition. She stays for many hours at her studio. Right now I don't know how to ask you this but I will just go ahead. I want to come to Maine soon to see you. I know it is winter there. Could I come for a week? My school has the winter recess. Mamma will let me come, I know. She does not like Fabio, my boyfriend, and would like me to get away. I really want to come. Hope you can help me. Can you email me your answer and then I will talk with Mamma.

Ti amo, Alcee

Elizabeth reread the letter. Why would Alcee write instead of emailing her this request? Was something seriously wrong? She wondered if Nell knew anything about her daughter's idea. Perhaps Nell was just getting too involved in her successful art career to notice. Perhaps Alcee just needed some warm grandmotherly love and understanding. Whatever it was, Elizabeth knew she could not ignore this plea for help. She left the letter out on the table. Tomorrow she would email Alcee and have a discussion with her housemates.

The next day the outside thermometer read twenty-six degrees as Catherine prepared to get the morning paper with Quigley. It had snowed during the night, but the temperature was rising. Though it was still snowing, Catherine feared sleet, or even rain, would come next. The Channel 2 weather forecaster predicted an ice storm — a small one, probably nothing like the Great Ice Storm of 1998, when most of eastern Maine was covered with a heavy, white ice crust and 300,000 people lost electricity. In that storm Catherine remembered Harold stacking logs beside the two woodstoves that kept the house warm. Neighbors without woodstoves were in serious trouble. Harold plowed and sanded the driveway frequently to keep ahead of the storm and invited chilled neighbors to come warm up. He went out several times to assist those with downed trees, and he responded when a chimney fire almost destroyed Billy Gray's home. The whole town pitched in to help folks who needed it. The radio station WVOM broadcast news updates to people isolated in their cold living rooms, listening to battery-operated radios. Unfortunately, three died, two from carbon monoxide poisoning while running generators inside and one from a fallen tree. It had been a challenge that winter.

"Do you think we should go into town this morning, before it gets any worse?" Elizabeth said to Catherine. She hadn't experienced a Maine ice storm. "My Highlander should do okay with snow tires and four-wheel drive. We could stock up on supplies, just in case."

"That might be a good idea," Catherine replied.

"Good, I'll check with Marty and Janet on things they may need, and we can make a list of staples and a few treats." Elizabeth wanted to be prepared.

"I expect school is closed today. I used to watch the school bus go by at my place, but we're a bit back off the road here."

"We are lucky to have the boys helping us out with the driveway and walkways. They're good boys," Elizabeth said. Briefly, she thought of her sons, Frank and Michael. She still missed them, even after all these years.

Outside, the snow fell gently.

At the grocery store people were stocking up. The aisles were packed, as often happened when the forecasters predicted a storm. Catherine and Elizabeth joined in the pursuit of staples. They made sure to have enough sugar, flour, and butter to do some baking. Their cellar was well supplied with winter squash and potatoes, but some green vegetables and salad makings suited them. Elizabeth suggested hot cereal and pancake mix. Catherine passed on the pancake mix, as she knew by heart her mother-in-law's old buckwheat-pancake recipe. She did pick up some Maine maple syrup, though. A gallon of skim milk and two pounds of ground coffee finished off the list. Elizabeth picked out a Chilean Shiraz and a Malbec from Argentina; she enjoyed trying new labels.

The ride home was tricky. The snow began to turn to sleet. Then Elizabeth and Catherine saw the flashing lights of Buddy Grindle's tow truck as it slowly pulled a familiar green sedan out of the ditch at Benson's Corner. Catherine looked closely to see if anyone was hurt, and then she recognized her old friend Pat, with her husband, David, standing on the side of the road. Elizabeth stopped gradually.

"Are you two all right?" Catherine inquired through the window.

"Hi, yes, we're fine. Just slid slowly into the ditch as we rounded the corner. Black ice, I guess. Unfortunately, we were just ahead of the sand truck."

"Do you want a ride home?" Elizabeth asked.

"No, Buddy thinks we can drive the car, but thanks," said David.

"Well, take care, glad no one was hurt. Might just be a big storm coming," Catherine added.

Slowly Elizabeth pulled away, glad that the sand truck had come by. The windshield wipers swept the sleet aside. Occasionally, however, an actual raindrop hit the windshield.

All day the sleet continued, striking the windows as the winds picked up. On the radio and TV, the highway patrol encouraged everyone to stay put and stay off the roads unless absolutely necessary. The speed limit for traffic on I-95 was reduced to 40 mph, but several accidents had already been reported. A tractor-trailer had jackknifed just north of Augusta in the southbound direction and temporarily closed off those lanes. The temperature vacillated between twenty-nine and thirty-three. A few times the lights in the house flickered, but they remained on.

Elizabeth, Catherine, Marty, and Janet were housebound, quite an unusual situation given all their routine scheduled activities. None of them could go out, so they began to settle in. There was no telling how long this storm would last. The news reported that the Buffalo area had received three feet of snow, paralyzing the city. This time New York was getting just rain. The weather along the Maine coast was hard to predict because of the warming effect of the ocean. An hour inland, conditions could be quite different.

Elizabeth took the opportunity to speak to everyone about her granddaughter coming to visit. As they gathered for lunchtime soup, she broached the subject, telling about the letter she had received.

"I'm not exactly sure why Alcee has made this request, but I do think it is a call for help, and God knows we grandmothers need to be there when asked," Elizabeth explained. "She can stay in the extra room, so it shouldn't cause any big disruption. She's really a very sweet kid."

"Well, I don't see any problem," said Janet immediately.

Catherine agreed. "You have been so generous to let us try out this Winter House idea; there's certainly room for your granddaughter."

"It's none of my business," Marty said, "but I think you have a right to be a bit concerned. Maybe she'll tell you more when you respond to her."

"Maybe," Elizabeth said. "Her school recess is only two weeks, so she won't want to stay here too long."

"Unless she prefers living with a bunch of old ladies," Janet added.

"Well, we'll see. I will extend the invitation to her today, and we'll put it on the calendar. It should liven up January a bit," Elizabeth said.

The sleet hit the windows harder. Beyond the porch a stand of tall, thin birch trees drooped over, a few of their tops imbedded in the snow on the ground. Elizabeth had never seen this before and feared they would snap, but Catherine assured her that in the spring, most of the trees would stand up tall again.

"Under the weight of the ice, the flexible trees will bend and survive, but the stronger, stiffer limbs of the oak can snap," Catherine added. When she was about eight, her Uncle Cyrus had taught her that, and he had insisted that one's life could be like that, too. It was years later that Catherine fully understood what he was trying to say, and then she tried to picture herself as a lissome, youthful birch tree.

Marty and Janet invited the other two to join them in the living room for some yoga. But Catherine wanted to start working on her income-tax form, and Elizabeth planned to email her granddaughter. Neither objected to a little quiet music, so the house filled with Puccini. Marty and Janet practiced their yoga standing positions. A sun salutation seemed a bit ironic, as no sun would be shining for quite a while.

Both of them had been making progress on their shoulder stands, but they decided to wait until Thursday to have Beth instruct and spot them. The gains that they had achieved through slow baby steps and stretching were impressive. Marty could now put her socks on with much less difficulty, and cutting her toenails was easier. Janet had never been able to sit on her knees without two blankets under them. Now she could rest comfortably on the back of her legs and experience no knee stress. There was little doubt that yoga was helping to maintain their flexibility, and in this small town it also added to their socialization. Getting to know Marty, at first through Beth's yoga class and now in the Winter House, had begun to pull Janet out of her hibernation. She really hadn't thought about it but avoiding alcohol now was much easier. Janet was slowly creating a life beyond John. She was faithfully using her full-spectrum sun lamp in the evening, and for her, living in the house with others was a positive change.

The telephone rang. Catherine, who was the only one without a cell phone, usually answered it first. "I'll get it," she said, as she turned toward the kitchen. It was Catherine's eye doctor's office.

The secretary spoke: "We just want to be sure you are all set with your transportation needs for the cataract operation scheduled for next week.

"Yes, I think so," Catherine replied. "My daughter will bring me in and one of my housemates is driving me home once Dr. Leonard says I am ready to leave. About how long do you think the operation and recovery period will take? My friend Pat was back by lunch," Catherine added.

"Yes, Mrs. Howard, if all goes well, you'll be home for lunch." Catherine had many friends who had had cataract operations. She had learned from her son Will, the ophthalmologist, that it was the most common surgery in people over the age of sixty-five. Catherine had been quite lucky to make it until seventy-nine before requiring the operation. For the last two years, she had limited her driving after dark, as oncoming headlights caused an irritating glare, creating a halo. This summer Will insisted that she not wait any longer, adding that some people deferred correction until it seemed as if they were looking through waxed paper. He told his mother that after surgery most folks were ready right away to have the other eye fixed; they wondered why they delayed so long. His encouraging remarks had made her move ahead.

Catherine double-checked her calendar. Yes, in big letters she had written CATARACT OUT. She had faith in Dr. Leonard and hoped all would go well.

By evening the freezing rain had not let up. Forecasts predicted the same through the night and possibly the next day. Power outages were occurring all around the Bangor area, as bending and snapping branches downed electric lines. Bangor Hydro was reporting over 15,000 people affected, and more problems were expected. The women of the Winter House were safe and warm, and at least three of them were somewhat accustomed to the variation in weather. The well-known January thaw was right on course. Amazing what the difference of a few degrees could make. An old rule of thumb that Uncle Cyrus preached was "one inch of rain makes ten inches of snow." Ever since she was little, Catherine loved snow, the more, the better. Even now she found the white blanket of Maine winters exquisitely beautiful. She also knew that "April showers bring May flowers" — another of Uncle Cyrus's favorite sayings — but rain in January was an unwelcome guest at her table. It could wash away all the snow, or soak it and then freeze solid into ice.

"Anyone for Bananagrams?" asked Elizabeth, wanting to get her mind off the weather and off her granddaughter, Alcee, who had not yet responded to her grandmother's email.

"Sure, I'll play," said Marty.

"Me too," added Janet. Catherine joined in as well, and for an hour or more, the crossword game distracted the foursome.

"Peel!" Marty called out, and each of them drew another letter, fitting it into her words. Elizabeth and Catherine, who loved crossword puzzles, were facile at using up their letters. Marty struggled with making longer words. Unlike Scrabble, Bananagrams went much faster and kept everyone's attention. Before they knew it, it was a reasonable hour to go to sleep. The lights flickered occasionally but still remained on. The generator had been checked in the fall, and Elizabeth hoped it would do its job and turn on, if necessary. Cliff had been determined when they winterized the house that he would not be caught without TV and a wireless connection — or the furnace, for that matter. Elizabeth was glad to have this fallback, which was somewhat of a luxury.

Catherine didn't walk Quigley too far in these conditions. The sidewalk was extremely slick, even though they had thrown some salt crystals on the walkway. She noticed the branches of the apple tree by the back door coated with a thick layer of ice. One apple that had stayed on the tree glistened like a crystal ball, reflecting the back-door light. Quigley quickly sprinkled the snow bank and came back to the door. The wind continued to gust from the northeast as Catherine shut the door. January was playing its wintry tricks.

"Good night, everyone," Catherine said, walking down the hall to her room. The other women collected their things and made their way upstairs.

"Let's hope that tomorrow the weather will break," said Elizabeth.

"It would just be so much better if the temperature dropped for snow or rose for rain. This ice mixture is rough," replied Marty. Missy ran upstairs first to find her favorite spot on Marty's bed.

"Well, good night. See you in the morning," Janet said. The Winter House lights went out one by one as the women prepared to sleep.

Elizabeth checked her email one more time. Alcee had responded, and now Elizabeth lay in bed thinking about her granddaughter, who had requested a visit next week. Alcee asked if she could stay ten days and then return on an Alitalia flight, which would get her back in time for the last semester. It would be good to have some quality time with her granddaughter. Alcee could take the bus directly from the Boston airport to Bangor, saving Elizabeth about a ten-hour round trip, and who knew what the winter driving would be like next week. Elizabeth planned to call her Boston-based children, Michael and Libby, to check their schedules.

The gusts blew against her windowpane. Elizabeth counted sheep.

At 5:30 a.m. Catherine woke to a loud humming sound that appeared to be coming from the backside of the house. She tiptoed out to the kitchen, trying not to disturb Quigley, who was still sound asleep on her bed. As she approached the kitchen door, she figured it out. The generator must have come on in the middle of the night. The kitchen light worked, and the stove clock was blinking. The thermostat read 64, so the furnace was working too. It was still dark outside, and the wind had subsided a little. Catherine turned on the radio at a very low volume.

"Well, so far, this isn't exactly the Great Ice Storm of '98," the announcer proclaimed, "but we do have at least 50,000 people out of power at this time in the greater Bangor area and western Hancock County. Emergency crews are out trying to get the lines back up. Unlike what happened in 1998, we predicted that this ice might cause power outages, and the teams were prepared. And luckily," he went on, "the temperature will begin climbing into the upper thirties by tonight before the rains end. Then we'll drop back into more seasonal temperatures."

Catherine wondered how many folks in Brooks Harbor were affected. She would call her daughter in a few hours. Her good friend Pat and her husband, David, always seemed to lose their power, Catherine remembered. Unfortunately, they had only an oil furnace — no woodstove because of David's asthma. Catherine wondered if they were warm enough.

The radio announcer continued, "Several power lines are down. Please stay clear of the downed lines. Crews are trying to get to these first, as soon as they can. Do not try to drive under a live wire. We are now broadcasting from an alternative tower, as our lines on the Brewer towers are down."

"What's going on?" Marty asked, as she entered the kitchen a bit earlier than usual.

"The power's out in many places, and we are now on the generator," Catherine replied.

"Ah, that's lucky. I had contemplated getting a generator last winter but postponed it. I guess Elizabeth's husband made a wise choice for this house. We are quite a way down Spruce Point Lane. It may be a while before we get our electricity back."

"Well, we should see if we can call Bangor Hydro and put our address on the list."

Catherine lifted the phone. "We do have a dial tone. I'll let Elizabeth call and report it when she gets up. Probably no rush." Catherine went to make the coffee. Quigley stretched, doing his "downward-facing dog", then right leg back, then left leg back.

Later that morning the Blakey boys came over to check on the ladies and perhaps to warm up a bit. They enjoyed the hot coffee and some warm cinnamon rolls that Catherine had thrown together. They reported having removed several branches that had fallen across the driveway. Jerry speculated that one limb had stretched the electric line, triggering a shutdown. The south side of town was completely out, though, and the north side had some spotty outages. Jimmy, who usually said very little, described almost poetically the appearance of the icy coating on the trees. He felt it was a sparkling wonderland. Jerry was more concerned with the slick roads and seemed eager to get back to help the volunteer firemen clear the roadways.

"Glad your generator is working for you," Jerry said. "We need to keep our woodstove going, but we are lucky the temp is supposed to rise and not fall. If the temp were dropping, we'd all have trouble with our pipes...well, not you, ladies. I'll be sure to check on Mr. and Mrs. Sullivan and send them over to warm up." Jerry smiled at Catherine and reached for the doorknob. Jimmy followed.

"Thanks for the roll and coffee," Jimmy said.

All day the temperature stayed right at freezing, but by evening, as predicted, it rose to thirty-six and things began to melt. Catherine and Quigley ventured outside for some fresh air. The boys returned to say that half of Brooks Harbor had gotten the electricity back on. It turned out that a major supply line had gone down when a large, rotten pine had fallen. They predicted the rest of the town would have power on by morning. The crews would work through the night before the temperatures dropped again. According to Jerry, Pat and David were glad to have had their heat restored by afternoon and sent their regards.

Elizabeth had prepared a Pad Thai meal using some frozen shrimp. She loved the hot, sweet-and-pungent Thai flavors and always tried to keep flat rice noodles on hand. As Marty poured Elizabeth and herself a glass of Sauvignon Blanc, Elizabeth's cell phone rang. She looked at the caller ID and smiled.

"Hello, Eve" Elizabeth said to her sister.

"Oh, dear Lizzy, I am so glad to reach you. We've heard that lots of folks in Maine don't have any electricity due to the big ice storm. I hope you are keeping warm somehow. I told you that you should not live in that godforsaken place.

Why don't you pack up and come down to Florida, where it is 79 degrees and just lovely?" Eve inhaled.

"We're doing just fine, Eve. Actually, we find it rather adventurous to have no heat and get bundled up. Our food rations may dwindle soon, but we will survive. You know how tough and crazy your little sister is." Elizabeth laughed and took a swig of her wine.

"Are you kidding me?" Eve asked. "I think you are really nuts!"

"Well, in truth, Cliff had a generator installed, so we ladies are living comfortably in the lap of luxury. We are just fine, really."

"Oh, that makes me feel better. I just hated to picture you all freezing up there."

"No, nothing like that. We are warm and cozy and just sitting down to dinner," Elizabeth had little more to say to her sister. "But thanks for calling."

"Well, you are welcome, my dear. I won't keep you any longer. Give my best to all your housemates." Eve hung up.

Elizabeth laughed with Marty. Funny, how Florida was paradise for some, while others found it too hot and flat.

"Dinner's ready," Elizabeth called. Janet and Catherine came to the table, and the women sat down to dinner. As they rose to clear the dishes, the lights blinked once and the generator humming stopped.

Catherine and Janet were just finishing the dishes when the phone rang. Catherine answered and heard: "This is a recording from Bangor Hydro. Your service should now be on. Please call if you have any further difficulties. Good-bye."

"Well," Catherine said, "I guess the Winter House has successfully made it through this ice storm. She hoped the other residents of Brooks Harbor had their power back too.

About a week later Elizabeth's cell phone rang. "Nonna, I made it!" Alcee declared over the cell phone. "I'm getting on the bus now and should be in Bangor in about five hours."

"Great, honey, I will meet you at the bus station. So glad you're here. See you soon." Elizabeth tidied up the guest room one more time. She fluffed the pillow and resituated the little, stuffed animals — a black bear and a brown moose — that her children used to play with. On the bedside table she placed her favorite photo of Alcee, Nell, and herself, taken in Italy in November. In this picture Elizabeth could see the clear family resemblance.

The hour drive to Bangor to meet the bus gave Elizabeth time to think. On the return trip she wanted to talk with Alcee and find out just what had precipitated this rather urgent visit. Elizabeth cautioned herself to be patient and let her granddaughter address the reason in her own time. Patience was not one of Elizabeth's strongest characteristics, but she continued to work on it; in fact she had been working on it for years.

Elizabeth thought about Nell, Alcee's mother, and the friction the two had had during Nell's teenage years. It had been tough. Nell, the youngest, was a handful, for sure, and her father was gone often with his work. Nell had been her own person from the moment she was born. The colic lasted for months, it seemed. Then there was the stage when Nell would go to preschool only if her father took her. That was a challenge for their schedules, but they worked it out somehow. At Greenwich Country Day School, Nell was tiny, feisty, athletic, and bright. Her teachers loved her, but she was a moody child at home. Libby, who was six years older, connected with Nell the best, but then Libby left for her freshman year at Yale just when Nell was entering junior high school — a period that was hell for Nell and worse for Elizabeth.

Abruptly, Elizabeth was pulled back to the moment. The truck driver ahead of her came to a sudden stop, and she slammed on her brakes, stopping just in time. Luckily, the roads were clear of ice, or she might have hit him. "Damn it!" she swore, not knowing the reason for the stop. Then she saw the yellow bus with its flashing red lights. Two little boys ran across the street to their mobile home. Their mother waited on the other side to greet them. The blinking lights stopped, and the school bus moved on.

Elizabeth looked at her car clock: 12:15 p.m. She had another forty-five minutes until Alcee's bus arrived. It would be close, and she wanted to be there waiting for her granddaughter. With only three traffic lights between Brooks Harbor and the Union Street bus station in Bangor, she was confident she could make it, barring any more school buses.

Elizabeth returned to her thoughts...

Nell had thrown herself into art class at Darien High School, neglecting her studies. Though Elizabeth certainly understood this love of art, she insisted that Nell do well academically to get into a good college.

Her daughter fumed. "I don't need to go to college. Van Gogh never did!"

"Well, you are not Vincent Van Gogh, and you are going to college. And that's it," Elizabeth shouted at Nell.

"Daddy won't make me," Nell replied, heading out of the room.

"We'll see," Elizabeth retorted.

Nell continued trying to divide and conquer. In the end,

for senior year, her parents sent Nell away to Kent School in Connecticut, where a skillful and sensitive art teacher convinced her to go to Rhode Island School of Design. That lasted three semesters until she took off for a semester-abroad program in Rome. Living a bohemian lifestyle with five other students, Nell was enchanted with Italy and Italian men. When she got pregnant, she kept it a secret from her parents for a long time. Actually, Nell first told her sister, Libby, who later broke it to her parents. It wasn't terribly shocking, but the unexpected surprise was that Nell planned to keep the baby, though she had no intention of marrying. To be completely honest, Nell wasn't sure which Italian lover was the father. She just knew she wanted the child.

When a baby girl arrived, Nell named her Alcina, meaning "strong willed" in Italian. Elizabeth and Cliff flew to Italy to help out. Nell seemed happy to see them. Sometime after that, Nell's attitude toward her parents, especially her mother, began to soften somewhat, and they had grown closer slowly over the next eighteen years. Perhaps it was the Atlantic Ocean that gave Nell her own space. From a distance, she seemed to have done well with motherhood. Of course, in the first several years Giuseppe and Anjelica, Nell's landlords, helped out often with Alcee. They were like foster grandparents. Nell's reputation in modern-art circles grew in time, and she gained a confidence and sophistication that Elizabeth admired. She thought her daughter and granddaughter had a pretty good life abroad.

At five minutes to one o'clock, Elizabeth arrived at the bus station. She parked and hurried inside to the ladies' room. Upon exiting, she saw the Concord Trailways bus pull in. Standing outside the bus, she thought she caught a glimpse of Alcee through the tinted glass; at least, some-body was waving. Several people disembarked before Al-cee stepped off the bus, carrying a small purple backpack, wearing a red hat and a long black coat. Her high, black-leather boots reminded Elizabeth of some she had bought in Italy several years ago.

"Nonna," Alcee said, as she gave her grandmother a big hug.

"Welcome back to Maine, my sweet," Elizabeth replied, kissing her on both cheeks.

"I have another small bag. *Un minuto, per favore*," Al-cee said, as she went to get the suitcase from the pile by the bus.

The sun poked through the clouds as grandmother and granddaughter climbed into the Toyota and headed back to Brooks Harbor. They spoke about the flight and the bus ride, which had all gone well. Alcee expressed appreciation for her grandmother's paying the airfare and allowing her to come.

"I'm just delighted that you wanted to visit me," Elizabeth said.

Alcee asked about the ladies who were now living with her grandmother. "What is it like, having such a change? Does everyone get along?"

"Well, it's different. Not exactly like having Papa around, and I do miss him," her grandmother replied.

Alcee missed her Papa Cliff, too. He had really been the only father figure Alcee had known except maybe for Giuseppe.

Elizabeth continued, "We all seem to be doing okay so far, and they stay busy with many outside activities. I'm trying to get back into painting after all these years."

"Really?" Alcee said, with a rather flat affect.

Elizabeth reached for her sunglasses while Alcee struggled to pull off her heavy coat. Both looked ahead.

"You have very little traffic here," Alcee said. She was thinking of the crowded avenues back home.

"Yes, I must admit I do not miss the traffic jams in New York City," her grandmother replied. "Maine has a slower pace and a lot more open space, and I'm getting to appreciate it."

"Yes, I suppose one could," Alcee agreed. Sweat dripped below her armpit. She was nervous and knew that her grandmother was waiting to hear why she had come all this way from Italy over the school break. Alcee thought of her grandmother as a very perceptive person, and when she was little, she used to believe that Nonna could read her thoughts. Now she wondered if her grandmother had already guessed the reason for her coming. Elizabeth turned on the radio at low volume. Alcee looked out the window. "It is white and beautiful here." Alcee said. "This year we have had much rain and cold at home. I remember only twice when it snowed in Siena, and it melted fast."

"We just got over a small ice storm, but otherwise it hasn't been too bad for my first winter in Maine." Elizabeth's stomach growled, and she realized she hadn't asked Alcee about lunch. "Are you hungry, dear?"

"I could use a little something, but anything will do."

Elizabeth pulled into a Subway sandwich store that had just opened on the outskirts of Bangor. "Do you have Subway shops in Italy?"

"Oh, yes, we do."

They ordered a foot-long chicken cordon bleu and split it. Alcee took her half with jalapeño peppers and hot mustard sauce, while her grandmother asked for mayonnaise — no onions, peppers, or hot sauce. They sat at the small booth, smiling at each other.

"I'm really glad you're here," Elizabeth said.

"Me too."

Both were hungry and finished off their halves. Alcee wiped her fingers after consuming most of the barbecue chips.

"Shall we continue home?" Elizabeth asked.

"*Andiamo!*" Alcee knew her grandmother loved to hear Italian and thought she'd surprise her every once in awhile. Here in America, however, she wanted to speak mostly English.

"*Bueno, andiamo!*" her grandmother replied.

Back in the car there was silence. Elizabeth had decided to stop making small talk and see if Alcee would open up. Silence can be a powerful tool. Alcee dug into her bag for her sunglasses. The glare of the sun on the snow was intense.

Alcee's pulse increased. "Nonna," she said, "I'm sure you are wondering why I wanted to come to see you. I want to tell you my problem, but it is difficult, and I feel so bad."

Elizabeth kept her eyes on the road. "I'm ready to hear, but you must feel ready to tell. Take your time."

Alcee turned to face her grandmother, who continued to look ahead. Then the girl let out a long sigh and took a deep breath. "I'm pregnant, Nonna," she said, as though apologizing, "and..." Alcee choked up. She wanted to be honest with her grandmother, and the next statement was going to be the hardest. She turned from her grandmother and looked out the side window. Elizabeth said nothing. Alcee sighed again. Her chest ached and her heart pounded inside. "And...I want to get an abortion here." There, she'd said it...she believed it...well, maybe she believed it...she needed to believe it. How much should she tell her grandmother...how much *could* she tell her grandmother...her mother's mother? The circle had gone around...like mother, like daughter...history was repeating itself...and yet she wanted to control her own destiny.

"I don't want to do what Mamma did," Alcee blurted out. She glanced at her grandmother for a reaction. There was none. She looked again out the side window and whispered softly, *"Un bambino ha bisogno di un padre."* She wiped her cheek, sniffled, and leaned her forehead against the window.

Elizabeth understood. A kid needs a father. She paused and then asked, "Is it Fabio?"

"Oh, yes, Nonna, the father is Fabio, and I love him, but he is not ready to be a father, he says, and I'm not sure I am ready to be a mother. It was a stupid mistake. We were trying to be careful, really. I don't want Mamma to know." She sniffled.

Elizabeth's mind flooded with memories, but she wanted to filter them. She heard her own mother saying in her warning tone, "You should save sex until you're married. Good girls don't fool around." Her father told her once if she got pregnant before marriage, he would send her to Sweden for an abortion. Her older cousin had told her about the rhythm method of birth control. Nell hadn't asked her mother about sex—or abortion, for that matter. She wanted the baby. She insisted she could do it. Maybe she wanted some love that she hadn't gotten from her own parents. What did Elizabeth feel about abortion? Cliff and she had never faced that question, either before marriage or after.

Alcee tried to collect herself. She had gone round and round about this trip, this plan, their plan. Fabio was the eldest of nine, five sisters and three brothers. The family was poor and needed support from Fabio, who could make good money at sea as a merchant mariner. He had almost completed his training and would soon explore the world and send money back home. But he could not support another family or stay home to be a father. Alcee had her own dreams too, and they did not include being a mother at eighteen. In fact, she was not sure she ever wanted to be a mother, and certainly not a single mom.

"Unfortunately, accidents happen, honey." Elizabeth said. She wondered if Alcee had used any type of birth control but didn't ask.

"We love each other, Fabio and me, really...I mean, for now...but I don't see marrying him, and I would want my baby to have a normal family." She started to cry again, putting her head in her hands. "It has been hard, Nonna," she said softly. And then she was silent.

Elizabeth wanted to give Alcee a big hug and promise her that things would work out. Maybe having this discussion in the car wasn't the best place, but it was too late now, and it had provided the private space for Alcee to talk and cry. She reached her hand over to Alcee's lap, and they joined hands. Elizabeth gave a firm squeeze.

Years ago another car conversation had ended in tears. Cliff and Elizabeth had landed at LaGuardia after their visit to be with Nell and her newborn. It had been so hard to return to New York that spring. Elizabeth had wanted Nell to move back to the United States after she had her baby, but Nell would have none of that. She wanted to stay in Italy, and at twenty she felt she could handle things on her own.

Despite his concerns for his daughter and granddaughter, which were mostly financial, Cliff had insisted that they respect Nell's wishes. Elizabeth had contemplated moving to Italy, but Cliff's job was tied to Wall Street. She had wept in the car all the way back to their home in Darien.

As the years passed, her granddaughter grew up across the Atlantic, and Elizabeth had seen Alcee only a few times a year, if that. She regretted getting such a narrow view of her granddaughter's childhood — and her daughter's life, for that matter. The two summers that Alcee came to Brooks Harbor had been wonderful, and their bond was sealed, but by then Alcee's childhood was ending, and she was becoming a teenager.

During Elizabeth's childhood in Vermont, her grandparents lived in the next town. Gramps had taught her how to collect maple syrup, identify trees, dig for worms, and catch pollywogs, while Grams instructed Elizabeth on baking perfect oatmeal-lace cookies. Grams would also help Elizabeth fold the fluffy egg whites into warm tapioca pudding. Just about every Sunday for many years, her extended family had come together for dinner. But that was almost sixty years ago, and times had definitely changed. This was a mobile society now. Many families lived apart, way apart, in other states and other countries. Around here only the Maine natives could claim four generations within twenty-five miles, if not five miles, of each other.

After quite a long silence, Alcee asked, "Are we almost there?" Her grandmother appeared lost in her own thoughts.

"Oh, oh, yes, dear...it's just another five or ten minutes. How are you doing?"

"Well, I'm getting a little sleepy. I couldn't sleep too well on the plane, and then on the bus I was just nervous and excited." Alcee yawned.

"You can lie down really soon. I've fixed up the guest room for you, and you can sleep as long as you want. We'll all try to be quiet."

"I have my earplugs anyway, and I don't think anything can keep me awake." Alcee paused and then added, "We need to talk more about this week, but maybe after I have had some sleep."

"We can do that, for sure," her grandmother said.

As they rounded the corner at Martin's Cove, Elizabeth saw Alcee's head hanging forward. She had fallen asleep. Elizabeth turned onto Spruce Point Road and then down her driveway. Alcee's exhaustion had overwhelmed her anxiety.

When the car pulled into the garage, the tired traveler awoke.

"We're here," Elizabeth whispered. "Let's get you to bed, honey."

Catherine's car was gone. Elizabeth remembered this was Catherine's afternoon to read at the library, and Janet would be over at Simon Kirby's place, reading him a classic. Janet was a dedicated hospice volunteer, and she found it a pleasure to read *The Iliad* aloud.

Quigley barked when Elizabeth and her granddaughter entered, but he quickly stopped and went right up to Alcee for a pat. Catherine left her dog at home when it was too cold for him to be left in the car. Quigley had his special spot in the living room on the red stuffed chair, where he watched the driveway, awaiting Catherine's return.

Elizabeth showed Alcee the guest room, pulled back the bed covers, and pulled down the blinds to shut out the bright afternoon sun. Alcee took little time to drop her bags, take off her black jeans, and climb into bed.

"Have a good nap, dear," her grandmother said. "You can meet the others when you are rested.

"Thanks, Nonna." Alcee rolled over with the blanket covering her head.

Elizabeth closed the door and headed upstairs to do a little reading or take a nap herself. It had been quite an exhausting afternoon. As she passed Marty's room, Elizabeth noticed her housemate working on her computer. Marty liked keeping connected to her friends and even corresponded with a few former patients. She turned to greet Elizabeth.

"I see you made it back," Marty said. "How is your granddaughter?"

"She's exhausted from the trip, and I've just put her to bed. She'll be more ready to meet you all a bit later."

Marty's concern and curiosity took over. "How are you doing? You look worried."

"Yes, I am afraid it is going to be quite a visit." Elizabeth wanted to tell someone about the situation. She was acutely aware of not having Cliff to discuss this family crisis with. Alcee had told her that she was determined not to tell her mother about her plans for an abortion. She was afraid it would hurt her mother to know that her own daughter did not want to follow the same pattern — keep the child and raise the child alone. Though Alcee dearly loved her mother, she could not forgive her for bringing her into the world without a father present. Elizabeth felt that Nell should know about the pregnancy and that Alcee should be the one to tell her. Elizabeth didn't have a firm opinion on abortion, thought each case was unique, but felt that the decision should be up to the pregnant woman, ideally along with the father's agreement. She knew, for sure, that being wanted from the start was important. Alcee was eighteen. If she were convinced she loved her boyfriend and wanted to get married and keep the baby, would Elizabeth object? Or if she wanted to keep the baby and raise it as Nell did, could she object?

"Do you want to talk about it?" Marty asked. She could see the stress lines on Elizabeth's face. Her years of practice as a caring physician had honed this skill.

"That might help. It might be good to bounce this off someone, like you, with experience." Elizabeth sat down on Marty's bed. Missy hopped off. "I know you sensed something was wrong when Alcee's letter arrived. I had a hunch but tried to play down my concerns. But, you were right; it's big. Alcee tells me she's pregnant and wants to get an abortion now, while she's here. She hasn't told her mother. Nell is apparently in the dark about this. I don't know the first thing about abortions. When I was a senior at Middlebury, rumor had it that the assistant women's soccer coach had gone for one after getting pregnant by a married professor."

Marty raised her eyebrows.

Elizabeth continued, "But really, Marty, do you know how one gets an abortion these days in Maine? And what should we do about Nell? Have you counseled young women on these issues?"

Marty was trying to figure out where to start to advise her housemate, and at the same time, she couldn't help but relive what she herself had gone through many years ago. Not until she met Abigail, her closest confidante, had she told anyone about her own abortion. She never spoke of it, not even to her mother or father. She used to have dreams about the baby she could have had but never did. Back then, she saw no other choice; her marriage had failed, and she wanted to follow her dream of medical school. Her successful and satisfying medical practice convinced her that it had been the right decision for her. But there was still no denying that for her it had meant keeping a long and lonely secret.

Marty began, "You should be pleased that Alcee feels close enough to you to share her situation. It seems you have successfully stayed in her life, even living across the Atlantic. Do you think she has really thought this through?"

"She and her boyfriend, Fabio, have discussed it, so that's good. Neither feels ready to be a parent. Fabio comes from a large family and helps his parents with the younger brothers and sisters. He wants to travel on the seas, and Alcee doesn't want to have a baby without a willing father. She is quite adamant about it. I guess being raised by Nell alone was harder for Alcee than she ever let on. Even though the definition of family has changed over the last few decades in some circles, her vision of a family is a mother and a father with a child wanted by both." This made Elizabeth think of the name Nell had chosen for her daughter, who now was indeed quite determined and strong willed.

"Well, certainly that has been the most traditional concept of a family," Marty said. She was well aware of other permutations, including gay marriage and artificial insemination. "What do you think Nell would think about all of this? She might be quite hurt that her daughter has elected not to confide in her."

"Nell has been very involved in her art and the new gallery that she is trying to open. She's always been very determined and may just have her priorities a bit out of whack. Now that Alcee is eighteen, I figure Nell might want to just live her own life, having had to be Alcee's sole parent. Oh, Nell's had significant boyfriends on and off but never found a strong enough man for her. Well, that's my opinion, for what it's worth. Her art career has always been her driving force."

"Elizabeth, you could talk to Alcee about telling her mother. Somehow, from experience in my practice, I find the bond of the mother-daughter relationship usually strengthens over this issue, though I have dealt with some exceptions." Marty thought about her mother, who died from ovarian cancer about ten years after Marty's abortion. Her mother suffered from depression, and Marty had tried to spare her any stress. It was her father, a busy surgeon, whom Marty usually confided in, and later, when they had medicine in common, conversations were easy. But she never could quite discuss the abortion with her father, even though he would have completely understood her desire to go on to medical school.

"I suppose I should at least try," Elizabeth agreed. "I think Alcee will be willing to tell her mother, but I don't know if she will do it before or after the abortion. Because she's eighteen, I don't think she needs any parental permission."

"Well, that's right. In fact, as far as I know now in Maine, parental consent or notification is not required for abortions, even for minors. Other states have different rules. But I think, at least, notification is preferred."

"Do you have any idea where she could get an abortion,

and how long she can be pregnant to get a first-trimester abortion?" Elizabeth inquired.

"These days they do both medical and surgical abortions in the first trimester. My experience was only with the surgical or suction-aspiration type. Those can be done any time before fourteen weeks of gestation. In Vermont we did them in our office after the Roe v. Wade decision of 1973. Before that, abortions were done for decades in the shadows," Marty said. Her mind flashed to the back staircase on Willard Street in Burlington so many years before.

"Where could she have it done?" asked Elizabeth.

"There's a women's health center in Bangor where women go for these particular needs. I know a physician's assistant who has worked there in the past. I could call her and get some more information if you'd like."

"First, I guess I should just speak more with Alcee about this. If she's agreeable, maybe you could even talk with her. You sure are more familiar with all this than I am," Elizabeth said, and yet she had no idea just how familiar Marty really was with it. "I'm going to make some tea. Would you care for any?" Elizabeth inquired.

"Sure, I'll be down in just a minute." Marty wanted to clear her brain and push the old images back into their closet. More than fifty years ago she had made her own decision. Imagine, she thought, her child would be almost fifty-two. Amazing. Her eyes watered a bit, even after all these years. For her it had been the right decision, but it hadn't been easy.

Catherine and Janet arrived home at the same time. Both chatted about their afternoon reading. The children at the library had been full of energy but listened well to

Catherine's reading of *Now We Are Six*. It was one of Catherine's favorite old-time children's books. The love of Christopher Robin for Winnie-the-Pooh was tender, and Walt Disney had certainly brought the story alive. One little boy said he liked Eeyore best.

Janet smiled at the contrast between Winnie the Pooh in *Now We are Six* and her reading aloud of *The Iliad* to Simon Kirby, now in his nineties. Today they had discussed Achilles, the great Greek warrior, and the origin of the phrase *Achilles' heel*. Simon had spoken of the myth of Achilles' mother, Thetis, dipping her son into the river Styx to make him invulnerable; yet in dipping, she had failed to protect his heel. This partial weakness ultimately led to his death. Ah, Simon had such a sharp mind.

As Janet and Catherine entered the kitchen, Elizabeth said, "Just in time for tea." Marty came downstairs, and they all gathered at the kitchen table. With their busy schedules, the four women had not sat down for tea very often, but it was the depth of winter, and the warmth of the kitchen brought them together.

That evening Marty prepared a roasted chicken, sweet potatoes, and green beans covered with toasted almonds. Alcee woke to the aroma of chicken and emerged from her slumber. At dinner she met Elizabeth's housemates, who all voiced their pleasure in having her visit. Marty remarked that Alcee's green-colored eyes resembled her grandmother's. Conversation centered on the trip, the weather, the snow, and the meal. After dessert Alcee could not conceal her yawning or keep her eyes open. Her grandmother encouraged her to go back to bed. It had been a long trip.

"Good night, everyone," Alcee said. "Thank you for having me. I will see you in the morning."

"Good night, dear. Sleep in as late as you'd like. I'll be here all morning," Elizabeth said. Alcee kissed her grandmother on both cheeks, just as she had done for so many years. Elizabeth was happy to have her here but knew they had many things to do in the morning.

Catherine was up early, ready for her cataract surgery. She had slept well after talking with her son Will, who reassured her that everything would go just fine. In a way, she wished he were doing the operation. He had a stellar reputation in northern New Jersey, but she trusted Dr. Leonard, who had been her ophthalmologist for about five years. Patients described him as "New Age" because his office had all the bells and whistles, and he was trained in the newest surgical techniques. Dr. Martin, an ophthalmologist she had seen for thirty-five years, had collapsed one day sitting on his stool in the office. Heart attack, they said. He'd changed her prescriptions for glasses for years, but he didn't seem to be keeping up with the times. Catherine chuckled to herself. Dr. Martin used to call himself a "dinosaur,"...kind fellow, though.

She wasn't allowed to eat or drink anything, so she just took a slightly slower walk to the mailbox with Quigley for the newspaper and then awaited the arrival of her daughter, Sarah, who would drive her to Ellsworth. This outpatient procedure fascinated Catherine, and she was certainly ready to say good-bye to her cloudy lens and obtain a new clear view of the world.

Knocking first, Sarah walked into the Winter House kitchen. Her mother pulled her coat back on and picked up her hat and gloves. "I'm just about ready, dear, " Catherine said. "You're right on time, as usual." Sarah was now manager of DownEast Trust Bank, and efficiency and promptness probably had something to do with her success. Catherine patted Quigley on the head, gave him a dog biscuit, and promised she'd be back soon.

Janet reviewed with Catherine the address of Dr. Leonard's office. Picking Catherine up after the procedure would be no inconvenience, as Janet was training some hospice volunteers until about noon in Ellsworth.

"Thank you for driving my mother home after her surgery. I can stay until she gets to the recovery room, but then I'll have to get back to the bank," Sarah said.

"No problem, we'll have her back here this afternoon, good as new." Janet smiled.

"We're off," Catherine chimed in. "Wish me luck!"

"Good luck, you'll do fine," Janet added. As a nurse, Janet knew that the outlook of the patient played a significant role in the speed of recovery, and few people were as upbeat as Catherine.

"Good luck," said Marty. "See you for lunch."

Quigley ran to his favorite vantage point and watched Catherine leave. He might not budge from that spot until she returned safe and sound. Janet and Marty poured themselves some coffee. They divided up the *Bangor Daily News* and began to read.

Marty checked out the sports section for the Boston Bruins hockey score and skimmed the local reporting for any news on the Blue Hill Hospital. Serving on the board of directors of the hospital was turning out to be a challenge, as Marty was only one of three physicians currently functioning in that capacity, and a takeover by the regional healthcare system was in the works. Of course, she was probably a bit more old-fashioned than the two younger docs, though she had the advantage of having worked with hospital administrators for many years. The only woman on the board, she sometimes felt outnumbered. Nevertheless, she was respected for always calling a spade a spade and identifying the elephant in the room.

Janet read the obituaries and noticed that many listed Hospice as a charity for donations. Hospice Volunteers of Hancock County had been established more than thirty years ago, and Janet had been volunteering ever since she had moved to the area. In fact, she recalled it would be twenty-five years in March. Again she remembered that she had first met Catherine when she was assigned to Harold, Catherine's husband, about twelve years ago. Catherine had been so strong, and Harold such a dear man. Janet had met many special people and their family members, all faced with end-of-life issues and the loss of a loved one. Even through her own personal struggles, Janet continued working with these families. That work had kept her going after her divorce, those rather lonely single years before she met John, and then during these past three years since his death. Giving to others was a gift to herself.

"Looks like a beautiful winter day today," Janet said. "Maybe we should go out for a cross-country ski this afternoon. Are you going to be around?"

"I should be here unless something comes up," Marty replied.

"I am picking Catherine up after her surgery, and then we will be home. If it stays sunny, it would be fun to just go around the Websters' field for a bit of exercise. If it clouds up and gets colder, maybe we should do some at-home yoga, as Beth suggests."

"Okay, good plan. I'll catch up with my correspondence this morning." Marty liked checking her emails.

Janet finished her toast and went back to her bedroom, greeting Elizabeth at the stairs. "Good morning, Elizabeth," she said.

"Good morning, Janet," Elizabeth replied, as they crossed paths.

In the kitchen Elizabeth greeted Marty. "Hi, How are you this morning?"

"Well, I've been better."

"Yes, me too. I bet we are both fretting over the same thing."

"I imagine we are."

"Have you heard any sounds from the guest room?"

"Not yet."

"When my kids were teenagers, they had an immense capacity for sleeping in," Elizabeth said.

"Teenagers have a lot more REM sleep than we do," Marty said, "and Alcee is just making up for her sleep debt. I bet she has had some sleepless nights over this decision. It's good she's still resting."

"Do you think she is doing the right thing?" Elizabeth asked.

Marty did not respond right away. This was such a natural question to ask. She doubted that it was possible to know for sure if this life-changing intervention was the right choice, at least not for a long time. Marty knew it took courage to make such a decision. She wanted to help Alcee and Elizabeth, but there were no easy answers.

Elizabeth boiled an egg, popped an English muffin in the toaster, and made a new pot of coffee. She couldn't help wondering what Nell would think. How hard should she press Alcee to tell her mother? Elizabeth decided at least to address the issue; she felt she had to. Maybe she was being selfish, trying to keep her own relationship with her daughter on good terms. Elizabeth would mention it to Alcee in a gentle, caring way.

Janet came through the kitchen on her way outside. "I'll see you two later, hopefully having Catherine back for a late lunch." And she was gone, carrying her purple-and-white hospice-volunteer training bag.

Marty offered to call a few medical friends who might know the specifics of obtaining an abortion. Elizabeth eagerly accepted the offer. Then they could be more helpful to Alcee once she awoke.

"Oh, damn it!" Elizabeth cussed. The smell of burning English muffins permeated the kitchen. She pulled the hot, charred morsels out of the toaster and began scraping the black coating into the sink. Immediately, she thought of Cliff, who had detested that smell and become cross with her whenever she absent-mindedly burned toast. In fact, Cliff recalled that once his mother had melted an aluminum coffee pot on the electric coil, and those were the days before smoke alarms. It was lucky their house never caught fire. Cliff's mother had had no sense of smell, so his childhood memories were filled with burnt toast and coffee. Elizabeth applied butter to the pathetic, scraped English muffins.

Marty had been thinking about her secret. She'd tossed and turned all night, wondering about revealing it to Alcee or Elizabeth or both. Once Abigail died, Marty had been again alone with her secret, and at her advancing age, she yearned to share it if it could help another. She sipped her coffee slowly and decided to talk with Elizabeth now.

Marty began, "Since last night when you told me about Alcee's pregnancy and desire for an abortion, I've been stewing a bit. Remember when you said you were glad to have someone around who's had experience with this type of situation. You meant my professional life, and you were right. But what you didn't know, and what I want to tell you now, is that I have had experience in my personal life too." Marty paused.

Their eyes met. "Oh, Marty, I had no idea."

"I know. Nobody knows. About ten years ago, after almost forty years of keeping it to myself, I finally told Abigail. But she's gone now, and the secret rests with me again. I never told my parents, my brother, or my ex-husband. He certainly wouldn't have cared. Actually, he would have encouraged it." Marty's bitterness toward her ex-husband had waned over the years, but that was not to say that the hurt of his having an affair with a student, after they'd been married just over a year, was any less painful. "I found myself pregnant one year into my marriage with a husband who had cheated on me and with a Middlebury student, at that. Oh, boy, I woke up and realized that for those few years I had put on hold my dream of becoming a doctor. I had been wooed by a handsome economics professor, diverted my attention from my goal, and had fallen for the Romeo, even married him, only to be rather quickly ditched. It was a very hard fall." Marty took a breath. This was difficult. "I had heard about a doctor in Burlington who did abortions, and I arranged it. Back then everything was through the backdoor, almost literally."

"I'm sure it was hard and scary to handle that all by yourself," Elizabeth said.

"I was pretty determined to move on, and Tufts Medical School was willing to accept me for the next fall. Luckily, I had all the premed courses I needed. Putting the brief marriage behind me wasn't too bad — marriage isn't all it's cracked up to be, at least that marriage wasn't — but there have been times when I have wondered about my being a mother. I've delivered a lot of babies and watched them grow up, but I can only imagine the joy of having your own child." Marty drank a sip of cold coffee.

Elizabeth wasn't exactly sure how to respond. She wanted to be honest but not cause Marty any further pain. It was obvious that she had moved on from the abortion so many years ago and had created a successful medical career for herself, even finding a special relationship with Abigail. Still, the inflection in her voice showed a hint of regret.

"For me, it was a definite joy to have children but an amazing challenge as well. Oh, I was thrilled with our first-born, Frank Jr., and then we had our little girl, Libby. The third, Michael, came along unplanned, but he was just so adorable and so playful. Cliff wanted one more because he had come from a family of four kids. My parents had only two girls. I remember Cliff pushing for the fourth, but he was gone so much of the time at work, I knew it would be once again all me." Elizabeth took a breath. "Well, we went off to Bermuda for a vacation away from the three kids, and just like that I got pregnant. He was thrilled; I was less so. I can't say that I ever seriously considered an abortion; it just wasn't in my sphere of thinking, but I wasn't all bubbly, as with the first one." Elizabeth was quiet. "Nell was hard from the moment she arrived on the planet: colic, school phobias, and teenage rebellion." Elizabeth sighed, "We certainly got more than we bargained for with our last."

"Well, from what I have learned in these last few months, you've remained pretty involved with your children, even as adults. And now you have the joys and challenges of grandparenting," Marty added.

"Yes, my family has played a major part in my life, that's for sure, and I really am touched that Alcee reached out for help."

"If she is as strong as I think she is, she will do okay, and we can be here for her now. As I said last night, I bet Nell will be very understanding if she is given the chance," Marty said.

"I hope you are right." Elizabeth reached over and touched Marty's arm. "Thank you for sharing. I know it is still a hard memory."

"It felt right to tell you, and we can share it with Alcee if the appropriate time arises," Marty replied. They each warmed their coffee in the microwave and listened to the radio. Flurries were expected tomorrow but little accumulation.

A little later, Alcee came into the kitchen, wearing black tights, a baggy sweater, and a blanket wrapped around her shoulders. Her dark hair hung around her face, and her eyelids were puffy.

"Good morning," she said as she sat down at the kitchen table.

"Would you care for some coffee, dear?" Elizabeth asked. "I could make some Italian espresso."

"Oh, Nonna, you don't have to go to that trouble. I can drink American regular," her granddaughter replied.

'It's no problem, really. I'd like to do it. How about some toast and jam?"

"Thank you. That's would taste good, Nonna."

Elizabeth busied herself with preparing the espresso and toast. Marty decided to speak. "Your grandmother shared with me your reason for coming to visit. I hope you don't mind. She thought that I might be able to help you. I am a retired doctor and have worked with many young women over the years."

"Oh, I guess I knew it could not be kept a secret from her housemates, and after meeting you all last night at dinner, I feel comfortable here," Alcee said. "If you can help me, I would appreciate that."

"I'm sure you have done a lot of thinking about this. I know it's a difficult decision to make, and you have your very own personal reasons," Marty began.

"Yes, I do, and in my mind I have weighed my options, like keeping the baby or giving it up for adoption. I've wrestled with it...but really I think an abortion would be the best for me and my boyfriend, Fabio. My mamma may feel different," Alcee added.

"You have not discussed this with her?" Marty knew the answer to this but thought it best to have Alcee open the topic for discussion.

"No, I do not want to hurt her. I am just choosing a different path," Alcee said.

"That's true, I understand that, but have you thought that it might be a bigger hurt that you did not confide in her?" Marty paused to let that sink in.

Alcee looked up at her grandmother, who was just

listening to the conversation and cutting the toast. Alcee looked back at Marty, "I guess I didn't think of it that way. I mean she probably will find out at some point and then that could hurt her."

"And maybe that hurt would be more intense," Marty added.

Alcee looked again at Elizabeth, who was now looking at her granddaughter, giving a subtle nod.

"Mamma has been working so hard on her art and getting the gallery ready. I guess I wasn't sure if she had time for me or even cared what I was up to. I know she doesn't really like Fabio, but without him I would have been alone a lot.

Elizabeth spoke: "Your mother may be busy and distracted, but I know she loves you very much, dear." She placed the toast in front of Alcee.

"Do you think I should call her?" Alcee said. "My plan was not to hurt her, but you both think not telling her would hurt her more?"

Marty said, "It's really up to you, Alcee. I don't know your mother, and I'm not a mother, but I would imagine telling her sooner rather than later would probably be best. What do you think, Elizabeth?"

"Alcee, your mom has always been a very independent child and is still independent, for that matter. I think that she would respect your independence. She elected not to tell us about her pregnancy for quite a long time, but eventually it came out. I guess we learned from your Aunt Libby, who was the first to know."

"Well, if my mother learns about it, I want it to come from me," Alcee declared. She spread some blueberry jam on her toast, took a bite, and swallowed. "I know she loves me and has always tried to do what is right for me, even though at times she's been less involved than I would have liked."

Elizabeth admired her strong-willed granddaughter.

Marty added: "As we grow up, Alcee, we learn to be more patient with our mothers. It's a fact we learn with time, that our mothers are human and cannot be all things to all people, much as we thought they could when we were very young,"

Elizabeth laughed, "Oh, yes, we mothers are far from perfect!"

Alcee smiled at her. As far as she was concerned, her Nonna was doing a great job of grandmothering.

"Then I will call my mother this afternoon," Alcee said.

"I think that is a very wise choice," Marty said. "And if you want me to, and you are sure you want to go ahead with this, I can call and see what we have to do to get an appointment for you at the clinic in Bangor."

"I would appreciate that," Alcee replied, "and do you think you could tell me more about the actual procedure? I have looked online but hearing it from you would be better."

"Sure, I can do that. Let's chat a little later this morning. I have a few things I need to attend to upstairs," Marty said. She left the kitchen.

Elizabeth turned to Alcee, "Why don't you shower and get dressed, and we can enjoy a bit of fresh winter air. I'm always trying to get a little natural vitamin D, and the sun is bright today. I have extra gloves and a warm scarf and hat for you." Elizabeth loved feeling needed.

That morning on the drive to the ophthalmology

appointment, Sarah decided to ask her mother how the Winter House arrangement was working. She had been quite surprised that Catherine had elected to try out this change. Sarah had worried a lot about her mother after the death of her father twelve years ago. Her parents had been a close couple, waiting on each other and openly adoring one another. Sarah was always a bit embarrassed when her father would walk out of the room and her mother would say to visiting guests, "Isn't he just the cutest guy?"

Some years earlier, Sarah had asked her mother to move in with her family in Blue Hill, but Catherine would hear none of it. "I'm not ready yet to give up my independence," she said. "I'll be fine and just knowing you are nearby gives me a great feeling of safety." Catherine had lived twelve years alone and had made quite a life for herself in the town, involved in many activities. When someone suggested she run for selectman — or selectwoman, as she said — she briefly considered it but preferred to work more with the children. She said she'd leave all that paperwork and town politics to the younger folks, though most of those in office were no longer young. Dick Dixon was pushing seventy and had been town selectman for almost thirty years.

"How are things going at the Winter House, Mom?" Sarah asked.

Catherine replied. "I'm actually really enjoying it, dear. Oh, the four of us are quite different in our own ways, but that's the fun part. It's only been seven weeks, so maybe we are still in our honeymoon phase." She chuckled. "But then again, there are three months to go, so maybe it's more like an affair." She laughed again, knowing that some of her neighbors wondered about the Winter House activities. "I'm even learning some yoga, and we have had fun playing

Bananagrams. Your old ma's pretty quick with the words. Elizabeth has only beaten me once." Catherine was proud of her ability, given that she was the oldest and Elizabeth, the youngest housemate. "And, my, it is just wonderful to have my meals prepared for me — a dream come true, really. You know how I used to struggle to get something on the table for all those years. Your father was such an understanding man; our menu was pretty standard, centered on his meat and potatoes. Now I eat quiche, ratatouille, or Chinese noodles with stir-fried shrimp. Last night Marty prepared a yummy roasted chicken with sweet potatoes and green beans covered with toasted almonds. Those two gals, Marty and Elizabeth, just love to cook, and you know me, I just love to do the dishes!" Sarah and her mother both laughed.

"Oh, your Aunt Ethel taught me some of her special recipes, like her delicious meat loaf with hamburger, cornflakes, canned tomatoes, eggs, and dried onion-soup mix, but as far as me actually enjoying taking the time to create meals, I've long since given up trying." Catherine's stomach growled, reminding her that she had had nothing to eat this morning. As they approached Ellsworth, she felt a twinge of anxiety over the coming surgery.

Sarah felt her mother's apprehension. She had always been good at reading her mother's emotion level. "You'll do just fine, Mom. I've heard it will be over in no time."

"I know. Your brother told me to just relax and marvel at what can now be done with modern technology. I remember my grandmother's last years. She went blind from cataracts. We've come a long way, that's for sure."

They pulled into the Downeast Eye Clinic parking lot, just five minutes ahead of schedule. The receptionist ac-

knowledged Catherine's arrival. "We'll be with you short-
ly," she said. Sitting on comfortable cushioned couches,
Sarah and her mother waited along with about eight others. Catherine had heard that it was like a modern assem-
bly line: pop out the old cataract, slip in the new lens. Her
daughter skimmed the *Ellsworth American*, turning to the
editorials and letters. Catherine thumbed through an old
Reader's Digest, stopping at the word-power section. Slowly
the patients were called into the operating suite. Catherine
waited patiently for her turn to join the line.

After a shower and a walk outside with her grandmother, Alcee went up to find Marty, who had been on the phone
for the last half-hour. It was a comfort to Alcee to know
that this housemate was a doctor. As she knocked on the
half-opened bedroom door, Alcee saw the chaos on Marty's
small desk and her clothes thrown over the chair. On the
desk was a framed embroidered sign that read: "Come in,
sit down, converse. My house doesn't always look like this.
Sometimes it's worse."

"Oh, come on in, dear," Marty said. "Please excuse the
mess. I've been working on some hospital-board projects
and have kind of spread out a bit. Besides, I guess I'm just
not the tidiest person in the world. I'd much rather be talking with people than straightening up."

Alcee immediately felt at ease and wondered why more
doctors couldn't be like this.

"Did you have a good walk?"

"It's colder here than my home in Italy, but today the
sun warmed us and sparkled off the bay."

"Good, well, I have called the Bangor clinic, and they
can see you tomorrow morning. I've made a tentative ap-

pointment for you, but we can always cancel it."

"My grandmother and I have talked more about this on our walk, and I do feel ready to make this decision and also ready to talk to my mother. She will be home after about seven or eight, her time, so I can call her this afternoon."

"Good, Alcee, I think that is a good idea." Marty had reviewed the details of the procedure with the nurse at the clinic and was amazed at how simple it sounded, compared with the back-door operation that she had had to endure almost fifty years ago. But though the procedure would be simple, the emotional aspects still could be hard.

Calmly and clearly, Marty walked Alcee through what to expect at the clinic and reassured her that her grandmother and she could stay with her throughout the procedure, if she wished. Alcee wondered if it would be painful. Marty stated that usually the pain is brief and more like menstrual cramps or a strong pinch. Pain medication is given, as well as antibiotics to prevent infection.

"And after?" Alcee asked.

"You can expect some bleeding, though that varies from patient to patient. Some have a little spotting for a few days, while others can have heavier bleeding. If it is quite heavy, you would probably need to be rechecked."

"How long will this all take?"

"The procedure itself takes only about ten minutes, but the initial intake time — for filling out papers, learning about options, a history and physical exam, blood tests, and an ultrasound exam — takes an hour or more. It will be okay, dear."

"I hope so. I'm a bit scared, but with you and Nonna there, it will be much easier."

That would be true. Marty would have given anything

to have a supportive, mature relative around when she had taken this step. Trauma and fear were etched into her mind, and even decades later her autonomic nervous system reacted. Her palms sweated as she remembered the event. She had decided not to tell Alcee about her personal experience. It really wasn't necessary. Alcee had made her decision. And besides, for Marty, revealing her abortion to Elizabeth this morning had relieved the pressure of the secret, leaving her feeling better. Now she just wanted to support this young girl.

"We'll be right there with you, Alcee," Marty added,

"Thank you. I'm so glad I came here, and I will be ready for tomorrow, thanks to you." Alcee went over to Marty and gave her a short hug. She felt safe and knew it would be okay.

"Let's go and find your grandmother. It's almost lunch time."

Downstairs Elizabeth had finished making a salad with avocado, carrots, oranges, spinach, and goat cheese sprinkled on top. The leftover mushroom-cauliflower soup from a few days before would be enough for everyone. Janet had called from Ellsworth to say that Catherine and she were on their way home and that all had gone well with the cataract surgery.

Marty noticed Quigley still sitting by the window and knew he would soon be rewarded for his loyalty. Even before seeing a car coming up the driveway, he could sense its approach and would perk up his ears, barking to announce the arrival. When Catherine came home, however, he wouldn't bark but instead whined and spun around a few times, wagging his fluffy tail. She's home! She's home! Let me out! Let me out! The housemates had learned to appease him by opening the back door, whereupon he would charge out to the car. Catherine always opened the car door for just a moment, allowing Quigley to hop onto her lap, kissing her face. This routine had developed over the past two months because there was generally someone inside to let him out. When Quigley and Catherine lived alone, he had to wait patiently until she walked into the house. Marty thought about Missy by comparison — much more the cat personality but still a soothing companion in her own way.

"Beautiful day today," Elizabeth said to Marty. The sun shone into the kitchen. The outdoor thermometer read thirty-five, and the icicles hanging off the porch roof were dripping. "Sometimes thirty-five even feels warm once you've been experiencing the single-digit temps." Elizabeth could not imagine her sister enjoying any of this.

Quigley sat up and started to whine and spin. "Guess they're back," Marty said, watching the whirl of Quigley's tail. She opened the door, and Quigley ran out. "He's been waiting quite a while."

Janet and Catherine came in. Quigley followed. A small, black patch covered Catherine's right eye, but a smile filled her face.

"Just in time for lunch," Elizabeth said.

"Great, I'm hungry!" Catherine replied. "It went well, and I am so relieved. That place is just amazing! Some folks would call it slick. They are quick, efficient, and pleasant. They put you in a recliner and wheel you around from room to room. The procedure is remarkable, with very little discomfort, and, poof, you're in the recovery room and then set to go home. I even had to wait for Janet," she laughed. "I think I'll be ready to do the next one right off."

"I'm so glad it went well," Marty said. "Maybe I should go with you next time and see how this medical factory really works. So many things have changed in eye care since I took a rotation in ophthalmology many years ago. Do you have to wear the patch for a while?"

"Oh, this. Well, it is just to remind me not to rub or scratch my eye, but I can take it off tonight. I have several drops to put into my eyes at different times of the day. It's all written down for me," Catherine commented.

Marty said, "I'd be glad to help you put the drops in."

"Thank you, I may just need some help. I have never been good at aiming them into the eye. If you're around, that would be great."

"No problem," Marty replied, always liking to help.

The conversations continued as they enjoyed their soup and salad.

Later that afternoon Alcee called her mother. Elizabeth would have loved to listen in on the conversation, but she knew that this was an important mother-daughter communication, and her granddaughter wanted to do it her way. Nell usually spoke frankly and rarely held back. A child with determination and a strong will can be a challenge for parents, but these are often admirable characteristics in an adult.

Elizabeth knew that she would be filled in on the conversation if Alcee wanted to. She could wait. Elizabeth retreated to her bedroom, where she kept an easel. She had skipped Bob Chester's art lesson because of Alcee's arrival but wanted to be prepared for the next week's assignment. They would be working on charcoal sketches of nudes. Bob had explained that a young man from Stonington would pose for them to earn money for his lobster license. Elizabeth would have expected something like this in New York City, but it amused her to think of nude modeling going on in the little village of Blue Hill — with a lobsterman, at that. Although many artists flocked to Maine in the summer, some hearty souls stayed throughout the year; Bob Chester was one of them.

On Cliff's dresser, now filled with her summer clothes, stood a reproduction of the Medici Venus. Cliff had bought the figurine in Rome on his first trip to Italy, knowing from his college art-history class that this was the most well-known nude sculpture of the goddess. Ever since the purchase, he had displayed the nude prominently in their Connecticut home and more recently in their New York apartment living room. Elizabeth had brought her to Maine when the apartment was rented this fall. She didn't imagine the statue had any material value, as small Venus figurines were readily available in Italy, but it remained a valuable emotional connection to her deceased husband. He had always told Elizabeth that her breasts were the perfect shape, just like those of Venus. At first, as a new bride, she blushed, but later, over the years, they both laughed. Elizabeth looked at the statue now and pictured herself in the mirror. Perhaps now Cliff would be stretching the truth if he continued to make that claim. Her breasts had dropped, ever so slightly.

Elizabeth readjusted her Strathmore sketch paper, picked up a soft charcoal pencil, and began sketching Venus. Her fingers held the charcoal with a delicate touch. As the smooth form took shape, the work of the moment carried her thoughts back to memories of Cliff.

She recalled that special Memorial Day in Vermont, a week before her Middlebury graduation. The sky was a Vermont blue, a vibrant deep blue. Cliff claimed the weather was perfect for a hike. He had completed his MBA at Harvard Business School, graduating second in his class, and had just captured a starting position as an associate at New York's Booz & Company, the oldest management-consulting firm in the business, known for its aggressive training of their new entrants. Cliff was ready to leave Boston and move on to New York City, "where the action was." But on this day he wanted an outing into the mountains.

Though Elizabeth had done only a little hiking in college, and Cliff probably even less, they both thought it would be fun to climb along a ridge and see some panoramic views of Vermont. The day was clear, providing great visibility. As Cliff drove his 1960 red Chevy Corvair convertible along the Governor Peck Highway, Elizabeth's long hair tossed in the wind. She felt alive and almost free from the restraints of college. The future was hers to seize. The early light green leaves of that late spring and even a few patches of snow, clustered on the north side of the woods, caught her eye. Cliff had checked in at the ranger's station along with a few other day hikers, and then, with a trail map, they left on the Sunset Ridge Trail, a three-mile climb to the summit of Vermont's highest mountain, Mount Mansfield. About a mile up the trail Cliff suggested that they stop for a snack and water. The upper campground was filled with a troop of Boy Scouts who had spent the night and now were eager to climb the rest of the way to the summit. Cliff had seemed disappointed that there were so many people around.

Elizabeth and Cliff continued hiking up the trail, stopping only when Elizabeth felt a blister coming on. She told Cliff to go ahead, and she would quickly catch up. He took off, wanting to stay ahead of the Boy Scout troop and knowing she would be safe with the boys coming up behind her. Elizabeth dug into her small pack for a Band-Aid. Once she had applied it to the hot spot, pulled her sock on, stepped into her left sneaker, and tied her laces, she was back on the trail. Cliff had taken the only map ahead. When she came to a **Y** in the trail, she was unsure of the route, but the left path appeared more worn. Both signs with arrows read "Summit." She went left and continued for quite some time, wondering if Cliff would just go all the way without her. Cliff had gone right, instead. After first waiting to let Elizabeth catch up, he began to backtrack, worried that something might have happened. He passed by the **Y** without thinking that this could have been a problem for Elizabeth. When he ran into the Boy Scouts group and none of them had seen a woman with a yellow shirt and blue backpack, he figured he had missed her somehow. Elizabeth had become worried because it was not like Cliff to abandon her, especially since he had been so attentive to her recently. For a few moments she sat near a stream and tried to think what would be the best thing to do. Maybe she should have gone to the right at the junction. Cliff would be quite worried about her not catching up with him.

Cliff turned back up the mountain. Elizabeth headed back down to the junction too and got there ahead of Cliff. She then took the trail to the right whereas Cliff returned to the junction and went up the left trail in search of her. The Boy Scouts stayed right along the shorter trail to the summit, and when they met the woman in a yellow shirt, they told her that her hiking partner was searching for her on the other branch of the trail. Cliff had instructed them to encourage her to continue up to the summit with them, and he would meet her at the top. Elizabeth wasn't sure that was such a good idea, but the troop leader insisted it would all work out and that she should stay with the group.

As she and the Scouts arrived at the rock pile on the summit, they could see a figure coming up the ridge from the left side. It was Cliff. When he was a little closer to the group, he saw Elizabeth and waved. She scrambled down to him. Initially, Elizabeth was concerned he might be upset with her, but relief showed all over his sweaty face. He enveloped her with his strong arms and kissed her.

"I'm sorry, honey, I'm sorry. I never should have headed off without you," Cliff said.

"Yeah," Elizabeth replied, "We didn't exactly have a peaceful, romantic hike together to the top. But it's okay, now." She ran her fingers through his hair.

As they sat down on a large rock away from the Boy Scouts, Cliff dug into his backpack, pulling out a small jewelry box. Turning toward her and opening the box, he whispered, "I never want to lose you again. Will you marry me?"

A gentle knock on the door startled Elizabeth. For a brief second she assumed it must be Cliff, but in the next second she regained her bearings. "Nonna, it's me, Alcee. Can I come in?"

"Of course, dear, come on in." Elizabeth quickly wiped her eyes, erasing the vivid mountaintop scene. She was needed here in the present moment.

Alcee told her grandmother of the long-distance conversation. Alcee's mother had had a suspicion and thus was not too shocked by her daughter's news. Alcee believed Nell was upset but not angry. Her mother had apologized for being so distracted with the art gallery and regretted having been overly opinionated about Fabio, but she just couldn't see Alcee and her boyfriend together for the long run.

"So we both agreed on that." Alcee took a few breaths. Elizabeth waited. "She just wants me to be sure of my decision, so we talked it through, all the options. Mamma wanted me to know that she never had any regrets about keeping me, and in many ways, she said, I was the best thing that ever happened to her. That made us both cry." Alcee paused. "Mamma did admit there were many hard times being a single mom, especially living so far away from you and Papa, but still she has no regrets." Alcee paused again. "But in the end I think we both decided an abortion is best for me and Fabio. Mamma wants me to go on to college and pursue my dreams. And we both hope children will be in my future some day."

"Sounds like you and your mother did some great sharing," Elizabeth said.

"Yes, I'm glad I called her. Thank you for encouraging me to do that...Oh, and she wants to be sure that I appreciate all the help you're giving me. She said she wasn't always so appreciative for all you did for her in her wild and younger years."

Elizabeth smiled. Wasn't it beautiful that mother-daughter relationships can continue to grow?

The following day, from the moment that Alcee, Elizabeth and Marty entered the women's health center in Bangor, they felt cared for. The pale purple and soft mint green walls and comfortable furniture created a feeling of welcome. The sensitive and compassionate staff completed the history, physical, and laboratory tests with a calm efficiency. Everything was clearly explained to Alcee, and at several junctions she could have changed her mind, having been presented with all her options. Throughout the entire time, Marty and Elizabeth were allowed to be present. Alcee experienced little discomfort but squeezed her grandmother's hand for most of the procedure. When all was finished, deep sighs came from each of the participants.

Alcee left with instructions to return if heavy bleeding occurred. Some spotting would be expected. She was to take it easy for a few days and not do any heavy lifting. A prescription for antibiotics to prevent infection was given. No follow-up appointment was necessary unless there were complications. Part of the education included a review of birth-control methods, and Alcee promised to visit the clinic in Italy for this, but for now, she wasn't thinking of future sexual activities. The nurse understood her immediate response but still strongly encouraged her to use safer protection in the future.

As they got into Elizabeth's car, Marty suggested a stop at Clyde's, a small deli just outside of town on the road home. "I'm ready for some lunch," Alcee said.

"Me too," said Elizabeth.

None of them talked further about the morning visit but instead listened to WERU's folk hour. Elizabeth was relieved that all had gone well for her granddaughter, with no apparent complications. Alcee now wanted to focus on a brighter future. Marty marveled at the change in abortion safety and ease that had taken place over fifty years. For this bright eighteen-year-old, Marty silently hoped for the best.

For the next several days the Winter House occupants enjoyed companionship. One night all five of them went to the Opera House in Stonington to see the remake of *An American in Paris,* which originally came out in 1951. Alcee loved the music, almost all of which was completely new to her. Catherine still thought Gene Kelly's dancing and looks could not be beat. On the drive home the Winter House women sang and hummed some of their favorite tunes from the movie.

On Alcee's last night Marty and Elizabeth treated the group to a seasonal wonder — fresh Maine shrimp. They had recently learned the tricks of preparing these little morsels and pulled out the recipe for stir-fried shrimp with herbs and sun-dried tomatoes over linguini.

"Delizioso!" Alcee said.

"Ditto!" Janet added.

Catherine even asked for seconds. "A Mainer can't turn down a Maine dish," she said, "though it is a bit fancier than my mother's shrimp dishes." After dinner the dishwashing crew took over. Catherine and Janet actually enjoyed their job for the chance to catch up with each other. Dishwashing really was no work at all, especially after a satisfying meal.

Elizabeth and Alcee opted to take a walk, checking out the full moon and having some private time together. The snow was luminescent, bright like whipped cream, with just a hint of glitter. A small plume of smoke, silhouetted against the dark blue sky, rose from the chimney of the house. The moonlight cast deep shadows. All was very still. Alcee snapped a flash exposure of her grandmother, wearing a purple-and-red-striped wool-felted hat, a light purple scarf, and a black coat. Alcee laughed at the rubber-soled, insulated L.L. Bean boots that completed the costume. No boots like that existed in Italy, but she knew they were warm, for sure.

With a timed night exposure Alcee snapped a shot of the Winter House to show her mother. This trip had been one she would never forget, not ever. Before walking back into the house, they embraced — grandmother and granddaughter — two humans each growing a little wiser and closer.

Quite early the next day Elizabeth drove Alcee to the Concord Trailways bus station for her trip to Boston. Both were quiet, just waking up in the pitch dark of a winter morning. Much had happened in ten days, a major change in the trajectory of Alcee's life. She had begun to dream of her future and the possibility of even returning to the United States. Many years ago she had visited the United Nations on a trip with her Aunt Libby, Uncle Michael, and her mother — a mini-family reunion of sorts. Alcee had been impressed with the simultaneous translators in the grand conference rooms. She had told her mother that she wanted to do that someday. Now she was determined to major in languages and foreign relations at her university, in preparation for a job as an interpreter or a foreign journalist in New York, perhaps at the U.N.

But now, leaving her grandmother was going to be hard. Alcee worried about her Nonna's future. Oh, Elizabeth seemed fine now, but would she want to continue this living arrangement for the rest of her life? Her grandmother was so vibrant and lovely, and Alcee wanted her to find happiness.

"Nonna," Alcee said, "are you going to be okay without Papa?"

Elizabeth was silent. She sighed. "Well, I hope so. There really is little choice, is there?" A pause gave her time to consider, and she recalled that she had been so wound up in her granddaughter's immediate problem that she hadn't really been thinking of herself, which was probably a good thing. Oh, she had her days, sometimes feeling that she was taking two steps forward and three steps back.

"I can tell you one thing, though," Elizabeth remarked, "I hate the term 'widow.' I have had to check off that little box too many times, and I've overheard others describing me as a 'widow.' I detest the word and refuse to use it. I was married. I am now alone. I was a 'wife' and a 'mother.' These terms I love. 'Widow' I hate." Elizabeth squeezed the steering wheel rather tightly.

Alcee was surprised by this outburst, but it came across as healthy. There was that spirit that she recognized from her own mother. Maybe it ran in the Sloan women's genes.

"I have an idea, Nonna," Alcee replied, "why don't you think of yourself as a *vedova*? You know, 'widow' in Italian."

"*Vedova*? 'Widow,' in Italian. What a great idea! A *vedova*. It sounds quite sexy, really," Elizabeth laughed. It sounded rather like Lady Godiva. In England she had seen a statue of Lady Godiva, a beautiful long-haired nude riding on a splendid horse. And then there was Godiva chocolate, Cliff's favorite Belgian chocolate. "That's it!" Elizabeth banged her palm on the steering wheel. "I like it. Whenever I read the word 'widow' or hear it, I will translate it to *vedova,* and it will be so much better and even make me smile. Thank you so much, my dear."

"So glad I could help you out," Alcee said, smiling from ear to ear. She hoped in her heart that things would work out for her grandmother, who had always been there for her, even from afar.

The rest of the way to the bus, the two talked about university. Alcee wondered if she might be able to come to America to study for a semester or two. Elizabeth thought that might be quite possible. She was aware of a Middlebury exchange program with Italian and French universities. "You must do well in your first two years, dear, and then I bet you could work something out. That will be a good goal for you."

"I am going to study really hard, Nonna," Alcee replied. "I know I can do well, and I do love studying languages. Maybe I could even be a teacher here in the U.S."

"Maybe. We need good and dedicated teachers here. I'm glad you have some ideas about what you want to do. When you put your mind to something, I have no doubt you can pull it off." Elizabeth smiled. A few years ago she had read *The Seven Daughters of Eve* by Bryan Sykes and was astonished to learn that mitochondria, the little energy factories that all our cells require, are programmed by mitochondrial DNA inherited from one's mother. Fathers do not pass along the mitochondrial messages in their sperm. So, the same genetic information that Nell inherited from Elizabeth was passed on to Alcee — from grandmother to mother to daughter, all three expressing the same mitochondrial DNA. Here was a concrete biological link, and it was little wonder that Elizabeth felt a strong emotional connection.

The morning light appeared as they drove along Route 1A into Bangor. It would be a beautiful ride down to Boston. Alcee would be picked up by her Aunt Libby at South Station and taken out for lunch and a play. Uncle Michael and his partner, Mason, would join them for dinner at Legal Seafood. Then they would get her to Logan Airport for a late-night flight to Italy. What a trip this had been, and Alcee had her grandmother to thank for all of it.

At the bus station the driver collected Alcee's ticket and placed her small suitcase in the compartment under the bus. She and her grandmother embraced, holding on to each other for a long time. Elizabeth promised to come visit in September, one of her favorite times of the year in Italy.

"Don't worry about this *vedova*," Elizabeth said. "I'm going to be just fine."

"*Ti amo, addio*," Alcee said, and she hugged her grandmother once more.

Elizabeth was going to miss her so. What a beautiful woman her granddaughter was turning out to be. As Alcee climbed the stairs of the bus, the two squeezed hands for one last touch. Through the darkened coach windows, Elizabeth could not tell if her granddaughter was crying. Only after waving good-bye, with the bus pulling out, did Elizabeth wipe her tears away.

That evening Janet lingered in her bath, soaking in the Epsom salts. The day had been extra busy, and she knew her body and brain needed a rest. It was almost February, and she could not believe how rapidly the time was passing. Last year the winter had seemed so long. Now, though she was using a full spectrum lamp to alleviate seasonal affective disorder, her well-being was probably more affected by her Winter House companions as well as two new activities.

Janet's ukulele lessons on Saturday mornings were really fun. Several local folks gathered in the old theater loft in town and strummed the tunes they had learned with Lotti Lynstrom, an experienced instructor. Janet had mastered three chords so far, the easy ones, but with just those simple chords she could play many familiar folk tunes. Lotti encouraged everyone to practice because the group had been invited to play at the spring concert in Blue Hill.

It had taken some strong encouragement from Marty for Janet to join the tennis group. Oh, she had given all sorts of excuses, but Marty would have none of that. Janet had finally acquiesced and agreed to try it. Long ago she had really enjoyed tennis, but with her nursing schedule and then her duties as a minister's wife, tennis hadn't fit into her life. Janet chuckled. For the first few times her balls went flying or hit the net. Her backhand was miserable – well, almost nonexistent – and her serve barely reached over the net. But Polly and Sally, Marty's pals, remained patient. Fortunately, her strokes were improving; even she could see it. Her yoga classes, which she had attended for three years now, seemed to have helped with muscle strength and stretching abilities. Still, after each two-hour tennis game, her body felt as though she'd run a marathon. As a nurse, she knew that this exercise was good for her, would keep her weight down, and would stimulate her cardiovascular system. Equally important for her mental health was the laughing, and these four women occasionally dissolved into giggling, pure nectar for the soul. As seniors on the tennis court, they all played mostly for the fun of it, relishing their ability to move their old knees, hips, and shoulders. Janet had noticed that Polly fretted a bit when she wasn't making her favorite shots the way she used to. Polly clearly liked to win and once had been the New Hampshire women's 3.5 champion back in the '80's. But that was over thirty years ago, and time can be hard on old champions.

The bath water had cooled, so Janet added some hot water. Soaking felt good. The best part of her day, however, had been the arrival of an invitation to the annual Hancock County Hospice Volunteers celebration in March. Along with four other women, Janet would be recognized for her twenty-five years of continuous service to comfort and aid families in their greatest time of need. This organization had carried her through the rough times in her own life, helping her to look outward, to not get stuck in her own tribulations but to extend her hand and heart to others. The benefits went both ways. She had found John through this organization, and that gift was eleven satisfying years of a second marriage. Hospice volunteering had given her years of personal connection with neighbors, gaining new friends through compassionate service. She thought of Catherine and Harold and the amazing coincidence that now she and Catherine had become Winter House companions. Janet looked forward to accepting this award, and perhaps her newfound housemates would join in the celebration.

Drying herself off after climbing out of the tub, she remembered that she had forgotten to send a birthday card to her stepdaughter, Andrea. Darn, she thought, I had such good intentions. Her stepchildren, John's kids, visited every summer since his death — well, all but Steven, who refused to return after his father died. During the other nine months of the year, Janet heard little from them. They all had gotten along when her husband was alive, but how was this relationship supposed to continue after the source of the relation vanished? She had felt some vibes that the children wanted the house to be theirs, and the sooner the better as far as they were concerned. Though this hurt Janet terribly, she knew it was not an unusual predicament. In fact, she had once talked with a good friend who faced the same situation. Janet knew she needed to address the issue but how? It was her hope to keep the stepmother-stepchildren relationship open and friendly.

In a small file box Janet found several birthday cards that she kept on hand. Some days she would peruse the card aisle at Rite-Aid, finding some funny cards, which occasionally made her chuckle out loud. Then she'd purchase five or more and put them in the file box for future use. Thank goodness she had brought it with her. Janet located a hilarious card for a busy modern woman turning fifty. She figured if she mailed it tomorrow, it might be just a day late. That wasn't too bad for an aging stepmother. Janet put a stamp on the card, placed it on the floor in front of her door so she couldn't miss it in the morning, and climbed into bed. She opened her current novel, *Cutting for Stone,* and was quickly drawn back into the fictional tale. But after four pages her eyes grew heavy and muscles relaxed. The book fell from her hands, hit the floor, and startled her. No use fighting sleep. It was a good exhaustion. She turned off the light, calling it a day.

FEBRUARY

*T*he first day of February brought calm weather with brilliant sunshine. The twenty-two degrees on the thermometer, hidden by the shade of the nearby tree, belied the warmer temperature in the direct sun. Catherine and Elizabeth walked to the mailbox to get the afternoon mail and breathe in the crisp air. Catherine noticed the fine details of the pine needles and could see the islands distinctly in the distance. Her good eye had healed, and just as her son predicted, she was eager to have the other cataract removed. She wanted to get it fixed before May, while she still had her Winter House companions around to help with driving and eye drops. Having Marty to administer the medication had been a great benefit. With her doctor's busy schedule and the demand for this procedure, she thought she had better call for that appointment soon.

Quigley barked, pulling on the leash. The women spied across the way a little red fox with a long, straight tail, jogging peacefully down the road.

"Is it unusual to see a fox this time of year? I thought they hibernated," Elizabeth said.

"No, those little creatures don't hibernate but roam quite freely and hunt down enough food in the winter to survive. Billy Gray says he loses several of his chickens each year to those clever foxes," Catherine said. Quigley barked again as the fox darted out of sight.

On their way back to the house, Catherine commented on the snowstorm that had walloped the South. "According to the paper, North Carolina received thirty inches of heavy snow, and Washington, D.C., was essentially shut down with over two feet."

"I guess they just don't have the snowplow equipment Maine does and certainly not the experience in driving on snowy roads. My sister Eve called me from Charlotte last night. She had left Florida to go check on their house in North Carolina for a few days and now found herself stranded, staring out the window at endless 'white stuff,' as she called it. Eve said the plowmen were overwhelmed and just couldn't keep up. She doesn't even have a snow shovel, not that she would use it." Elizabeth laughed. "With these topsy-turvy weather patterns, maybe those south of the Mason-Dixon line will have to learn to live with a lot of the white stuff."

Catherine added, "I've read that global warming can change patterns as well as increase the temperature across the board."

The two women returned to the kitchen. Catherine divided up the mail. Elizabeth gathered her *New Yorker* magazine, a bill for her Verizon cell phone, and a letter from California. Marty's pile included the quarterly newsletter from Blue Hill Hospital, an Orvis women's catalog, and a letter from Tucson. Catherine had one letter that caught her attention. The address was in the lower right-hand corner, the stamp in the lower left, and the typing appeared to be from an old-style typewriter. Her curiosity caused her to open it immediately, a move she quickly regretted as she read the typed note. She quickly crumpled the paper and stuffed it into her pocket to open later in the privacy of her own room.

On the way back to her room, she noticed Elizabeth sitting in the living room, reading the *New Yorker*, which she always read cover to cover starting with "The Talk of the Town." Janet came down the stairs, passing Catherine in the hallway.

"Catherine, are you okay? You look a little pale," Janet said.

"Oh, I'm fine, just a little tired." Catherine went into her room and shut the door. Her hand shook as she pulled the crushed paper out of her pocket. The envelope was addressed to: Catherine Thomas Howard and your 4F Friends, Spruce Point Road, Brooks Harbor, Maine, with no zip code. She opened the crumpled note. On the faded scrap paper a typed salutation read: to Four Filthy Female Faggots. Then came the message in bold type:

GET YOUR FUCKING ASSES OUT OF MY TOWN!!!!!
SIGNED, A QUEER HATER

Catherine crushed the paper again. Who would do this? Her pulse raced. She moved weakly to the red recliner and sat down. This was her town, and she felt so embarrassed to learn there was anyone out there this raw and wrong.

She looked at the envelope. Who knew her maiden name was Thomas? It had to be an old-timer. She'd lived around this town all her life, and in her experience folks kept their thoughts to themselves, but occasionally a hothead stepped over the bounds of what most would call propriety. Catherine wondered. Could this be Anson Grange?

Her thoughts flashed back to that night on her porch after the junior prom. Anson, also a junior, had asked her out. It was her first and last date with that fool. Catherine wasn't even able to remember what she had seen in Anson or why she had accepted his offer to take her to the dance. He told her that night that he had wanted to date her for two years but hadn't thought she'd go out with him, she being so beautiful and smart. He was good-looking with a muscular physique. Maybe Catherine had felt sorry for him, as he didn't have many friends. In junior high some of the other boys used to bully him, calling him "stupid." He didn't do well in math or English, but in high school in shop class, he knew all about car repairs, having helped in his father's garage whenever he was not in school. The other boys respected him for that knowledge and stopped calling him names.

On the porch that night Anson grabbed the straps of her dress, pulled them down over her shoulders, and pushed her against the wall, leaning hard against her. He then forced his lips on hers — slimy lips, as Catherine recalled — and hugged her as she tried to squeeze away. When he finally withdrew, he blurted out in his husky voice, "There, Catherine Thomas, I been wanting to taste those lips for a long time." She slapped his face, almost an automatic response, as she had seen women do in the movies. He stepped back.

"Don't you ever touch me again, Anson Grange!" With that, she turned and went inside her house and shut off the porch light. She could hear his truck with the broken muffler speed off.

Catherine wiped the sweat off her forehead and felt faint. She sank back in the recliner, trying to block out any further memory of Anson. But she couldn't. He'd quit school before graduation to join the army and within the year was sent off to Korea. Three years later the Korean armistice was declared, and a homecoming parade was held for Anson. Two other Brooks Harbor boys had been killed in the war, but Anson received a hero's welcome, having fought in the battle of Pork Chop Hill and sustained significant injuries; he lost a leg. Many townsfolk said he was never quite right after the war and kept to himself down on Long's Cove. Some said he drank a lot. Eventually, somehow, Anson took over his father's business, married, and had three boys, whom Catherine taught in high school. Over the years she saw Anson around town, but he never spoke to her. In fact, he just plain avoided her and any of her family. But would he send this vile note? Catherine wondered. Why would anyone hold onto a grudge for that long?

She got up to go to the bathroom and felt faint again. Maybe she should just lie down and let this feeling pass. As she lay on the bed, Quigley jumped up to be next to her. Catherine never took naps, so perhaps her faithful dog found this an unusual behavior and sensed something out of line. He licked her face. Strange, but Catherine could almost see worry in his eyes. "Don't worry, Quigley, I'll be fine in a little while. She stroked his fuzzy white head and compact body. What a friend he was.

JOAN MACCRACKEN

When she didn't come out of her room, and the door remained shut, Marty and Janet grew worried. Catherine rarely shut the door, and it had been more than an hour.

"Should we knock?" Janet asked Marty.

"Well, I don't think it could do any harm. She rarely takes naps and it's getting closer to supper, and if she was as pale as you described, maybe we need to have a look-see." They approached the door and heard nothing.

Marty knocked. "Catherine, are you okay?"

There was a moment of silence, and then she responded. "I think so," she replied, " but you can come in." Marty opened the door and saw Catherine and Quigley on the bed. Marty's medical training took over.

"How are you doing?" Marty asked, cocking her head and wrinkling her brow.

"Well, I've been better." Catherine had no desire to talk about the letter. "I'm just feeling a bit light-headed."

"How long has this been going on?"

"It started this afternoon."

"Have you ever had this feeling before?" Marty sat down on the side of the bed.

"Maybe once or twice when I have gotten up quickly, but nothing for this long," Catherine said.

"May I check your pulse?" Marty inquired.

"Sure," said Catherine, who respected her house-mate's experience.

Marty placed her fingers on Catherine's wrist and looked at her own watch. The pulse was not strong and was rapid, around 160 beats.

"Are you experiencing any chest pain?" Marty asked

"My chest feels a little funny, but I wouldn't call it pain. But I felt so dizzy and tired that I thought I should lie down. Maybe it's my blood pressure. It has been high in the past, though I take my blood pressure pills regularly," Catherine added.

"Do you have a family history of heart disease?" Marty asked.

"My father and his sister, my aunt, had heart failure in their sixties.... I hope that is not what I've got."

Marty didn't want to alarm Catherine, but she knew full well that heart attacks in women can present with fatigue and light-headedness, even sometimes with back pain. Often chest or arm pain that men experience with a heart attack do not show up in women. Marty did not like Catherine's pulse, which was weak and rapid. In her younger years Marty might have just put Catherine in the car and driven to the hospital, but in this circumstance she knew that further evaluation was necessary and that transportation to the hospital should probably be done by ambulance. The EMTs could get an electrocardiogram and send it ahead to the hospital, and the diagnostic process could continue from there.

"Catherine, this may be nothing or it could be something more serious. I really suggest that we call 911 and get you to the Blue Hill emergency room for evaluation. And I suggest we do it now." Marty was always up-front. Janet moved closer to the bed and stood by her housemate.

"I agree, Catherine, it is better to be cautious. We aren't getting any younger, you know," Janet laid her hand on Catherine's shoulder.

"You're right, I am pushing eighty in two months, and I'd really like to get there."

"You will, don't you worry," Marty added, squeezing Catherine's hand before leaving the room to dial 911. She explained the situation quickly. She knew that if it were a heart attack, time could be important. In minutes the ambulance would be on its way, but it would take about fifteen minutes to get to the house. Luckily, with the new GPS equipment, locating the house would not be a problem. Once that call was completed, Marty phoned the Blue Hill ER to talk directly with the on-call staff. The more they knew, the better they could be ready for Catherine. With their direct telemedicine connection to Bangor's cardiologists, quick decisions could be made. Marty appreciated this advance in medicine, even though she had concerns about other aspects of modern medicine. When her father, a practicing surgeon in Vermont, had his heart attack, there was no 911 or direct line to a medical center. He died before anyone could save him. But he hadn't suffered, and he died doing what he loved, checking up on his patients.

Elizabeth helped gather a few things that Catherine wanted in her bag. Marty called Sarah, Catherine's daughter, in Blue Hill and suggested she meet her mother at the hospital. Catherine insisted on speaking with her daughter. "Sarah, I'll be just fine, dear. I'll see you at the hospital. I'm just feeling tired and dizzy."

While her housemate remained resting in bed, Marty noticed some perspiration appearing on Catherine's forehead and upper lip. Janet gently patted the sweat and made a quick glance toward Marty. They were speaking the silent medical language of concern.

After what seemed an endless wait, the ambulance arrived. The EMTs quickly brought in a stretcher and conducted a brief history, as well as a cursory exam with vital signs recorded. They elected to move Catherine to the ambulance and communicate with the hospital while on route. Marty went in the ambulance to comfort the patient, but she let the experienced EMT personnel run the show. Janet drove along behind at a slightly slower pace. Elizabeth stayed home with Quigley and Missy and prayed that Catherine would be all right. Unlike Marty and Janet, Elizabeth had never liked hospital scenes, not even on TV.

By ten o'clock in the evening, things were falling into place. Several test results had returned, and the doctors had determined that Catherine was in atrial fibrillation, giving her the rapid, erratic, and weak pulse. The possibility of a slight heart attack was raised, but so far, laboratory tests had not confirmed any cardiac damage.

The plan was to observe Catherine in Blue Hill, as the cardiologist in Bangor did not feel transfer to Eastern Maine Medical Center was necessary. Medications were started to lower the heart rate as well as to bring the rhythm back to normal. The need for the more aggressive cardioversion was ruled out. Anticoagulants to prevent stroke were administered, but a further discussion about their long-term use would take place with Catherine's primary-care doctor, whom she would see as an outpatient in a week. If needed, more in-depth evaluation of her heart muscle function would be pursued.

Sarah would stay by her mother's side all night in the hospital. The Winter House women headed home, feeling that their friend was in good hands and happy to know that the event, though somewhat frightening, was not as serious as it might have been. Marty's father and Janet's second husband had died of sudden heart attacks. Both women knew that heart disease was still the number-one killer of women over thirty-five, yet often presenting much differently in women, making it more difficult to diagnose. This time Catherine had been lucky.

Back at the Winter House, while waiting for news of Catherine's condition, Elizabeth opened the letter from her son in California. She hadn't heard from him in quite a while, but then she hadn't communicated with him either. It had been heartbreaking for Elizabeth and the rest of the family when Frank had refused to come to his father's funeral in New York. Elizabeth was having a hard time forgiving him, though she knew that this separation, emotional as well as physical, wasn't good for either of them. She longed for the old relationship they had had. He was her firstborn and had brought joy into her life. Prior to his birth, Elizabeth had no idea that she had any maternal instincts. No one could explain exactly what occurs when a small, vulnerable being, just out of the womb, is placed in a mother's arms. Her nurturing instincts blossomed overnight. Cliff had wanted to name the baby Clifford Franklin, Jr., but Elizabeth had refused to call him Junior, so they settled on Frankie, which he later changed to Frank, when he went off to college.

Cliff absolutely refused to talk with Elizabeth about the argument that he had had with his son. She knew that both Cliff and Frank were stubborn and a bit hotheaded at times, but in the past they had always been able to talk it out with Elizabeth's not-so-subtle encouragement. Not this time. Frank lived in California now, working for a nonprofit environmental group, and had recently had nothing to do with his father. Cliff saw no need to apologize or make any attempt to connect with his "wayward" son. For almost four years, their communications ceased. This estrangement had been extremely hard for Elizabeth. She checked on Facebook occasionally to see what Frank's son, Matthew, was up to. He was a graduate student in Seattle, and occasionally photos of Matt and his parents were on his Facebook site. Elizabeth longed to reconnect. She read the letter:

Dear Mom,

As the first anniversary of Dad's death is coming up, I have been thinking more and more about my actions, and I realize that because of my stubbornness, I hurt you. Michael and Nell might have seen my side of the story, but my selfishness blinded me from seeing the situation from the other side. Recently Matthew sent me an article on forgiveness, and it struck home. I realize it is too late for Dad and me to reconnect, but the disagreements weren't about you, and yet our relationship was so affected by Dad's attitudes.

What I am trying to say, really, is that I miss you and want to see you again, soon. I've talked with Libby and Michael, and they suggested we all meet in Boston in two weeks and reconnect as a family. I don't think Nell can make it due to her art gallery opening. Lib and Michael loved seeing Alcee recently. They say she is turning into a lovely young woman.

Perhaps someday I will actually go to New York and visit Woodlawn Cemetery to see Dad's grave. Maybe there I could feel a little reconnection. We did have many wonderful times together, but you know we could be stubborn.

I can fly out for a long weekend, just a simple nonstop flight from San Francisco to Boston. Maybe this would help to make the anniversary of your loss, our loss, not quite so hard. What do you think?
                                    I love you, Mom.
                                    Frankie

Elizabeth read the letter again. Tears dripped on the handwritten note. Why hadn't she reached out to her son first? Just what had stopped her? She had let her hurt blind her. Disengaging from one's own pain to connect with another's hurt takes courage, and often some kind of shove or little voice is needed. Perhaps, Matthew, a loving son, had nudged his father with some wise words, and that was what Frank needed — that gentle push to bring an awareness to the surface. She let out a huge sigh, holding the letter to her heart.

All these tears were not just over her relationship with her son. Elizabeth had been having vivid nightmares about Cliff's last words to her. She had told no one about the last conversation. It was too painful. And as the anniversary of his death approached, the mental video played again and again.

Cliff had flown to New York City from Bangor after a delightful President's Day three-day weekend. Elizabeth would drive back through Boston, stopping to visit Libby and Michael. She had brought up the topic of his fully retiring again, but Cliff said they could talk about it later. He rushed off to the airport for his afternoon flight to New York. When he called later that night, she made another comment about his retirement, and he exploded. He yelled, "Shut up, Elizabeth," and hung up the phone. She had burst into tears at the sound of those words, all-too-familiar words that pushed her buttons since she was small. Within minutes her cell phone rang. It was Cliff, but Elizabeth didn't answer. He left a message: "Elizabeth, I know you are there. I am so sorry. I didn't mean it. I just wasn't in the mood to talk again about my retirement. You know my consulting business is going through some rough times, and Mark Chandler just called to tell me our offshore deal fell through. You know how much that deal meant to me. Please forgive me. I'll call you in the morning." And those were the last words she heard from Cliff. A drunk driver turning onto 78th Street from Second Avenue hit him on a crosswalk around one in the morning. He died at the scene, they said. She didn't know what he was doing out that late, maybe drinking away the disappointment he was feeling; if only she had answered his phone call, given him some comfort, been a better wife, been more understanding. If only...

The phone rang, startling her. Elizabeth immediately picked it up. It was Marty. "Hi, Elizabeth, just wanted to tell you, we'll be home in about half an hour. Catherine is doing much better but will be staying overnight at the hospital. We'll tiptoe in, if you want to go to bed first."

"So glad to hear about Catherine. I probably will be in bed," Elizabeth replied. She felt mentally drained. "See you two in the morning."

"Sleep tight," Marty added. "Good night."

Elizabeth decided to take Quigley for a little walk before going upstairs. She found Quigley sleeping on Catherine's bed. At first, he was reluctant to go out without

Catherine, but he finally hopped down. Elizabeth used the leash. The night air struck her cheeks and chin, and she wrapped the scarf around her neck. The stillness and silence on Spruce Point calmed Elizabeth a bit. Lately, she noticed that she was getting more irritable with the living arrangements. Two days before, the yoga mats, blocks, and blankets lying around in the living room had bothered her. Marty and Janet had left them out absentmindedly. Though Elizabeth had felt like yelling, she instead went up to her room and cried on the bed. She wanted her old life back. She wanted Cliff's slippers by the door, not anyone else's. She longed for the aroma of his pipe and Old Spice. Elizabeth had read that the anniversary of a loved one's death could be tough, but she hadn't anticipated its toll on the household. She had considered just going away somewhere to be alone, but now with Frank wanting to reconnect, she realized the family had some significant sharing to do if they were ever going to be at peace with each other and themselves. Having her granddaughter around, even for a short time, had impressed upon her the need to keep the bonds tight with her own family. She realized a visit to Boston was just what she needed.

Elizabeth climbed into bed before the others arrived home. She wasn't up for late-night conversation. Not tonight. In her medicine cabinet she found some sleeping pills, which she hadn't taken since just after Cliff's death. Tonight she wanted to sleep and sleep without the recurrent nightmare. An unfinished crossword puzzle lay on her bedside table. Within fifteen minutes of adding some missing words, Elizabeth fell asleep. The pencil dropped.

When her two housemates returned, they checked on

Quigley, who was curled up on Catherine's bed. He looked up, hoping for his owner's return. "She'll be home tomorrow, Quig," Marty said. Upstairs, Janet said good night. Marty saw the light on under Elizabeth's door, but heard nothing. She opened the door, found her sound asleep, and turned out the bedside light. Then the Winter House was still. It had been quite a day.

A few days later, after yoga and lunch at the market, Marty and Janet returned to the Winter House. Both commented on the rather exhausting yoga class that Beth had led. They had concentrated on the spine and posture. Marty could hear Beth's enthusiasm in her comments and repeated them to Janet in the car. "Finding how to anchor your shoulders is strategic to a happy spine and a healthy life," Beth had said, as she placed her hand on the spine of each student, helping them locate the inner edge of the scapula. Marty had always had a problem with her shoulders flopping forward and had been following Beth's mantra. "Set your shoulders," she'd say and would demonstrate what she meant. "Up, back, and down!" Marty also had a troublesome ankle, and today she recalled another soothing statement from Beth: "Let your well side teach your healing side. You can release the restrictions with slow reprogramming."

That was it, Marty thought, slow reprogramming.

Janet spoke: "Beth didn't let us off the hook with our abdominals, either. Remember, she said, 'Coordinate your abdominal energy field to articulate your spine for greater spinal longevity.'"

"Wow," Marty remarked, "that was a mouthful for meaningful meditation." She laughed.

Janet laughed too, enjoying the yoga-session replay. She chuckled again, relishing the feeling of glee. What a difference a few months had made — her living in this new housing arrangement. Getting to share more than just a few hours a week with Marty was a significant bonus. Though still there, Janet's memory of the dark winter of last year was drifting off, diminishing with time.

The February early-afternoon sun grew warmer with each day. This was the month of more stable temperatures. The roller-coaster ride of temperature swings in January had passed, and as the days grew longer, the daytime temperatures reached a plateau in the twenties, very acceptable to Maine folk. The unknowing snowbirds who left for the winter months missed this fabulous time of brilliant sun and powdery snow.

As the two reached the driveway, they saw Catherine sitting out in the sun where the snow had melted. Quigley was on her lap also enjoying the fresh air and the warm sun. Catherine had been home a few days now and seemed as chipper as ever. She said she felt that she had been given another chance and planned to be better at exercising and eating right. She'd already given up her afternoon cookies.

"Good to see you outside," Janet said.

"Sure is a mighty fine day," Catherine replied. "Hard to stay inside with all this sunshine. I know spring is not really just around the corner, but it's getting closer every day." Catherine's favorite season was spring, always had been, ever since she was a little girl working with her mother in the garden, the same garden her grandmother had tended. Though dormant in the cold winter months, her perennials always returned, first slowly and then into full bloom. Catherine still had a dark-blue iris patch that went back four generations. Maybe this spring she would give Elizabeth a clump to decorate the Winter House's front yard.

"Yeah, a perfect winter day," Marty said. "I can't quite believe I am leaving next week, but it will be good to see everyone in Tucson. The little boys love visiting their grandparents' house there. You can't keep them out of the pool, and it's a good way for me to load up on vitamin D. You're getting some right now."

"Well, with only my face showing, I'll have to sit here awhile," Catherine replied.

"I suppose that's true. In Tucson I may even put on my bathing suit and splash around," Marty added.

"How long will you be gone?"

"Just a week, long enough to visit with my brother and sister-in-law, see the little boys and their parents, and hike a few trails in Saguaro National Park. It's a fun place for a family reunion, something to do for everyone."

"I've never been to Arizona, but I've heard it's a lovely place. Probably would be a bit too dry for me. I'd miss my ocean," Catherine said.

"Yes, well, I find it a lovely place to visit, but I'm with you — our water views are hard to beat, even in the winter."

They left Catherine and Quigley in the sun and entered the house. Elizabeth sat in the living room with her laptop, reading emails from the four children. They were all pleased that their mother had decided to come to Boston for a long weekend. Frank expressed happiness that this reunion would actually take place. He had struggled with writing the letter and was now relieved that he and his mother were connecting again. His son, Matt, rejoiced with the news and wanted to get away from his course work for the gathering, but he had a few big papers due and could not clear his calendar. "Be sure to email me photos," Matt had written his grandmother, "and maybe we can video chat." Nell was sad that she could not fly over from Italy to gather with them, but her new gallery was doing well, and she also wanted to be around for Alcee. Nell and Matt had both suggested that maybe a three-way video chat could be arranged. Elizabeth marveled at today's technology. Just imagine eliminating the distances between folks by placing a live screen right in the living room. This was science fiction not so many years ago.

"How are things?" Marty asked Elizabeth. Marty had felt a little chill around Elizabeth lately and wasn't exactly sure of the cause, though she and Janet had speculated that their yoga equipment was bothering Elizabeth. Over the last few days, they had made a big effort to put the mats and blocks away. Marty also poignantly remembered the first anniversary of Abigail's death and thought she knew what her housemate was experiencing. Elizabeth didn't seem to want to talk about it, so Marty had remained respectful.

"Things are okay," Elizabeth replied, as though she wasn't quite convinced of that. "I'm going to go to Boston over Presidents' Weekend and visit with my kids for a few days. Frank is going to fly in from San Francisco, and it's been some time since we've seen each other." Elizabeth couldn't remember if she had shared with the women that her elder son had been somewhat estranged for a while and hadn't come to his father's funeral. She opted not to mention it now.

"That's good news," Marty said. "I'm flying out to Tucson for a week with my brother and his family."

"So we'll both be gone for a while," Elizabeth said. "I'll just take the Concord Trailways bus from Bangor. It's quite a pleasant ride, with one movie and a snack. I find it more restful than getting into the snarl of airport delays, and around vacation time that always seems to happen." Elizabeth could drive to Boston, as she used to do quite often, but the bus was reliable in case there was a storm going or returning. Besides, parking in Boston wasn't easy. Getting around on the "T" was so simple.

"I've got a flight out of Bangor to Detroit and then on to Tucson, so I hope all goes well. If not, I'll just do some airport gazing. It's always amazing to notice what folks outside of Maine are doing. Seems like cell phones might as well be glued to everyone's head, and tattoos and earrings appear anywhere in any form on the body." On her last trip to Boston at Thanksgiving, Marty had seen a young man with fake padlocks hanging from his ears. However, it was a key tattooed on his forehead that really caught her eye. Amazing these fashions.

"Getting to see family will be good for both of us," Elizabeth said. "We don't want them to think we are all a bunch of hermits up here." She wondered to herself if she was actually hiding from the outside world.

The next weekend Janet came into the kitchen, having slept a little later than usual. "Good morning," she said to Catherine.

"Good morning. My, it seems empty around here, doesn't it?" Catherine poured a second cup of coffee. She had already walked Quigley, retrieved the Saturday paper, and read almost all of it. She hadn't yet begun the crossword puzzle. This slight feeling of loneliness was a bit strange to Catherine, who had been living alone for twelve years. Perhaps she was getting accustomed to speaking to more than just Quigley.

"I stayed up late last night, finishing my book," Janet said. "I just couldn't put it down, so I guess my body decided I needed to sleep in a bit longer," Janet paused. "Anything interesting in the paper today?" She knew Catherine devoured almost every word and then spent her time on the crossword puzzle.

Janet poured coffee, made herself an English muffin, buttered it lightly, and sat down. Catherine passed her the front section and started in on the crossword. Janet usually skimmed the headlines and read only what interested her. Catherine noticed that Janet was frowning as she read the front page slowly and flipped to the second page, staring intently. Then Janet dropped the paper on the table and left the kitchen, going upstairs without a word. Catherine thought she saw Janet wipe her cheek as she exited, but she wasn't sure.

What had upset Janet? Catherine had already read the entire front section. She looked again and quickly recalled the lead article: "Restaurant Owner Arrested for Sexually Abusing Minors." Was this the story that caught Janet's attention? In the article was a reference to the man's estranged daughter, who now lived in Georgia. The daughter was quoted as saying she could not believe that her father was not on the sexual predators' list. She demanded to know how that could be in this time of public disclosure. The article said that state officials claimed that the database was not yet complete, and they had been going retrospectively backward, adding names of offenders since the registry had come out. But it was in 1982 that this man had been found guilty of molesting his daughter and her best friend, and the database was completed only back to 1984. Thirty years later, long out of jail, he was still molesting young girls.

Was that what had upset Janet? Catherine wondered if she should go and see whether her housemate was okay. She waited a bit, but wanted to help and decided to go upstairs, holding tight to the banister for support and to protect her right hip. She knocked twice and Janet responded. Then she and Catherine had a very personal conversation.

Janet began, "When I was six or seven, my grandfather Al used to baby-sit for me and my older brother, Edward. Eddie used to play inside, working on his model planes and crystal radio. But, even at six, I liked to be outside and followed my grandfather around, watching him chop wood and repair engines. I liked hearing the stories that he told of his adventures in Alaska." Janet stopped telling the story and just looked out the window. Catherine said nothing. "Occasionally, when my mother was not around, my grandfather pulled out magazines from an old box on the top shelf of the tool shed and flipped through the pages, sometimes staring for a long time at the photos of naked children."

"You don't have to go on," Catherine said gently.

"I need to," Janet said. "I've kept this secret for too many years. I never told my mother. She never knew. I never even told my husband, John. I've tried to suppress it, sometimes even using alcohol to drown the memory, but that's not a healthy method, I know." She paused again. "It's a very deep pain, and I think bad secrets should come out." She grabbed a throw pillow and held it tightly. Catherine thought of her own recent secret — the hate letter.

Janet continued: "One day my grandfather asked me to take off my pants and sit on his lap, and while he told me a story about a beautiful white pony, he jiggled me up and down and touched me where he shouldn't." Janet now had tears in her eyes and began to sob.

Catherine put her arm around Janet's shoulder. "Janet, it's going to be okay. This was a long time ago; your grandfather was a sick man, and it was never your fault."

Janet went on. "He gave me candy after the story and told me never to tell anyone about our secret pony rides. And the worst part is that he gave me these rides for at least a year, but only when my mother was gone to town for the afternoon." Janet paused. "It seemed to stop when my brother started to keep an eye on Grandpa. I've always wondered if he did this to other children, or if he had done this to Eddie, who kept pretty clear of him. But I never spoke about it...never." Janet put her head down on Catherine's shoulder and sobbed. She cried for a long time, and Catherine held her, gently rubbing her back.

"Just let it all out," Catherine whispered. "Let it all out." Catherine's heart ached for Janet. She had known of a few cases of suspected incest with some of her own students. One father was actually sent to jail for sexually abusing his own daughter, a crime that had turned Catherine's stomach. The abused teenager, the mother, and a younger daughter moved away from Brooks Harbor soon thereafter. Catherine often wondered how the young teenage girl turned out. The curtain of secrecy and silence within communities did not help back then. Catherine knew that recently in a nearby town a support group had been created to help the victims of sex abuse. Most people, however, didn't want to hear or talk about it.

Janet's sobbing ceased. Catherine spoke: "I guess that article in the paper brought all your memories back. I think it is good that you have finally opened up. I will completely respect your privacy on this conversation, but maybe it would be helpful for you to meet others who have come out with their painful stories. There are support groups around."

Janet raised her head. "I've never felt I could speak about it. I felt embarrassed and guilty. AA meetings helped me with my drinking problem, so maybe you're right. I'll consider it, though it won't be easy, that's for sure, but just telling you feels better. No child should have to be exposed to this," she paused, "or have to live with such dark secrets."

"You're so right," Catherine said. "Trusting others to share your difficult story is a good start. Perhaps if there is more public discussion and awareness, children will be quicker to speak up." She hugged Janet.

"Thank you for being so understanding, Catherine."

"Listen, Janet, you helped me in my time of need with Harold, and now is my turn to help you." They smiled at each other. "Now, let's go down and get you some breakfast. We can warm up those English muffins and put on a fresh pot of coffee." Janet felt safe and cared for.

The two descended the stairs. Quigley, who was sitting outside the bedroom door, arose and led the way, prancing down each step. Perhaps a few crumbs of muffin would fall in his direction.

That evening Catherine decided to cook a meal. Without Marty and Elizabeth around, someone had to think about supper. Catherine prepared one of her mother's favorites, beef stew with dumplings. She used to help her mother drop the little balls of dough into the stew. To her amazement, the dough sank, disappearing into the broth, and then miraculously popped up like a submerged cork to the top, all light and fluffy. She remembered the three ingredients: water, flour, and salt. Her mother's hands would skillfully knead the dough. Catherine wasn't sure she had that technique mastered, but she was willing to try.

Janet volunteered to make a salad. In her childhood the definition of a salad to her mother was a pale piece of iceberg lettuce, a slice of canned pineapple, a spoonful of cottage cheese placed in the hole, and a bright red maraschino cherry on top. To Janet's credit, she had moved beyond her mother's concoction to master a spinach salad with mandarin oranges, dried cranberry pieces, whole walnuts, and feta cheese dressed with store-bought vinaigrette.

To their amazement the two women actually enjoyed the process of food preparation, perhaps because they each carried no pretense of being a superb cook and no expectations of the other's skills. When the meal was ready, they sat down to eat. Spontaneously, with a twinkle in their eyes, they raised their glasses of skim milk, clinked them together, and toasted to each other. Both hoped Marty and Elizabeth were enjoying their time away and looked forward to their return.

A few days later Janet and Catherine drove to Bangor, taking in a matinee of the new movie, *Iron Lady* with Meryl Streep, and wandering around the mall for a while. They met Elizabeth at the 6:10 bus from Boston. The bus was right on schedule. Then they chose to eat at Captain Nick's before driving home. Catherine had chicken Caesar salad;

Janet, a lobster roll; Elizabeth went for a bowl of haddock chowder with a glass of Chardonnay.

In the car on the way home, Elizabeth told of her wonderful visit to Boston. Though it was the anniversary of Cliff's death, the family tried to lighten the atmosphere and remember the good times in the earlier years, when Cliff had time for his family, and they vacationed in exotic places. They all remembered fondly their first trip to the Virgin Islands, where they had rented a fancy mansion with a gigantic pool. Elizabeth reminded everyone that Cliff had jumped in the pool with all his clothes on to rescue Nell, then just a toddler. Libby brought out the old photo albums, and Michael, Frank, and Libby told stories of their childhood and teenage years that Elizabeth hadn't heard before or didn't remember. Libby's two teenagers were all ears to hear Uncle Michael tell how he used to spy on his sister Libby when she was out in the backyard with her boyfriend. It seemed Libby and Michael had actually enjoyed annoying one another in their youth. Michael was three years younger but always tried to keep a step ahead of his older sister. Frank, the oldest, and Nell, the youngest, stayed out of this sibling rivalry and had their own adventures.

Elizabeth wasn't sure if she should tell all the events of the recent weekend. Some of the conversations had been tough. One night, after several glasses of wine, everyone had relaxed enough to bring up the harder issues. Elizabeth thought that these skeletons, now out of the closet, should be kept within the family. She was happy to have her relationship vastly improved with Frank. She respected his opinions and the reasons for his own actions. In the end there were a number of issues between Cliff and Frank that had broken their bond, including Frank's standing up for his gay younger brother. It had been good for Mason, Michael's partner, to hear about Frank's support. Elizabeth felt that now Mason and Michael could feel fully a part of the family.

Appreciating the virtual clearing breeze of this weekend with her family, Elizabeth wanted to extend that openness to her housemates. "I want to apologize to both of you for my crabbiness the last few weeks. I guess I hadn't realized how much the anniversary date of Cliff's death would affect me, and I have allowed that to put a strain on our environment. I have really appreciated having you all around, and it has made this winter pass much more quickly. I actually am not sure I would have had the courage to stay in the house all winter alone."

Janet concentrated on the road. Catherine piped up from the back seat. "Unfortunately, Janet and I both know about anniversaries of deaths of loved ones. Your reaction is entirely normal and to be expected. I can't speak for Janet, but for me the passage of time helps, but it was several years before the date slipped by without my mind calling attention to it. However, Harold's birthday I'll always remember."

"I've never been good with dates anyway," Janet added, "and I agree with Catherine that time does help, but the first year can be exceptionally hard. You have been very generous offering us the Winter House, and I think you have nothing to apologize for. We have made it through almost three months, past the halfway point, and for four independent women, I'd say we've done quite well."

"Well, you are great to say that. I believe it has been a good journey so far." She changed the subject. "When is Marty getting back?"

Janet spoke again: "She'll be back in three days, and I bet she's missed us." They all laughed.

The next day Elizabeth opened her mail, which Catherine had neatly piled up for her. A five-by-seven-inch envelope from Italy lay on the top. What could this be, she wondered. Inside her granddaughter had stuffed a note and three photos.

Dear Nonna,

I cannot believe it has been over a month since I was in Maine with you and your special friends. I'm doing well in my classes and my teachers are very pleased...so is Mamma...and me too. You told me I could do it if I tried. Thanks for having that confidence in me.

Fabio has taken off to sea. We've seen each other a few times, but it's not the same.

Enclosed are three photos for you. The last one captures the special place for me in my time of need. Thanks again for being such a wonderful grandmother.

Ti amo, Alcee

P.S. Please thank Marty for all her help. Hope all is going good there. Say hi to Quigley and Missy too.

The first photo was of Alcee and her mother, standing outside the new art gallery that Nell had been working so hard on. The expressions on their faces implied that they were close again and that the opening of the gallery had been a success. The second photo made Elizabeth laugh out loud. There she was in her black winter coat, purple scarf, and striped wool-felt hat, with her less-than-stylish L.L. Bean insulated rubber boots. Elizabeth pictured a label across the advertisement — *a Maine fashion statement*. The third photo was breathtaking, a magical scene. The full moon hung over the bay, casting its light on the water. Glistening snow covered the yard, the roof, and the trees. The warm yellow glow from the inside lights was in stark contrast to the deep blue of the winter night. Alcee's camera caught the smoke rising straight from the chimney. Elizabeth easily recalled that night and the warmth she had felt toward her granddaughter as well as toward the women inside the house.

Just then Elizabeth's cell phone rang, breaking her focus. She didn't get many calls and had recently seen most of her family.

"Oh, Elizabeth, this is Sarah. I'm glad to catch you. I assume my mother is out at the library, reading to the children."

"Yes, I think that is where she is," said Elizabeth, who really didn't keep track of Catherine's activities, as she was such a busy woman. But it was Thursday, so she must be reading. "How can I help you?"

"Well, Mom is having a birthday on April 28th, and it is a big one, her 80th. She has told me she doesn't want any fuss made over this. She says she will just be happy to reach it. I'm sure she will, but many folks in the town want to throw a big party for her to thank her for all that she has done for others over these years."

"Hey, that's a marvelous idea. I'd love to help you. What's your plan?"

"Well, to surprise her, we will probably have the party

the night before, so she won't be suspicious. We would like to keep it a secret for as long as we can, because otherwise Mom will fight it. Can you, Marty, and Janet think of something you could do with my mother on that evening, and then, instead of doing that, bring her to the community center? We'll have it all decorated and take care of the food and cake. Emma and Ella are really excited about the idea. I think I can get my two brothers, Harold and Will, to come up with their families. It should be a fun gathering of family, neighbors, and friends, old and new. I'm going to sneak over to Mom's place and make up some photo posters for display. I might also try to get some music for the event."

"Sounds like a great time. Count us in on the surprise," said Elizabeth. "I will tell Janet and Marty and see what ideas they may have."

"Great. I'll be in touch. Take care."

Elizabeth had only a small twinge of envy. How great for Catherine to have a daughter so near.

Janet sat by Simon Kirby's recliner. He was getting slowly weaker, and he knew it. She had read several pages of *The Iliad* as she neared the end of the book, but he seemed restless and unable to hold his concentration on the tale. At times he would doze off while she read, and at other times he asked her poignant questions on death and dying.

She respected this Harvard-educated man, a former professor at Vassar College, and an expert on Chaucer and Shakespeare. Simon had outlived his wife, also an academic, who had died of breast cancer, as well as his son, who had died on September 11, 2001 in New York City. At one time he had the command of seven languages. Simon had slowly lost much of his vision from macular degeneration, a cruel affliction for an avid reader such as he. When he received the diagnosis of aggressive prostate cancer with bone metastases, he had elected at his age of ninety-four to forgo any heroic treatments. His mind had remained sharp. At times he required narcotics to alleviate pain, but in general he wanted to face death straight on.

"Janet," he said, "I have a favor I would like to ask of you."

"What would that be, Simon?"

"I've been doing a lot of thinking about people with whom I haven't kept in touch over these years, and, Lord knows, unfortunately, some have already died. Some people I have hurt too. There is one special fellow I would like to write to before I die. I know he is not dead yet."

Janet listened intently to this old and wise man. During her hospice work she was accustomed to hearing folks actively reviewing their lives as they neared their death. Currently, Janet used a book, *The Top Five Regrets of the Dying,* by Bronnie Ware, as a supplement in her hospice-training course, and she knew it was an equally good reminder of how to live life, even before approaching death. Regretting the failure to keep up with friends and family, for whatever reasons, was a common disappointment. Near the end, it was not money, possessions, status or fame, but relationships that counted. Janet recalled the four other most common regrets. Many men wished they hadn't worked so hard, realizing that they had neglected their children's youth and their wives' companionship. Janet thought of Elizabeth and a regret that her husband, Cliff, might have had if he had lived after the accident. What had pushed him to spend so much time on the treadmill of work, slowly losing his family connections? Others regretted not having the courage to express their feelings. Janet admired Marty for being so up-front with hers. For years Janet had kept many feelings to herself and maybe had dived into the bottle just for that reason. But slowly she was finding it easier to share.

Simon continued, "After my twenty-fifth college reunion, I completely lost touch with George, my Harvard roommate. He moved out to California with his new partner, and our communications ceased. I had been shocked to find out he was gay, never having a hint of it in our three years of living together at college. I guess I thought this revelation reflected on me, and I wasn't prepared for that. At the tenth reunion he had brought his new wife. But I guess that relationship didn't work out. It all seemed strange to me. He even wrote me around the fiftieth reunion to see if I was returning, but I never responded to him, just didn't know what to say," Simon paused. "I went to the reunion, but he didn't come. He was my best friend at Harvard, and what a talented chap. You know, Janet, he won all the drama awards and even wrote plays for the Harvard Dramatic Club. Our years at Harvard were such fun, and we had some jolly laughs...once we all dressed in drag and put on *The Threepenny Opera*. It brought the house down." He smiled.

"Janet, I'd like you to help me write a letter. Would you get some stationery in the second drawer of my desk? There's a pen there too."

Janet found the Harvard stationery, a little yellowed with age. Simon probably had not used it for a while, given his poor vision, and his handwriting suffered from a fine tremor.

The last two regrets came to her: Those dying wished

they had lived a life true to themselves, and not a life that others expected. Simon's roommate had done that. In an age of closeted gays, George had openly come out at his twenty-fifth college reunion, had been rejected by many of his closest friends, and then moved to San Francisco, where the atmosphere was changing more quickly than on the stodgy old East Coast.

Simon began his dictation. Janet lifted the pen, listening closely to his words:

"Dear George,

I am on my deathbed, they tell me, and yet I luckily still have my wits about me. My eyesight has entirely failed me, so a friend is writing this down for me, just in case you don't recognize the handwriting. Before leaving this place, I wanted to reconnect and tell you how much I regret that I have not stayed in touch with you. Of all my friendships through these years, ours was the most fun, most creative, and most sincere. You made me laugh and participate in activities that I might never have chosen. I haven't acted in years, much less dressed in drag. I want to tell you that I admire you for following your own path and not worrying what others would think. How the times have changed over these seventy years, and I have too. I allowed my narrow upbringing to blind me to others' situations. Your personal choice of partners should not have affected our friendship, but I let it. And for that, I apologize.

I hope that you are doing well and that aging has left you still vital and engaged with life. Who

*would have believed we both would make it into our
nineties. Each day for me is still a miracle.*
                    My sincerest regards, Simon"

"How's that?" Simon asked.

"That's just fine, Simon," Janet replied. She could barely hold back tears. The final regret of many folks is to have
not allowed themselves to be happier. Near the end, they
begin to realize that happiness is a choice, and yet many
remain stuck in old habits and patterns. Yet, as life slips
away, many crave an openness and honesty to be themselves. "I am sure he will appreciate your letter, Simon.
Why don't you sign it right here." Janet guided his hand
on the paper.

"You'll find stamps and an envelope in the second drawer. In the blue index-card box on my desk is his address
under H for Hallowell, George Patrick Hallowell." As Janet
prepared the letter for mailing, she noticed that Simon had
fallen asleep, having taken care of one regret.

Elizabeth drove to Bangor to pick up Marty at the airport. Marty's Detroit-Bangor connection had been delayed,
which gave Elizabeth time to stop at the Art For All store
and buy some new art supplies. In her art class the night
before, Bob Chester had decided to move on from charcoal
sketching, which everyone seemed to have enjoyed, to oils
— a greater challenge. At Middlebury Elizabeth had tried
her hand at oils but found watercolor easier. Bob insisted
that everyone should give the medium of the Old Masters
a try. He wanted each student to bring in a photo to work
from. Almost immediately Elizabeth knew the picture she
wanted to paint, the one that Alcee had sent. Maybe she

could capture that magical moment on canvas. Bob had given the students a list of supplies to get them started, and Bangor was a good place to pick them up. She purchased an array of Windsor and Newton colored oil tubes, concentrating on the dark blues, purples, blacks, and a few different whites with such names as Snow White, Titanium White, and Pearl White. From college she recalled that artists used reds and yellows beneath the more obvious colors. Though these materials were expensive, Elizabeth hoped to make painting a significant part of her life now.

Her cell phone rang. It was Marty. "The eagle has landed," Marty said, making reference to a Michael Caine movie from the seventies. Elizabeth got the picture.

"I'll be there in a few minutes. I'm on Union Street. I'll meet you outside the baggage claim door."

"Okay, see you soon," Marty replied. Bangor was a small airport, which made for easy pick-ups. No traffic jams or lines of taxis or hotel limousines. No, it was very convenient, though occasionally more costly for flights. Its main claim to fame was the group of dedicated troop greeters who continued to meet U.S. soldiers going to and returning from Iraq and Afghanistan. A documentary on these greeters, called *The Way We Get By,* had come out a few years ago. The film had even been nominated for an Emmy award. Elizabeth and Cliff had gone to the film's grand opening in New York, and both of them had choked up during some of the scenes.

As Elizabeth pulled up to the curb where Marty was standing, she noticed three or four soldiers dressed in desert fatigues standing outside, smoking cigarettes. Some were talking on cell phones that had been given to the troops to call home. Elizabeth only hoped that someday these young soldiers would all come home for good.

"Hi, Marty, I'm so glad the plane made it, finally," Elizabeth said.

"Thanks for picking me up. Leaving Tucson was fine, but some mechanical problem in Detroit delayed us. Glad it wasn't the snowstorm yet. How are the roads?"

"Oh, not bad really. We just had a dusting last night, and all the roads have been cleared or sanded. But they're talking about a foot or two for tomorrow night."

"Well, I'm up for a little winter fun. It's good to be home. Tucson is pleasant, and it was great to see my brother and family, but I was ready to get back to winter. How's everyone?"

"We're good, we're good," Elizabeth said, and after her Boston visit with her family, she certainly felt much better than she had when Marty left a week ago.

MARCH

*T*hat snowstorm came, and then another one followed in a week. The piles by the sides of the roads built up into high mounds. The Blakey boys, Jerry and Jimmy, returned several times to shovel the walks and push back the sides. Luckily, the snow had been light, causing some drifting but no ice to speak of. It was a winter wonderland.

The women enjoyed staying inside together. School closed for one day during the first storm and two days, the second. Several activities in the community had been postponed after the second storm. But all this was quite normal for the season.

Folks used to try predicting the last storm. Just when you thought spring was around the corner, the arctic jet stream would dip down and throw in another blizzard. Mainers handled them as they came. By the end of March, however, most wanted winter to stop.

Janet and Marty made ski trails down toward the Point and ventured out most afternoons. Though Catherine and Elizabeth admired their housemates' outdoor activities, each had inside projects. Catherine had catalogues to peruse, while Elizabeth spent hours upstairs working on her oil painting. She wasn't willing to show it to anyone yet, but she had definitely caught the passion again.

On the Wednesday between the two storms, Marty attended a board meeting at the local hospital. As with other small community hospitals, operating costs were increasing, and the board felt it was time for some drastic changes. Recently the board had been split on whether to join the regional healthcare system. Several local hospitals had thrown in the towel, unable to survive as solitary entities in the modern medical environment, just as many physicians had given up their traditional solo shingle or small group practice and been almost forced to become employees of the hospitals. Times had certainly changed during Marty's life. Both she and her father had worked as physicians in their own communities, each considering the medical practice a calling, never imagining being salaried and regulated by hospital administrators. Certainly, they never envisioned being tied to a computer screen — checking off little boxes — too rushed to be able to look into patients' eyes to read their emotions or to sit at their hospital bedside during the greatest time of need, when the involvement of their personal physician mattered most to them.

All these medical changes were supposed to increase efficiency and accuracy and cut costs. But at what expense to the patient/doctor relationship? The hospitals, the states, and the country face great pressures to cut medical costs. The well-known journalist T.R.Reid, author of *The Healing of America,* has alerted Americans that the United States has the most expensive healthcare system and yet does the poorest job among all the industrialized countries of caring for patients. Of these countries, only the United States, the richest nation in the world, fails to cover all its citizens for medical care. Fifty million people have no medical insurance. Marty believed this was an atrocity, but she had little hope that in her lifetime universal healthcare coverage would become a reality.

Marty was not convinced that joining the larger medical system was necessary for the local hospital, but many other board members, mostly businessmen, believed it was financially the only way to go. Even though some holdouts on the board had clung to their spirit of Yankee independence, revering the hospital's ninety-year history, the members eventually voted eleven to five to join the larger regional healthcare system. On the drive home, Marty hoped for the best in this decision, concluding that if a merger could prevent the financial collapse of the hospital and provide access to modern medical technologies — all without losing its personal touch — it would be a win-win for everyone on the peninsula.

As the snow kept mounting outside, Catherine came into the kitchen for her morning coffee. She and Quigley had slept in a little longer than usual. Marty had already made the coffee and brought in the *Bangor Daily News.* Somehow or other, the paper, just like the mail, almost always made it, no matter what the weather.

"Wow, this is looking like it's going to be a big one," Catherine said.

"The paper says we'll have quite an accumulation."

Marty had scanned the paper already and checked the weather report. One obituary had caught her eye. A handsome, seventeen-year-old boy from Brooks Harbor had "died unexpectedly" at home. Marty knew that was often a euphemism for suicide. Many years ago a suicide-prevention study had shown that kids tended to copy-cat suicides reported in the newspapers, so the policy in many papers was to not mention the cause of death, with the hope that this would cut down on suicide contagion. Marty asked Catherine, "Did you know Tyler Simmons? It says he lived in Brooks Harbor."

Catherine wrinkled her forehead. "I met his mother at the library once. They are fairly new in town. I think the father's an architect," she replied. "Why?"

"The boy died at home," Marty said. "That's a shame. He was so young."

"Was it an accident?" Catherine asked.

"Doesn't say so here," Marty said.

Catherine and Marty reflected on their experiences with suicide. In her career as a high-school teacher, Catherine had had two students who had taken their own lives, and she knew that obituaries didn't use the word anymore. "We know so little about suicide, and it is such a tragedy for those who are left behind," Catherine said. "Some folks never get over it, or if they do, it takes a lot of support from friends and the community." Catherine remembered the relatives of these two students. One family had left town, but the other family still lived in Brooks Harbor and had built themselves a new life.

Marty couldn't help thinking of a young patient of hers who had hanged himself in the basement of his home. He'd left a note for his parents, saying he just couldn't stand to be different anymore and didn't want to be an embarrassment to them or be bullied in school. They were devastated. Their religion claimed that homosexuality was a sin, and they had prayed every night that he would repent. Marty poured her second cup of coffee, slowly stirring the cream and sugar.

"I had a young patient once who committed suicide. I'll never forget him." Marty paused. "There was something about him I admired. He dressed in his own way, though his parents insisted he wear a coat and tie to church and go every Sunday. He loved to write poetry and suggested books to me that seemed way beyond his years." She paused again. "On his last visit to my office, he had just turned fifteen and insisted on seeing me alone, without his mother. He told me he was feeling isolated from his peer group at school and misunderstood by his parents. When I tried to delve deeper, he clammed up, perhaps afraid that I would speak to his mother. I suggested he come in again, if things didn't get better...and obviously things didn't get better, but worse." Marty swallowed hard. "He killed himself two weeks later. As a physician, I failed him, not being able to probe his tortured teenage mind and ease his pain." Her throat tightened. "I probably should have asked him straight out if he was considering suicide. We know now that asking that question does not put thoughts into their minds but instead may help and even open up the conversation." Marty shook her head and sipped her coffee. "If only back then, I had told him that things improve with time." She thought of the recent online video "It Gets Better," produced by a gay man in response to a tragic event at Rutgers University — a freshman committed suicide after being exposed on the Internet.

Marty continued, "Many studies have shown that gay teens are at a higher risk for suicide than heterosexual teens, although some folks argue over the statistics used to prove this. I don't know if anything I could have said would have influenced his actions."

Catherine had seen that online video and had read a lot about homosexuality, but she had never discussed it openly and never directly with a lesbian. Nor had she ever talked with Marty about her partner, Abigail. She had seen Abigail a few times in the market but hadn't really known her. Most of the time Marty and Abigail stayed at their house, gardening and sailing. Catherine was curious about Marty and Abigail's relationship. Years ago, in the high school where Catherine taught, a single male teacher, whom Catherine assumed was gay, kept his private life pretty much to himself. In those days teachers could be fired for being gay, so they remained in the closet. Parents had fears that a gay teacher would influence their children. Some folks even equated homosexuality with pedophilia. From her reading Catherine had learned they were not the same, but there was much confusion in the public mind.

"How did you and Abigail meet?" Catherine asked.

"Oh, I began working in an outreach medical clinic in Burlington, and she was the intake nurse. I had been practicing medicine for several years, and medicine was my life. Abigail was divorced too, and we just started talking and sharing our situations. Something about her made me feel so comfortable. So we began seeing each other outside of the clinic. And in time we realized we were falling in love," Marty said.

Catherine hadn't expected Marty to be so candid, but then Marty was direct about everything else, so why should she hold back on this aspect of her life?

"She brought me great happiness," Marty continued. "I'm not one for labels and feel that much harm is done trying to label 'love.' Am I bisexual or a lesbian? I thought that I loved my husband, at least for a short time, but maybe that traumatic and abrupt ending channeled me to look for comfort from a woman."

Catherine said, "Personally, as I near the age of eighty, I have less and less tolerance for intolerance. Just whose business is it, really, who loves whom? A few years ago Reverend Perry gave a sermon about accepting gay marriage, and three members left the church and never returned." Catherine paused, thinking about that hate letter she had received. "About five years ago at the annual town meeting, Brooks Harbor passed a resolution calling for no discrimination based on race, religion, sex, or sexual orientation. After one emotional plea from a local woman, the vote was 87-4, winning by an overwhelming majority." At first Catherine smiled, but the hate letter gnawed at her heart. Marty noticed the concern on her face.

"What's that look about?" Marty said. She had years of training in reading faces and knew when something bothersome was on someone's mind.

At that moment Elizabeth and Janet came into the kitchen to have their morning coffee. The falling snow continued to accumulate, and no one was going anywhere.

"Oh, sorry, did we interrupt something?" Elizabeth said. Catherine and Marty were slow to respond.

"It appears that we have," Janet said.

Catherine took a deep breath and quickly decided to tell all the housemates about the letter. She knew it wasn't good to keep the upsetting note to herself. After all, stress wasn't good for her health. "No, no, I have wanted to talk with you all about something," she paused. "Do you remember several weeks ago, just before I was taken to the hospital?"

"Yes," Janet said, "the afternoon you looked so pale."

"Right, well, I received a horrible letter in the mail that day, and it really upset me." Catherine wanted to get the matter out in the open but didn't want to speak the filthy words. "Let me get it," she said, and she went to her room.

"Wow, it must be something. She's kept this a secret for almost a month," Janet added.

Catherine came back with the crumpled note that she had stashed in her bedside drawer. She handed it to Marty, who read it silently and passed it to Janet, then to Elizabeth.

"Do you have any idea who wrote this? I'd say the author has a mental problem." That was Marty's best guess.

"Well, I'd second that. This is hardly the predominant sentiment in town," Janet said. "Good alliteration with the F words, though."

"Catherine, this is just some mixed-up person who wanted to get your goat. It's actually a snail-mail type of bullying," Marty said.

Elizabeth spoke: "It's what goes on over the Internet in chat rooms and social networks all the time. I think you know that my son, Michael, is gay, and he struggled with coming out to us. In high school he had seen how brutal his peers could be to the openly gay students, so he hid his sexual orientation until his thirties. I think he knew how his father would respond too."

No one said anything for a few seconds.

Then Elizabeth continued, "We had worried about him; I had my suspicions. Cliff just kept saying he hadn't met the right woman yet. When finally Michael met Mason, he wanted to introduce him to us. Cliff had a really hard time with it. I just wanted Michael to be happy. I tried to get Cliff to read the book called *Much More Than Sexuality*, which Michael had given me, but unfortunately Cliff, like most people, wouldn't even look at it. The book certainly did help me understand better." Elizabeth paused. "Then, when Mason and Michael wanted to get married in Boston, Cliff just couldn't go along with it. But Michael didn't care at that point. And I just learned that his brother, Frank, stood up to Cliff, and that was the last straw; their relationship really went to hell," Elizabeth's eyes moistened. "It was just so hard. I just wanted my son to be happy."

"He is now, isn't he?" Catherine said gently.

"Yes, you're right, and now my family is united. And Mason is a part of it," Elizabeth said. She wiped away tears.

"Catherine, I'm really glad you showed us this letter and voiced your distress. We all know who we are, and at our age, do we really care what others think?" Marty said.

"The concept of older women deciding to live together when they are single, divorced, or widowed is strange and new to many. Some women would prefer to live alone, even though they know that companionship is important to health," Janet commented, thinking how positive this experience had been.

"Maybe some folks in town think of us as an expanded *Boston marriage*," Elizabeth laughed, "or that we've just reverted to a five-star dormitory life." She recalled a bumper sticker that she had seen on her trip to Boston: *"Small communities do not have to equal small minds."* It made her think, but she figured she wouldn't put that on her bumper.

"I say just let them think what they want and fantasize all they want. They just don't know what they are missing," Janet added. Then she asked, "Anyone for eggs and bacon?"

The week before, Janet had returned to Simon Kirby's and noticed a change. He slept most days, though he woke up for her. She asked if he would like to have some singers from hospice come and give him his own concert. A dear friend of Janet's had helped to start the Evensong Singers several years before, and she had heard them by the bedside a few times. She thought Simon would enjoy it. He agreed.

Today was the day. About eight volunteer singers arrived and came into the sunlit bedroom. After introductions the leader started them off with the oldie "Take Me Out to the Ball Game." This delighted Simon. He had shared earlier with Janet, also a Red Sox fan, that their team's winning the World Championship in 2004 was one of his biggest joys. It had been a long wait, but he had remained loyal despite his father's talk about the Curse of the Bambino. In fact, the last time his team captured the title was in 1918, the year Simon was born.

"Thank you," Simon said, almost tipping his imaginary baseball cap.

Janet had given the group a little background on Simon's history. When they broke into "Men of Harvard," she was not surprised. Simon, in his weakened state, mouthed the words. Tears came to his eyes as well as to Janet's as the group ended with the final verse: "And when the game ends, we'll sing again. Ten thousand men of Harvard gained vict'ry today." Then Simon requested his mother's favorite hymn, "Be Still My Soul," and the singers knew this well. The room filled with a peace that Janet had rarely felt. His last choice was for "Amazing Grace," the most commonly requested hymn. His eyes closed as the singers' harmonies filled the room: "I once was lost but now am found, was blind but now I see." He slept. Janet walked the group to the door.

Saturday was a busy day for the four women. Elizabeth had invited them all to go with her to experience the Metropolitan Opera screen performance of Handel's *Rodelinda* at the Grand Theater in Ellsworth. For several years now operas had been brought to Maine with live simulcasts. Initially, only serious opera buffs went, but as their popularity grew and spread by word of mouth, these performances became a Saturday afternoon ritual for many. Marty's father had loved opera and listened to it on the radio when she was young, so she was familiar with much of the music. She had never heard *Rodelinda*. When they lived in New York, Elizabeth and Cliff had attended many performances at the Met, and now she enjoyed these simulcasts immensely, as the camera lens brought the audience up close to the performers and the orchestra. Janet and Catherine had not seen any live opera and readily accepted their housemate's invitation.

On this overcast day the women drove to Ellsworth for the four-hour screening. Upon entering the theater Janet recognized a few people from her years of work in Ellsworth. Marty chatted briefly with the chairman of the board of the hospital, while the other women found their seats on the left side about halfway down. Catherine had been to a few movies at the Grand, but now the spectacle of the theater's red and gold accents made it appear more alive. On the screen was the elegant interior of the Metropolitan Opera concert hall. The audiences chatted in New York and Ellsworth, awaiting the arrival of the maestro in the orchestra pit.

The lights darkened, the curtain opened, and *Rodelinda* began. Handel's opening piece, the overture, had set the stage. Catherine was delighted that the actors' words appeared at the bottom of the screen. She had had a hard time reading the program notes describing the acts, involving many characters with unfamiliar Italian names. She was most thrilled to hear the soprano Renee Fleming for the first time.

At these simulcasts no binoculars were necessary. Everyone had a good seat. The music and lyrics affected Marty, much to her surprise. She had a tough shell and had thought she was over the loss of Abigail. Fleming's acting and singing so successfully captured the tragic loss of Rodelinda's husband, and then the joyful romantic reuniting, that Marty allowed herself to ponder what was next in her own life. When she heard "Return my greatest treasure, the hope which fate had taken from me. My hope is restored. Love will conquer all past sadness," a tear fell down Marty's cheek. She tried to conceal wiping it away, but Janet, sitting next to her, noticed, reached her arm around Marty, and gave a gentle squeeze to provide her friend comfort. Loss and love were powerful themes in the opera.

The performance flew by for Catherine, though sitting for four hours had been hard on her hip. The two intermissions made it bearable. As she walked to the car, Marty hummed her favorite aria. Fleming's tone and range were astonishing. Elizabeth commented that she had heard Fleming at the Met several years before in this production. Janet was quiet on the way out. Though she had enjoyed it, her mind kept wandering back to Simon Kirby. She knew he would die soon and wasn't quite sure she was ready for it. No matter how old someone was, the final separation was painful. Janet remembered her fellow hospice volunteer Anna sharing that she was continuously awed by the meaning and the mystery of those last moments between life and death. Simon exemplified all the things Janet's father was not — not educated, not sensitive, not real. What demons had her father held inside to keep him so distant? She could only imagine. When her parents died, their dark secrets went with them.

"Janet, are you with us?" Elizabeth asked, as all four climbed into the Toyota.

"She's probably thinking about tonight. It's so wonderful you are getting recognized for all your hospice work," Catherine said.

"I admit I'm both honored and nervous. I'm certainly not used to public attention," Janet replied, "and I don't want to get overly emotional in front of people."

"You'll do just fine," Marty replied, sensing a bit of sadness in Janet's voice and wanting to repay her kindness in the theater. "Are you worried about Simon?"

Janet appreciated Marty's sensitivity and caring. "I think he will die soon, and I need to prepare myself. As hospice volunteers, we can get pretty close to those we visit. After all these years there are still some connections that are more intimate than others. As a nurse I tried to stay objective or have a little guard up, or I would have burned out quickly. I do believe it is in the giving of ourselves that we receive." She realized she was almost quoting the Bible.

"Well, you have been such a help to him," Catherine replied. Catherine had known Simon for quite awhile. She'd always wondered how he managed with no family around. "You've provided much solace for him in these last two years."

"It's been a mutual admiration society," Janet answered.

"And as for tonight," Catherine said, "we'll all be there for you. Having given much to our community, you deserve this recognition."

Later, at the annual hospice-volunteer recognition dinner, Janet and three others were presented with plaques. Because of Janet's twenty-five years of service and her recent interest in adding travel to her hospice experience, she received a copy of a book titled *Hospice Care on the International Scene.* Janet had been looking into traveling to Nicaragua with a group she had heard about, but she knew she'd have to brush up on her high-school Spanish — a review that would actually be like starting again.

Being new to the year-round community, Elizabeth was impressed with the turnout for this event. The large meeting room was filled with people whom she had never seen before. That should have been no surprise; most summer folk, and she had been one, usually stuck together, partying, sailing, and enjoying their precious summer moments in Maine. Those were the faces she knew. But here Elizabeth was becoming aware of another community, a giving community that was at this moment recognizing their own.

Elizabeth had done some charity work during her time in Connecticut and New York. Cliff was always being asked to be on various boards. He usually offered his wife's services, and Elizabeth had dutifully accepted. She realized that it was their money and name that organizations wanted. She never became overly involved, however — just served on some ad-hoc fundraising subcommittees, which didn't bring her much satisfaction. As she listened to descriptions of the work that hospice volunteers were doing in Maine, she made a commitment to herself to join in on the ground level of some charitable organization right here.

Marty was very proud of Janet. How many people stuck with an organization for twenty-five years? She recalled, from her own practice in Vermont, the need for assistance with end-of-life issues. At one time doctors in general had not been very accepting of hospice programs. In medical school young physicians were trained to save lives, not to end them. Desperate measures were taken to keep patients alive, and she recalled the common personal challenge during her residency: Don't let a patient die on my watch. Over the years Marty learned that death should not be looked upon as the enemy or as a failure. In fact, everyone knew they would die sometime. Significant progress had been made in accepting hospice as a mindful, reasonable, and perhaps more humane alternative to dying in the hospital, where sometimes useless, expensive, and inappropriate last-ditch measures to sustain a life were implemented.

Janet beamed as she walked up to receive her plaque and book. She knew it had been this program and her ability to give of herself that had been paramount to her surviving single life after the difficulties — divorce and alcohol abuse — that had contributed to her utter loss of self-esteem. Since John's death, she had continued to be able to help others, and that had helped her to heal from the loss. On the way to the podium, Ruth Bishop, one of the hospice volunteers who had played a significant role in Janet's mother's final days, extended her hand and voiced her congratulations.

At the podium Janet spoke: "Thank you everyone for this recognition. However, it is I who must recognize Hancock Hospice for these wonderful twenty-five years that you have given to me. Hospice volunteering has given me the opportunity to stay vital and alive and connect with special people in their time of need." She took a breath and continued. "There is no doubt in my mind that this organization provides a win-win opportunity for us all. Thank you, thank you." Everyone rose to give her well-deserved applause as Janet threw a gentle kiss out to the gathering, bowed with her hands together over her chest, and walked back to her seat. Marty, Elizabeth, and Catherine each loved this special woman in their own way and were delighted to have shared the experience.

As March moved along and the snow began melting, daytime temperatures rose, heralding the return of spring. In the morning Catherine observed small, deep-blue snowdrops poking up through the snow cover on the sunny side of the house. The fresh smell of the pines reappeared. Quigley sniffed the bare spots on the path as if some creature had recently been there. Then she noticed the metal rod that held the tubular plastic bird feeder, the one she tried to keep filled all winter for the hardy remaining black-capped chickadees. The rod was completely bent over, and the bird feeder lay on the ground with large puncture holes in the plastic. The metal top was still on the feeder, but no seeds remained inside. Catherine supposed the seed had all been shaken out. Only a bear could have bent the one-inch steel rod and bitten into the plastic. The bear had come out of hibernation, a sure sign of spring.

At breakfast Elizabeth was shocked to be told about the bear. She had heard at the market that a bear had been spotted digging in someone's compost pile but had never imagined one would come so close to her house.

"I've only seen a bear in the zoo," Elizabeth said.

"We have quite a lot of black bears around, and now they must be hungry and might have a cub or two to feed. I probably should have kept the bird feeder inside during the night. Those little chickadees will soon have easier foraging as spring comes along." Catherine had loved the black-capped chickadees ever since she was a little girl. "Did you know that those chickadees are the designated Maine state bird?" Catherine said. "I remember Uncle Cyrus telling me that when I was small. My husband catered to my fondness for bird feeders and birdhouses and made many creative contraptions to keep the squirrels and chipmunks away," Catherine laughed. "Some worked, some didn't."

As Catherine read the obituaries, she found Maeve Blakey listed. She had heard at the library that Jerry and Jimmy's mother had been found dead in bed. Maeve had not been well, but still it was probably a shock to the young men. Catherine made a mental note to call them.

When Marty and Janet returned from their yoga session, they were excited to tell their housemates of their progress. Neither could actually believe that they were getting closer to a complete headstand. For weeks their final exercise of the session was practicing on setting their base correctly. Beth, a patient instructor, knew full well that to obtain the ultimate position the students must have a proper base for stability. Otherwise, there could be the risk of injury. Well into their seventies, neither woman wanted to do anything dangerous, but they were both progressing and beginning to comprehend that a headstand actually has little to do with the head. It all depends on forearms and shoulders. Today each had advanced a baby step, and they were thrilled.

"Janet almost has it," Marty said to Catherine and Elizabeth.

"No, I don't think so. I'm still a long way from doing the complete inversion," Janet quipped. She had been doing yoga for a while and had faith in her teacher.

"Well, Beth won't let us try the complete inversion until she believes our core, shoulders, and arms are strong enough. Even if we don't do a complete inversion, we're doing pretty well for our age," Marty added.

"Yes, the others are much younger and have been doing yoga for years. They do make it look easy," Janet said.

"Well, you two amaze me. Just your determination to keep at it is impressive," said Catherine, who never really exercised except for walking Quigley. For her heart health she knew she should do more.

Elizabeth had noticed that she had put on a few pounds. It was true she wasn't doing any exercise. In Manhattan she had walked everywhere, even in the winter, and weight had not been an issue. But Maine winters presented a challenge, especially to those who didn't ski. She was considering signing up for the Zumba classes that were starting in April at the community center. After all, she still wanted to look good in a bathing suit.

When Elizabeth returned from her late-afternoon painting class, she noticed that instead of arriving back home in the pitch darkness, there was now a hint of twilight, a sure sign the days were getting longer. After pulling into the garage, she saw that Marty's car was gone, and there were no lights on in the house. She opened the door to the kitchen and flipped on the switch. The house was empty, but a note lay on the kitchen table.

Marty's scribbled handwriting read: "We've gone to Brewer with Quigley. A porcupine got him, and we must get the quills out. Hope to be back soon." Poor dog, Elizabeth thought. She turned on a few more lights. She hadn't been alone in the house for almost four months, and it felt odd. First bears, then porcupines. Wouldn't her sister, Eve, enjoy this menagerie of wild things?

She went back out to the car and brought her canvas inside. Her painting session had gone well, and Bob Chester felt she was really capturing the scene. He had given her a few suggestions, which she appreciated and planned to work on. He wanted her to enter the Belfast Art Festival competition. For several years now many local artists had submitted the fruits of their winter labors. Bob remarked that Belfast had created a popular spring event to greet the return of the snowbirds from their southern hibernation.

Of course, Elizabeth was flattered and thrilled by Bob's encouragement. The deadline for submission was March 31. She would do it, just for the fun of it. Wouldn't Nell be amazed to hear that her mother was entering the world of art? And Cliff would have been quite surprised too. He always urged her to get back into it but also said he doubted she ever would. He had also believed that she wouldn't like living in Maine in the winter. Well, he was wrong — wrong on both counts.

Her cell phone rang, interrupting her thoughts.

"Oh, hi, Elizabeth," Marty said. We're all set with Quigley. The vet had to knock him out to pull out the quills from inside his mouth. He's a bit sleepy, but we're bringing him home."

"Poor little fellow," Elizabeth said. "How's Catherine?"

"She's fine. But we are all a bit hungry so we'll probably stop at Wendy's for a quick bite. I hope you can find something to eat," Marty said.

"Don't worry about me. I'm on a diet, remember?" Elizabeth was trying to watch her carbohydrates and limit wine to one glass a night, a way to cut calories and decrease her risk of breast cancer. She had just read about that recently. She pulled out a can of Snow's clam chowder and made a simple green salad. She'd skip the crackers. As she sat down in front of the TV to eat, she turned on the Nightly Business News. Elizabeth then recalled that she hadn't eaten alone since December 1, marking almost four months of communal living. Eating alone now seemed odd and lonely, even more than it had before. She was not sure she wanted to return to that phase.

Around eight-thirty everyone came home, and Janet carried Quigley in. From his expression, the dog looked as if he had learned his lesson the hard way.

"Well, that was a small diversion," Marty said, jokingly. The round-trip drive, plus the hour at the vet's and a short stop for a quick meal, had taken almost four hours.

"And an expensive one at that. That emergency vet hospital sure has high prices," Catherine said.

Janet repeated for Elizabeth's sake the joke she had heard a few years ago: "So, this summer visitor's dog ran into a porcupine, and his owner raced the dog to the vet, who pulled out six quills. When the bill was presented to the summer visitor, he looked astonished. It was three hundred sixty dollars, or sixty dollars a quill. 'Wow,' the shocked owner said, 'What do you folks do in the winter time?' The vet smiled and replied, 'Raise porcupines!' " Elizabeth laughed, and the other three chuckled too. Fortunately for Catherine, the price wasn't quite that high, but it was certainly not insignificant.

"I'll just have to keep him on a leash in the evening when those pesky porcupines are wandering around," Catherine said.

"Probably a good idea," Janet said.

"Well, I don't know about you, Elizabeth, but I'm up for some dessert," Marty said.

"Me too," said Catherine. Marty dished out a small bowl of vanilla ice cream with chocolate sauce for Janet, Catherine, and herself. Elizabeth passed on dessert.

Daylight-savings time arrived on Sunday, but Catherine forgot and arrived at church an hour late. The service was just ending. She laughed at herself and went in for coffee, anyway. There she found a few others who had missed the time change. Reverend Perry joked, "No worries, Catherine, it happens every year and, besides, most of the congregation who made it here were asleep in the pews."

Catherine realized that none of the other women at the Winter House had remembered either. It seemed early for the change, as she always thought of it being on the first Sunday in April. Then she recalled that that had shifted about five years ago. The first year daylight savings occurred in mid-March, she didn't like it. Oh, she liked the longer afternoons, but the mornings reverted to a later sunrise. Still, by all indications, spring was on its way.

That afternoon Catherine spent time looking through garden magazines, choosing new colorful perennials to plant. This always happened in March. And now with the days getting longer, she had the itch to dig, plant, and tend to her flower beds.

For the next two weeks Elizabeth worked hard to complete the oil painting of the house, still keeping it a secret from her housemates. She fussed with the whites of the snow on the trees, trying to catch the shadows from the moonlight. The smoke from the chimney rose straight up, indicating the stillness that Elizabeth recalled even now. Alcee had been gone two months, yet it almost seemed like yesterday.

Usually Janet practiced her ukulele with the door closed, trying to get the fingering of the chords correct as well as to keep the rhythm consistent. Lotti, her teacher, had introduced some new rhythms, like the rumba, and also some new methods of picking the strings. This wasn't coming easily to Janet, but she absolutely knew that mastering new things, like learning a language or playing an instrument, was a good stimulus to the brain. Use it or lose it, folks often say. Though Janet wasn't convinced that mental exercises would prevent Alzheimer's, it probably helped keep the normal aging memory functioning better. Her mother had done crossword puzzles for years and played golf weekly, but still she ended up with dementia. Janet couldn't help wondering if, in her lifetime, a cure for that mental robber would be discovered. Pharmaceutical progress seemed so slow.

Refusing to call a plumber, Marty spent time fixing a

leaky faucet in her bathroom. She considered it a challenge to replace what she figured was an old washer. The dripping had become irritating. As a child she'd seen her father do it many times. He had believed that as a surgeon, he should be able to diagnose and fix plumbing problems. Only once that she could recall did he get in over his head, eventually having to call in a licensed plumber. To him that was a humiliation.

Elizabeth received an email from her real-estate agent: "Elizabeth, dear, your renters have inquired as to whether you are willing to sell the apartment. They just love the location and convenience and would prefer to own instead of rent. Have you given selling any thought? Hope you are doing well in Maine. Do let me know ASAP. Always, Sonia."

Elizabeth had given it some thought, quite a bit. Much to her sister's surprise, Elizabeth very much wanted to sell the apartment and say good-bye to the city. She was finding life in Maine just what she had hoped for and even more. Though Elizabeth had enjoyed suburban living and the big-city experience, now for her next several years, she was ready for the rural tempo of Maine.

At lunch Elizabeth presented her housemates with an idea. "I was wondering if you would all like to come to New York City with me. We could make it a road trip of sorts. I need to go to see Sonia, my realtor, and sign some papers. I'm probably going to sell the apartment soon."

"When would you think of going?" asked Janet.

"Well, this year Easter is earlier in April, so I thought maybe we could go then and see the Easter parade in Manhattan. It really is quite an event if you have never seen it," Elizabeth said.

"I think it would be fun," Catherine said. "Maybe we could meet up with my son and family, who live just across the Hudson River in New Jersey."

"Maybe we could get tickets to the Radio City Music Hall performance. I've only seen the Rockettes once, and that was for my sixteenth birthday, a long time ago," Marty commented.

"Will we all be able to stay at your apartment?" Janet asked.

"Yes, the couple renting it are going away on vacation for two weeks, and we'll only stay a few days. We can easily all fit in there," Elizabeth answered.

"Sounds like a plan," Marty said.

"When do you want to leave?" Catherine asked.

"We could take off on Good Friday in the morning, drive to Boston, have lunch, and then on to New York for dinner. Many fine restaurants within blocks of the apartment await us," Elizabeth said, smiling.

"Should we take Easter bonnets?" Catherine asked. She had watched the parade on TV a few times.

"Well, I don't even own a bonnet," Marty quipped.

"Watching is just as much fun as strutting around, but I'm sure we can find some fun hats if you want to wear something." Elizabeth drank a swallow of milk. "So, I take it you are all on board."

"I think you're right. A road trip for the Winter House women would be a great treat as we go into our last month together," Janet said. Her voice sounded a little nostalgic. The move-out date had been set for May 1 back in November, when they originally hatched this plan, and as far as everyone knew, that remained the date.

"Good, then we will take off two weeks from today. I'll let Sonia know we are coming. She can probably reserve some tickets to Radio City Music Hall for the Saturday matinee. Think about what else you want to see in the city. I figure we can return on Monday and maybe stop in Boston on the way home to see my kids. All that can be arranged later," Elizabeth said.

"I'll call my son and see if he and his wife can come to meet us for Saturday night, or maybe they would want to take in the parade," Catherine said, "and I'll have to call Pat and see if she will watch Quigley for the weekend."

"Missy will do fine here. I can just leave out enough food," Marty said, glancing over at the cat, sitting on the top of the living room couch, her favorite daytime spot."

Thus a road trip was planned, and excitement filled the house.

Hospice was now on a twenty-four-hour vigil with Simon Kirby. Janet hoped to stay with him through much of the time remaining. He had stopped eating about seven days before but was able to take water with assistance. At one point he opened his eyes, looked at her, and said, "You know, this really isn't so bad," and then drifted off again. She wondered what he meant. Was he coming in and out of this world? Was his life flashing in front of him like an ongoing movie? Could he see his wife waiting for him, calling him? Did he believe he would soon be joining her? Just what had he meant by "This isn't so bad?"

Oddly enough, he still was aware of her reading. He had whispered that the reading soothed his soul.

Sitting next to his bed, she read to the last page of *The Iliad*: "Now, men of Troy, bring timber into the city, and let not your hearts fear a close ambush of the Argives..."

The doorbell rang, interrupting her words. Janet jumped, expecting no one at this time. She told Simon she would be right back, as they appeared to have a visitor. He nodded minimally. At the door Janet saw a man with a full head of white hair. He was slightly bent over, holding a cane.

"Hello, I'm George, Simon's old roommate," he said. "Am I too late?"

"Oh, my goodness, hello, George," Janet replied. "No, he is still with us but fading in and out. I'm sure he will be glad you've come. Please come in," Janet said. "Let me take your coat."

"Thank you, dear." As the unexpected visitor handed his overcoat to Janet, she noted his old crimson sports coat and Harvard-insignia bow tie. Once a Harvard man, always one, she thought. He followed her into Simon's bedroom and went directly to his side. Simon appeared to be sleeping, breathing heavily.

George bent over, speaking softly, "Simon, it's George, your old friend." Simon's hand lifted slowly and went in the direction of the voice. George gently reached out, and their hands joined. Both Janet and George noticed a smile on their friend's face. George felt a slight squeeze that he gently returned.

Simon opened his lips to speak, but nothing audible came out. He placed his other hand over their united hands. Janet saw a tear roll down George's cheek and a tear in the corner of Simon's eye. She couldn't keep from tearing up either. What memories returned to these two old men? How beautiful was it for this reunion to occur, though so late in their lives.

"It's so good to see you," George whispered. For several moments no one moved. George stood vigil. Simon's breathing slowed. Janet recognized the breathing pattern. The end was near. She returned to her reading aloud. At last she came to the final sentence of Homer's *Iliad*: "Such was their burial of Hektor, breaker of horses." Janet quietly closed the thick book as she watched Simon's top hand slip down and drop to his side. At that moment she knew he had drifted off to the eternity beyond.

JOAN MACCRACKEN

APRIL

*C*atherine's second cataract operation went well. Within days she marveled at the clarity of her vision. As her son predicted, she wondered just why she had waited so long. This summer would be special, returning to her the intensity of color of the perennials in the garden. Even now, in early spring, the subtle light greens of the young mosses and lichen and the reds of the new buds caught her eyes. These had all been muted for several years. With each day she rejoiced.

One day on the way out the back door, Catherine noticed the green tips of daffodils just peeking out of the ground and a robin near the bird feeder. As the soil began to thaw, earthworms returned to the surface, and robins looked for a tasty meal. Catherine took Quigley to visit with Pat and David, who had agreed to watch him over the Easter weekend while the Winter House women traveled south on their road trip to New York City. They had kept him once before, but it had been a few years back, and they were glad to become reacquainted.

"He's getting older now," Catherine said. "I take him for a walk twice a day. Usually the afternoon walk is longer if the weather is good."

"How often do you feed him?" Pat asked.

"Oh, one scoop in the morning and one scoop at night, and he likes a little doggie biscuit before bed." Catherine said.

As David scratched the top of Quigley's fuzzy white head, the dog seemed to be listening to every word.

"If you have any trouble, Sarah knows him pretty well. If he gets sick or anything, I use Blue Hill Vet," Catherine said. "I'll leave the number."

"Oh, don't worry, dear, he will be just fine," Pat said.

"So you leave next Friday?" David said, still stroking Quigley's head.

"Yes, we are going to get an early start, so I probably should drop him off on Thursday night, if that's okay," Catherine said.

"That's just fine, dear," Pat replied. "We'll be ready whenever you get here."

Pat and Catherine had been good friends for many years. Catherine could still picture their elementary-school graduation almost seventy years ago. The line from a Girl Scout song came back to her: "Make new friends but keep the old; one is silver, the other gold." Pat was gold, for sure. Catherine left, feeling reassured about Quigley's mini-vacation. He was going to be in good hands.

Elizabeth had finished her oil painting and driven to Belfast the day before the deadline. In a brief email to Nell and Alcee, she said that she had thoroughly enjoyed her art class and had been encouraged by her instructor to submit a painting to a juried art show. She herself thought the painting really wasn't so bad for a mere beginner. Alcee sent back a quick response: "I'll keep my fingers crossed and I know, Nonna, that you have many hidden talents and aren't exactly a beginner. And can you possibly come to my graduation? Alcee."

What a sweet granddaughter, Elizabeth thought. Maybe she should think about going to Italy to see Alcee graduate. Elizabeth had a very good feeling about this young woman.

Later, Elizabeth spoke on the phone with Michael. Her son was busy teaching on Friday, the day the women would leave for New York City, but he could cook a dinner for them on their return trip Sunday evening. He suggested that they spend the night and get an early start back the next morning. Maybe two of them could stay with Michael and Mason, and two could sleep at Libby's. It sounded like a good plan. Elizabeth could tell that Michael wanted to show off their new apartment.

"You'll like my friends, Michael," Elizabeth said. "We've gotten along pretty well up here. We have a bit of cabin fever, so strolling along Fifth Avenue in New York will be good for us."

On Thursday afternoon Janet drove by Simon's house, now empty. She had helped him with his obituary, which appeared in the *Bangor Daily News*. Simon had instructed her to submit a photograph of him as a young college professor; perhaps those had been his happiest years. In lieu of flowers, the obituary asked that people donate to hospice or to the Brooks Harbor library. Simon chose to have no funeral. He had no family left, having lost his only son in the World Trade Center tragedy and his wife a few years later.

Janet thought of her own demise. Would she be so alone? After John's death, she had decided not to move to Colorado, where her son lived. She spoke with Peter on the phone once or maybe twice a month, but she hadn't seen him in almost two years. Peter had hated seeing her drinking after his parents' divorce. Then, a few years ago, he had been the one to figure out quite early that she had started drinking, yet again, after John's death. Peter never felt welcomed by John's children and had little connection to Brooks Harbor, preferring the Rockies to Maine. But after watching Simon Kirby die with no family members, Janet was rethinking her situation, especially the emotional and physical distance from her son.

Janet thought about the upcoming road trip to New York with gratitude. She needed to get away and do something fun and adventurous. Her hospice volunteering with Simon and the training classes, which she had led for several years, kept her busy and pretty much tied down to Brooks Harbor. She had never really been a traveler, but "getting outta Dodge" appealed to her now.

As the women prepared for their getaway, packing for the road trip brought on an atmosphere of anticipation in the Winter House. It wasn't every day that Maine folk traveled to New York City. Elizabeth explained that they would be gone three nights, two in New York at her apartment and the last night in Boston with her son or daughter. They all thought it a good idea to start early, so they could stop off in Freeport, the outlet capital. Many Maine folk refused to go to Freeport in the summer, leaving space for the tourists who packed the stores for bargains; for the same reason, locals didn't usually go to Bar Harbor in the summer. April, however, was a good time to stop at L.L.Bean and the other outlet stores in Freeport, where spring sales would be going on.

Elizabeth had checked the weather forecast for the next five days, and all signs looked good: pleasant spring temperatures and little chance of precipitation.

"Good," Marty said, "we can leave our raincoats and umbrellas behind."

"I suggest good walking shoes too. We'll probably stroll down Fifth Avenue with the Easter parade crowds," Elizabeth said. "When it's sunny weather, lots of people turn out, and you never know whom you'll meet. My friend Sonia found four tickets for Radio City Music Hall's Spring Easter matinee. I figure we can go to dinner wherever you'd like. New York has so many great restaurants that we can eat any type of food. You name it. The choices are endless — Italian, Middle Eastern, Thai, Korean, if any of those appeal to you." She paused. "I'd like to get to the Museum of Modern Art. There's an exhibition of Diego Rivera's murals on display until May 14, but you all may have other things you'd prefer to see. Of course, if we stayed for a week, we'd have more time. This will just be a teaser for us."

"I'm up for anything," Janet said.

"Me too," said Catherine.

"Me three," said Marty.

"Great, let's finish packing and get a good night's sleep," Elizabeth suggested. "Should we plan to leave by seven or seven-thirty? Janet, do you think you can make that?"

"If you can, I can," Janet quipped back. The late sleepers laughed at themselves, and Catherine and Marty just smiled.

The next morning they were off by quarter past seven, but getting to New York was not uneventful. In Freeport Elizabeth pulled into the expansive L.L.Bean parking lot, which was filling up even at ten-thirty in the morning. Marty remembered shopping at Bean's once at 2 a.m. on her way back from a Boston trip. To the amazement of many tourists, the Freeport store was open twenty-four hours a day, seven days a week. The women decided to spend no more than an hour looking around, stretching their legs. Marty went to the Patagonia outlet for sales on winter ski jackets. Janet rushed over to the L.L.Bean discount store to replace her worn rubber boots. Elizabeth and Catherine had no particular needs or ideas and thought they'd just watch the people milling around.

As Elizabeth pushed the automatic lock button and closed the door, a split second of horror struck. She had just left her keys on the seat, right there in plain sight.

"Damn, oh no! How could I have done that? How stupid!" she growled.

Catherine had made this mistake herself once and tried to console Elizabeth. "Sometimes things like that just happen, especially after driving three hours," Catherine said.

"Well, at least I have my purse," Elizabeth said.

"I'm sure we can call some garage to come open it." Catherine said. "Harold used to just slide something into the window and pull up the latch. But these newfangled electric locks are harder to open, I think."

"Well, I can call AAA. I'm still a member. Cliff used to

insist we carry their coverage. He never wanted me to have to change a tire by myself," Elizabeth said.

As she was mumbling about the waste of time this was going to cause, she searched in her wallet to get the AAA number. She flipped through all her credit cards, Medicare insurance card, license, airline cards, and AARP membership card, finally coming to the AAA card. The 800 number for road service was on the back. Her cell phone had good coverage. As she was about to dial the number, Elizabeth remembered Cliff's secret. He had always kept a spare key hidden on the fender for just such an occasion. Elizabeth had momentarily forgotten this. But which fender? Catherine watched Elizabeth as she felt above the tires. The car had gone through an entire winter's sand and spring mud, so she wasn't confident it would still be there. On the last fender she checked, tucked high up, she felt a bump covered with caked mud. She yanked the magnetized box out and, with some pressure, slid the top off. Voila! The spare key to her Toyota.

"Oh, thank you, Cliff, thank you," Elizabeth said, in a joking fashion.

"Imagine, Elizabeth," Catherine said, "he is still looking after you. And we still have time to do some window-shopping."

Around eleven-thirty they all met back at the car, and Marty volunteered to drive. En route to the highway Elizabeth told Marty and Janet about the incident with the key, and they all talked about the silly things they had done recently. Marty admitted to driving all the way to the tennis court and leaving her sneakers at home. Janet had received a warning from the local sheriff for being overdue on her car registration and not having a copy of her insurance available in the car. Catherine mentioned arriving at church an hour late by failing to turn the clock ahead for daylight-savings time. Many years ago, after Harold's death, Catherine had absentmindedly put her purse in the freezer.

"Well, I can top all of you for silly, absentminded things," Marty quipped. "I drove over my laptop computer and crushed it. Now that was expensive and stupid, besides being silly."

They all admitted their minds were not always in full gear before proceeding. Everyone but Marty thought this was an aging problem. Marty realized that she had struggled with that quirk all her life. She could hear her mother admonish her: "Slow down, Marty, dear, and take your time. Be more patient."

In preparation for the long trip, the women had decided to listen to a book on tape to help pass the time. They had chosen *The Help,* after having heard about it from several friends and reading the full-page advertisement in the *New York Times*. It had been on the best-seller list for months, and the movie had won many film awards. Marty put in the first audio disk, and the travelers settled into the story just as they crossed the bridge into New Hampshire.

The voice began, "Aibileen, Chapter One: Mae Mobley was born on a early Sunday morning in August 1960. A church baby we like to call it. Taking care a white babies, that's what I do, along with the cooking and the cleaning."

Elizabeth couldn't help thinking of her Aunt Reta, who had lived in Birmingham, Alabama. At nineteen she married a cigar-smoking southerner who lived on an old plantation. Once, when Elizabeth was thirteen, she and her parents had visited Aunt Reta and Uncle Thomas. Elizabeth hated the pungent smell of his cigars and fought the instinct to hold her nose. She remembered the delightful taste of the fresh farm eggs gathered every morning, but she was acutely uncomfortable with the black maid serving her breakfast. Her aunt ordered Dotty around, with no pleases or thank-yous. Later Elizabeth's mother told her that in the South things were different. And that was in the '60's. Elizabeth hadn't returned to the Deep South except for Florida, and that didn't count. She wondered about the changes.

The reader's voice continued: "I go like she tell me to, even though they cups is full to the rim."

Catherine hadn't known any black people in Maine until about five years ago, when a young family had moved into town. The wife, a lawyer for Pine Tree Legal Aid, and the husband, a history teacher at the high school, brought their two little boys every Thursday afternoon to the children's reading group. They were bright children and eager to learn. But Catherine always wondered how it felt to be so isolated in the all-white community of Brooks Harbor. Back in the forties, when Catherine went to the University of Maine, she recalled only three black students, probably on sports scholarships, she thought. Even now, Maine was listed as the whitest state in the United States. The southern drawl remained an unfamiliar dialect to Catherine, for sure.

"Could you turn up the volume, just a little bit?" Catherine asked. She had been noticing a slight hearing loss.

"No problem," Janet replied. The narrator's louder voice continued.

As they traveled on Interstate 495 outside of Boston, Elizabeth asked, "Anyone hungry?" Janet stopped the recording so everyone could state her opinion.

"I could eat something," Marty replied. The other three women agreed.

Elizabeth noticed a Subway shop sign for the next exit. Marty drove there for a quick lunch stop, where they stretched their legs, hit the bathroom, had a sandwich, filled up the gas tank, switched drivers, and then headed to Manhattan. Janet took a turn at the wheel. Everyone agreed that *The Help* was a fun distraction on the long drive.

Later, in southern Connecticut, as Elizabeth looked out the car window, she noticed the three Greenwich exits, the familiar exits she had used during her family's years there. That was a phase of her life that she now rarely thought about.

The traffic picked up as they approached New York City on the Major Deegan Expressway. Elizabeth switched with Janet, who admitted being somewhat nervous driving into the city. Elizabeth understood this apprehension and felt a bit rusty herself at maneuvering in four lanes at high speed, but she figured the skill would come back quickly. Driving around Brooks Harbor certainly never prepared anyone for these traffic jams. Luckily the late-afternoon rush-hour traffic was going out of town while Elizabeth negotiated her Toyota south on the FDR Drive along the East River.

Catherine, Marty, and Janet were all eyes as a red tugboat towed a huge freighter down the tidal river. Yellow taxis darted in and out of lanes, many bringing passengers from LaGuardia or JFK. Elizabeth passed the turnoff for Spanish Harlem and took the next exit onto 96th Street. She drove west to Second Avenue, a major southbound thoroughfare for the Upper East Side.

"We are almost there," Elizabeth announced.

"I'm excited to see your apartment," said Catherine, who had never been inside a New York City flat. The contrast between living quarters in a modern Manhattan apartment on the Upper East Side and Catherine's Brooks Harbor hundred-year-old cape would be considerable.

The attendant on duty in the underground garage of Elizabeth's building recognized her immediately. "Welcome back, Mrs. Sloan," he said. "Will you be staying for a while?"

"Just for the weekend, Mickey," Elizabeth replied. She was surprised that she remembered his name, but he had always been helpful in parking their car, and Cliff used to say Mickey was too smart to stay a parking attendant. It was a job, though, and he was good at it.

"Oh, just leave the bags," Elizabeth said to her friends. "They'll bring them up on the dolly."

Elizabeth pushed the button, and the shiny silver-chrome elevator carried the four smoothly up to the 30th floor. A large mirror greeted them as the elevator door opened. Everyone looked bedraggled after the nine-hour journey, but they were all smiles. Elizabeth knocked to be sure the renters weren't there; she had the key and knew they were away on vacation.

"Well, here it is, our temporary residence. Make yourselves at home," Elizabeth said. The apartment did look different with a mixture of her furniture and the renters' things. Most all of her personal belongings were gone except the tall grandfather clock in the corner. Getting that clock into the apartment many years ago had been a challenge, but the effort was worth it. Elizabeth had always loved hearing the Westminster chimes announce the hours when the clock resided in her grandparents' Vermont farmhouse. Now she tried to envision its place in the Maine house.

"What a beautiful clock," Marty said. "Does it chime?"

"Oh, yes, if you keep it wound, but sometimes the hourly chimes can keep you up at night," Elizabeth remarked.

Janet had already walked to the other side of the apartment and was appreciating the skyline. "This is an amazing panorama," she said. "Can you identify most of these buildings?"

Catherine spoke up. "I think that's the Empire State Building."

"You're right," Elizabeth said, and she proceeded to point out the spire of the Chrysler Building and the slanted roof of the Citicorp Building, initially designed for solar panels. "See that triangular one? It's the new Hearst Building. Cliff told me it has no vertical steel. Triangles are stronger than rectangles, supposedly. Isn't it amazing?"

"Really, you can see so much from here," Janet added. "I think I can see a plane landing at LaGuardia."

"You're right. Cliff used to say you could even see planes landing at JFK, but I never could," Elizabeth confessed.

"Could you see the Twin Towers from here before 9/11?" Marty asked.

"No, they were way downtown, and that big building blocks the view in their direction. But we could see black smoke rising for days. It went way up into the sky. It really was a horrible time for New Yorkers. Cliff had a meeting in one of the towers just the day before. We were lucky. I must say, I felt a real need to return to Maine, but I also wanted to stay and be supportive," Elizabeth said.

"Have you been down to Ground Zero?" Marty inquired.

"No, I haven't. I'm not sure I really want to visit the site. The whole episode was hard, and I'd rather not have to think about it again," Elizabeth confessed. She knew that the site was a popular tourist spot now, but she had decided to put the memory away and not dwell on it after more than ten years.

Janet added, "Simon Kirby's son died in the Twin Towers."

"Oh," said Marty, "how sad." There was a pause in the conversation, almost like a moment of silence.

Catherine decided to change the subject. "Elizabeth, what are the plans for tonight?"

"Well, I guess we have several choices, and it's up to you all. We could order supper in. There's a great pizza place around the corner, or a Thai restaurant that can deliver in three minutes from the time we order. Or we could go out to a restaurant," Elizabeth said. "What's your pleasure?"

Marty spoke first. "It's been a pretty long day. I would love to just stay here and relax. We can hit the city tomorrow, when we all have a bit more energy and don't suffer from road fatigue."

"Marty, those are my sentiments exactly," Catherine said. Her hip and back were aching. She was not used to long car rides.

"Well, I was hoping we would go out and party all night," Janet joked.

It appeared to be a unanimous decision to relax after the long drive and enjoy the evening skyline. They chose Thai food, and Elizabeth called in the order. She smiled as the owner on the other end of the phone barked out his usual questions: "Phonenumber?" "Whatchewlike?" She ordered. Then she heard, "Okaybye." In just over three minutes, the doorman called to say the meals had arrived.

"Send it up, thank you," Elizabeth said. Marty, Catherine, and Janet were amazed to see how this New York City version of fast foods worked. The world was certainly right at their fingertips.

Saturday morning dawned with the sun coming up over the East River. The early risers, Catherine and Marty, had their first cup of coffee out on the balcony. A constant din of traffic below was noticeable, particularly to those who usually heard only the early dawn chorus of morning birds in Maine. But the energy of the city was palpable, and with a good night's sleep, Marty and Catherine claimed they were ready to explore their surroundings.

After breakfast Elizabeth said she had some meetings with Sonia, her real-estate agent, and her lawyer. She listed several things the women could do in the morning. "You are only six blocks from Central Park and the Metropolitan Museum of Art. If you like museums, along Fifth Avenue is the Museum Mile, where you can find at least nine of the best, like the Guggenheim and Frick museums."

"I would personally love to visit the Metropolitan and walk through the impressionist section. At Middlebury I took an art-appreciation class and loved many of the impressionists," Marty said.

"Could we go see the Rembrandt paintings? I always loved his use of light," Janet added.

"There are several paintings of his in the collection," Elizabeth said. She used to go often to the Met when she lived here.

"I'd be happy to go with you as long as my hip holds out," Catherine replied.

"Well, we can take a taxi and save our walking for the museum," Marty said.

"No, really, I think I can make it, but I might be a little slower than the rest of you," Catherine said.

"No problem, we're just sightseeing," Janet replied.

"You can look down Lexington, Park, and Madison Avenues before you get to Fifth. Let's plan on meeting back here around noon. We can get some pizza and then head downtown for the Easter matinee," Elizabeth said.

"Should we just meet at the pizza place?" Marty said.

"Sure, good idea, I'll meet you there. It's across the street from here. Then we can come back up here if we need to," Elizabeth said.

"Sounds like a plan," Janet said.

Elizabeth felt she needed to have some time alone and get her head straight. She wasn't beginning to have second thoughts about selling the apartment, but coming back had brought to mind many memories of Cliff and their life together. They had had some great times in the city. It was really where Cliff flourished. He had so many connections and business associates. Having that type of network in Manhattan made things easier, and their social life had been active. Widowed now for over a year, Elizabeth was learning how it was to be without a partner. Thank goodness for Marty, Janet, and Catherine, who had helped her get through the first winter as a *vedova*. For that, she would always be grateful.

On her way out the door of the apartment, Elizabeth bumped into Hector and Rosa Gonzales, an elderly Ecuadorian couple, who were happy to see her. "Elizabeth, my dear, oh we have missed you," Rosa said.

"I have missed you too. Are you well?" Elizabeth inquired.

"Yes, but we are moving out."

"No, really? I cannot believe it."

Hector spoke up, "We are going to move over to Ridgewood, New Jersey, where our daughter lives. It is better that we be closer to family now that we are both pushing ninety," he smiled.

"I know how much you two love New York, but I can understand your wanting to be closer to Maria." Elizabeth had spent many hours with these two. They had always been there for her when Cliff was away on his long trips.

"So things change." The old man shrugged. "We will miss the city, but we are ready for a quieter life. You will sell your place, no?"

"Yes, my renters would like to purchase it, and I too must move on," Elizabeth admitted.

"Oh, they are a very nice young couple," Rosa said.

"Yes," Elizabeth agreed, "they seem happy here. They're in Cancun right now. Well, I unfortunately have to go to an appointment. So good to see you both." She gave each of them a quick hug.

In the elevator she ran into Alden, the son of a gay couple three doors down. He was carrying his cello.

"How's your music coming?" Elizabeth inquired. Alden had been playing since age six and now attended the Juilliard School.

"Very well, thank you. I'll be coming up your way soon. I have just been accepted to study at Kneisel Hall this summer in Blue Hill. I hope you will be able to come to our student concerts," Alden said.

"Oh, Alden, that is a real honor. I often go to the summer concerts and always enjoy them. Congratulations!" Elizabeth was impressed with this young man's news, knowing that Kneisel Hall, nestled in tiny Blue Hill, Maine, was one of the most significant chamber-music programs in the country. Obviously, he was doing very well at Juilliard.

The elevator doors opened and both exited. "See you this summer," Elizabeth said. "And please tell your parents to call me when they come up to see you."

"They would be happy to do that. I will tell them I saw you." Alden disappeared down the hall with his instrument.

At the Metropolitan Museum Marty looked at a colorful painting across the room. "That's got to be a Van Gogh," she said. "I think I recognize it from my art-appreciation class." She walked toward the wall and was happy to find herself to be correct. In this part of the museum, the impressionist section, Marty was delighted with the works of Monet and Degas and with Seurat's famous *Sunday Afternoon on the Island of La Grande Jatte*, painted in the artist's recognizable pointillist style.

Catherine and Janet looked at several well-known Picasso paintings and then wandered off toward the Rembrandt rooms, with Marty following slowly behind. She did not want to get separated, as it was quite easy to become disoriented in the maze of connected galleries.

"Aren't those faces magnificent?" Janet remarked to Catherine. The vast collection of Rembrandt's portraits of doctors, damsels, and dignitaries was remarkable. Janet had gone to Boston in 2006 for a special exhibition commemorating the Dutch artist's 400th birthday, and since then she had been fascinated by his style and technique. She had considered a trip to the North Carolina Museum of Art this past winter to see an exhibition of Rembrandts, but it hadn't worked out. Maybe someday she would travel to Europe and get a fuller exposure to the Master.

Marty, Catherine, and Janet left the seventeenth-century galleries and found themselves in the modern-art section. Some of the paintings had bright colors splashed or dripped onto canvas. In one fascinating construction, the artist had used bottle tops, wire, and aluminum cans to create a face. Amazing, Marty thought. Another piece, made of metal, captured random reflections, a magical effect.

In the gift shop Janet bought some note cards of Rembrandt portraits. Marty contemplated a book on the impressionists but decided it was too heavy to carry, and she could probably order it online.

On the walk back to First and 80th, they peeked into a few shops. All were shocked at the prices. New Yorkers seemed to purchase shoes for over two hundred dollars, and women's Coach purses started at over four hundred. It was another world outside of Maine. In one small shop Catherine noticed "Hello Kitty" purses that resembled the one that her granddaughter treasured twenty-five years ago. Catherine decided to get two small purses, special treats for Emma and Ella. "Hello Kitty" seemed to be passing down into yet another generation.

Elizabeth met them at the Italian Village Pizza, where one large slice for $4.95 was a reasonable and filling lunch.

A quick stop at the apartment and they were off on yet another adventure, to see the Rockettes.

The women flagged down a yellow taxi. "Good afternoon," Elizabeth said to the driver. "Radio City Music Hall, please." She jumped into the front as Marty, Catherine, and Janet adjusted themselves in the back seat of the cab. A small video monitor on the back of the front seat played advertisements and movie previews. Catherine couldn't believe that taxis now had TV screens. The volume was loud, and Marty punched the mute button.

"Where is Radio City Music Hall?" asked Janet.

"Oh, we are headed to 50th and the Avenue of the Americas. There will be traffic, but we've left plenty of time," Elizabeth said. The taxi driver cut left, then right, as he wove his way around the buses and slower cars. Elizabeth thought this traffic was just about normal for New York City. For the others, it appeared a nightmare. But by 1:30 p.m. the four left the taxi and found the line for the matinee. Even though they had tickets, they would still stand in a long line to get in. The Rockettes performed only at Christmas and at Easter. Many folks, including New Yorkers, came to the Easter holiday event, but it wasn't quite as packed as the Christmas show. No one pushed, and the line moved fairly quickly once the doors opened. The four women found their seats in the orchestra section, row W.

"These are great seats," said Marty to Janet. "W for Winter House."

"Right," Janet replied, as she moved in, allowing Catherine and Elizabeth to take their places in the row.

The majestic Wurlitzer organ music began. From her youth Elizabeth remembered the beautiful sound created by this pipe organ. Her children had loved to hear it played, and Michael had once wanted to be an organist just so he could perform at Radio City Music Hall. His piano lessons hadn't gone well enough to advance to the organ, however, and he moved on to other things.

"This theater is stunning," Catherine said, impressed by the ethereal, gold backdrop of curtains. The seats filled up, everyone anticipating the grand opening. In the dim light Catherine had a hard time reading the detailed program, but Elizabeth pulled out her smartphone and used the tiny flashlight to illuminate the page.

The 80th-year performance of the Radio City Music Hall Rockettes provided lively entertainment for the Winter House women. Dressed in white bunny costumes, thirty-six dancers displayed extraordinary precision with their world-famous high kicks. Marty noticed that all the pink-and-white rabbit ears remained erect during the entire dance. At intermission Marty told the story of her miserable first-grade experience, when she was a bunny rabbit — the only one whose ears flopped over during the play. It was a humiliation, but she didn't know that word. Her mother, who had been in the audience and had made the ears, tried to console her, telling her no one noticed. She knew that was not true. When the thank-you notes from the other grades arrived, almost all of the drawings had a lone bunny with floppy ears. She was horrified. Marty remembered going home in tears that day. Her father held her in his lap and told her that having the only floppy ears made her *unique,* and he said that was a good thing. That support from her father made her feel just a little better.

"You're still unique," Janet said to Marty, "and that's a good thing." They both laughed.

The second half of the show was equally entertaining,

the final act filled with people strolling down a stunning set of Fifth Avenue and singing a jazzy "In Your Easter Bonnet." The seventy-two legs of the perfectly synchronized dancers reappeared for the grand finale. The audience rose to their feet, clapping gleefully in time with the music. It truly was an Easter extravaganza.

"What fun, what fun!" said Catherine.

Marty and Janet agreed.

"I'm so glad you all enjoyed it. I do think that was one of the better Easter shows," Elizabeth commented.

Afterward they went to Florio's, a restaurant in Little Italy. Cliff had met the owner years before through one of his clients, and he and Elizabeth always received special treatment. Antonio recognized her immediately. "*Buonasera*, Mrs. Sloan. It's a-been a long time since you've a-come here," he said. "I was so a-sorry to hear about Mr. Sloan." She extended her hand.

"It's good to see you, Antonio. I've brought along some friends from Maine. I wanted to give them the experience of eating at the best Italian restaurant in the city," Elizabeth said.

"Thank you a-so much, Mrs. Sloan. We think it is. We think it is. Do come with a-me." Antonio led them to a table in the back, away from the noise of the bar.

The four women chatted, covering a variety of topics. Marty and Elizabeth each ordered a glass of Chianti Rufina, recommended by Antonio, while Catherine and Janet chose sparkling water with a slice of lemon. Each tried a sample from the antipasto plate. The fresh bread, dipped in olive oil, melted in their mouths.

Elizabeth knew that the entrée portions were generous and suggested they each have a salad and then split two entrées. She was right about that. The spicy pasta puttanesca, covered with black olives and cheese, made a generous dish, and the delicious rigatoni with lamb was much more than they were accustomed to eating. When Giovanni, their waiter, recommended dessert, the four ladies passed, though Catherine eyed the cheesecake. Florio's was a fabulous choice for their big night out.

The taxi driver headed north toward 80th on Third Avenue. When he started to turn onto 78th Street, Elizabeth gasped and asked him to go straight two more blocks. The driver did as he was told. No one in the cab but Elizabeth knew that Cliff had died just around the corner on 78th between Third and Second Avenues. She had been holding together visiting the city, but driving down that street would be just too hard. Still, after fifteen months, she had her ups and downs. Life was very different now.

Back at the apartment everyone collapsed. It had been a long day, and the trip was only half over. Within a few minutes Catherine climbed into bed. Her hip ached, but she hoped some ibuprofen would fix it. Marty and Janet decided to watch TV. Elizabeth said good night and disappeared into her bedroom. She needed to be alone.

"Tomorrow's another day," Marty heard herself say. That was a phrase her mother had uttered almost nightly when Marty was a child. What had that meant anyway? She always wondered.

Catherine woke early to once again see the sunrise over the East River as a lone tugboat pulled a cargo ship to sea. Looking over the railing of the balcony made her a little dizzy. Thirty stories up was awfully high. The early walkers down on the sidewalks looked like miniature figurines.

She noticed someone walking a pair of little white dogs, and she thought of Quigley.

"Morning, Catherine," Marty said, as she poured herself a cup of hot coffee. "Have you been up long?"

"No, just long enough to see the sunrise. I think it is going to be a beautiful day for the parade," Catherine replied. "I brought my pink hat just for the occasion." She held up the hat with white artificial flowers on the brim.

"Well, I haven't worn an Easter bonnet since I was probably eight years old. My mother used to buy a new one for me every year. Can you imagine?" Marty said. "I think I'll pass on the hats."

"Oh, come on, Marty. I'm sure Elizabeth has a few extra," Catherine laughed.

"What's so funny?" Janet asked, as she came into the kitchen.

"Marty refuses to wear an Easter bonnet. What do you think of that?" Catherine said.

"Well, that really doesn't surprise me one bit," Janet replied. "I can't quite envision her with any floral arrangement on her head."

"You're right about that, Janet. Did you bring a hat?" Marty asked.

"Elizabeth let me choose from her collection. It has quite a broad brim to keep out the sun's rays."

"You're kidding," Marty said.

"No, really, I don't want to get too much sun." Janet had already had two small basal-cell carcinomas removed from her forehead. When she was a young girl, she was outside a lot and had never used sunscreen.

Elizabeth came out of her bedroom after a while. She had spent some time putting on fresh makeup to give herself a little lift. The night seemed long, as she had some difficulty getting to sleep, thinking of Cliff and failing to keep the "what ifs" and the "if onlys" from replaying again and again.

Marty saw fatigue on Elizabeth's face. "Would you like some coffee, Elizabeth?" Marty asked.

"Yes, I could use some. Looks like another beautiful day."

"TV says it's going to be in the high 60s," Janet added. "What time does the parade begin?"

"We should be down on Fifth Avenue by 10 a.m. if we want to see the colorful strollers," Elizabeth replied. "It's all pretty informal but quite a lot of fun. Are you all still up for it?"

"You bet," said Catherine, as she placed the pink hat on her head. My son, his wife, and their son will meet us at St. Patrick's Cathedral around noon for lunch. Will said he would call your cell phone, Elizabeth, so we can find each other in the crowd."

"Great, I look forward to meeting them. After that we'll pack and leave for Boston," Elizabeth commented.

The four women sat and ate breakfast: delicious doughnuts picked up at the bakery around the corner. Janet liked the chocolate one with coconut on top. Marty poured a refill for everyone while Elizabeth planned the route. Catherine felt her hip was fine for a stroll down Fifth Avenue and looked forward to window-shopping at stores like Macy's and Saks. Mostly, though, they all just wanted to partake in people-watching.

On Fifth Avenue and 52nd Street the foursome from Maine paused to watch the parade walkers in their extravagant outfits. With the avenue closed to all vehicular traffic, it became essentially a mall of high-spirited people. One woman in a long, green fleece gown had a large globe perched on her head; written on a poster on her back was "Save our planet." An elegant couple walked hand in hand, wearing long, matching mink coats. Kids were everywhere. Twin infants dressed in furry bunny costumes rode in decorated strollers. Proud owners of dogs of all sizes displayed their canines' Easter sweaters and bonnets. One pug strutted with a white knitted sweater and silly-looking rabbit ears.

Marty snapped a photo of the other three, all wearing their hats. Elizabeth's bright yellow hat with pale purple feathers was nothing Marty would ever wear, but it suited Elizabeth's style and accentuated her long, brunette hair. Under a wide brim, Janet hid from the brilliant sun, and Catherine looked ready to attend church with her pink-and-white bonnet. When a young Chinese woman offered to take a photo of all four, Marty graciously accepted her offer. This might be the only documentation of the Winter House women on their road trip.

"Hey, Bags! Is that you?" Elizabeth turned to a voice from long ago. A handsome white-haired man in a sporty navy blue blazer stood to her right, several feet away. She smiled, not immediately knowing who he was. He pushed through the crowd to come closer. Then Elizabeth remembered those penetrating blue eyes from her first freshman-class socializers.

"Oh, Brad," she said, as soon as she recognized him.

"Bags, it *is* you. You've hardly changed. I was so sorry to read about Cliff in the alumni notes. That's a shame. I'm sorry," Brad said.

"Yes, it certainly caught us all by surprise. I miss him a lot."

Brad paused a second and then said kindly. "It does get better."

Elizabeth wondered how he knew. She had not kept up with his life after college. In fact, she couldn't remember much about him after their freshman year. As a sophomore, she had started dating Cliff, an upper classman, and missed much of her own class activities. In their first year, however, Brad and Elizabeth had spent quite a bit of time together.

"Do you still live here in the city?" Brad inquired.

"Well, no, not really. I've been living in Maine this winter but came down this weekend to finalize the papers on the sale of the apartment here. So I guess from now on, I am officially a permanent, year-round resident of Maine."

"Really, I forgot that Cliff's family summered there. It's a great state."

"You used to go up there, didn't you?"

"Yes, I started going to Maine when I was eleven, attending a boys' camp, and later, during college, I was a counselor. My parents bought a summer cottage in East Blue Hill, and now my sister, brother, and I own it, splitting the summer months. You're mighty adventuresome to spend the winters there."

"Well, this was my first Maine winter. Cliff was not quite ready to leave New York."

Brad waved to a group of women walking by in floppy pink hats. One woman and a young child waved back. Elizabeth wondered what the connection was, and Brad was quick to share the information.

"That's my daughter and my granddaughter. They're walking for breast cancer." Brad said nothing else. The adorable little girl of maybe five or six ran over to her grandfather.

"Poppop," she said, "Did you see me? I walked two miles with Mommy. Now, let's go see the Easter Bunny." She tugged on Brad's hand. "Come on, please, Poppop." Brad turned to Elizabeth.

"Maybe I'll see you in Maine sometime." Brad waved good-bye and turned away.

Elizabeth whispered, "Maybe."

When Brad was out of sight, disappearing into the large crowd, Janet spoke up: "Who was that handsome man, and what did he call you?"

"Oh, that was an amazing coincidence. In all this crowd in New York City, how could Brad Thornton, my old freshman boyfriend, find me?"

Marty piped up: "I have actually never believed in coincidences." She had read a book titled *Synchronicity,* and it had confirmed her opinions.

"Did he call you 'Bags'?" Catherine asked.

"Well, that was my nickname at Middlebury for the first two years. Cliff never liked it," Elizabeth said.

"Why Bags?" asked Catherine.

"Well, my full name was Elizabeth Anne Goethe, but my parents didn't want me confused with my Aunt Elizabeth, so they called me Betsy Anne, which I just hated. So my family nicknamed me 'Bagsy,' which was better, I guess. Then I shortened it to 'Bags' when I went off to college. When I started to date Cliff, he preferred Elizabeth, so I changed. Only a few people still call me 'Bags,' like my freshman roommate, whom I seldom see. My sister, Eve, never liked 'Bags' either, thinking it was not feminine enough. Eve preferred 'Lizzy' and stuck with that name, which I have never really liked."

"Maybe it's time we switch back to Bags," Janet quipped.

"Oh, I don't think so," Elizabeth replied quickly, but at that moment she wondered if a change of name might signal a change in her future journey.

At St. Patrick's Cathedral they met up with Catherine's family. Justin, her grandson, was currently a senior at New York University. In a crowded coffee shop they waited for a table for seven.

"Mom, how is your vision?" Catherine's son asked.

"Just great. You were so right about the improvement, and the procedure was really easy," Catherine replied.

"That's great, Gran," said her grandson. "I've sent in my applications to medical schools and should hear anytime now," Justin added.

"Wonderful," Catherine said. "Marty is a doctor, you know."

"Well, I was a doctor," Marty replied. "I retired several years ago."

"Once a doctor, always a doctor," Catherine quipped. She was thinking of all the assistance Marty had given to Alcee before and after her abortion as well as her astute diagnosis of Catherine's atrial fibrillation. There was little doubt that Marty's medical skills continued to be utilized.

At lunch Justin hinted to his grandmother that he would love to spend his last free summer in Maine, maybe as a sternman for Billy Gray. Catherine thought that would be wonderful and responded that she would enjoy the company.

By two o'clock the women were ready to depart for Boston. It had been a whirlwind forty-eight hours in Manhattan. Elizabeth had signed the final papers on the apartment sale. As the other three women went down to the car,

Elizabeth took a few minutes before locking the door. The old grandfather clock chimed. Soon it would be moved to Maine and some of the other furniture distributed to her children. This had definitely been Cliff's home, and she was leaving it for the last time. She closed her eyes and tried to picture him sitting on the couch. She spoke to him: "Cliff, our marriage wasn't perfect. We both knew that. But we worked on it and made it through fifty years. That was quite an accomplishment. We had many good times here." Elizabeth felt tears coming, but she continued. "I just want to say I'm so sorry for not picking up the phone when you called back. It was selfish of me. Maybe the accident would not have happened." She wiped away a tear. "Or maybe it was fate that we could not control." She then thought of their children. "And I want to tell you that I forgive you for your problems with Frank. I know you loved him, and you loved Michael too. Sons and fathers can have their clashes. You worried about them, but they are both going to be okay." Her eyes filled with tears as she stood there quietly. Then she whispered to the empty apartment, "Thank you, Cliff, for the times we had together, for our children, for exposing this Vermont girl to so much. I do miss you...but I need to move on with my life now." Another tear fell down her cheek. "I know that is what you would want me to do." She closed the door. It locked behind her with a crisp click.

Elizabeth drove out of the city as the afternoon turned gray. Catherine fell asleep in the back seat, while Janet worked on a sudoku puzzle. Marty held off on starting *The Help* to give some silence to everyone. She quietly skimmed the Sunday *New York Times,* only occasionally making brief comments to Elizabeth. At one point Elizabeth found herself completely alone with her thoughts as the others snoozed. She'd never been able to sleep in automobiles except when she was small and her father drove. That was a time before children's car seats and seat belts. Kids could lie down in the back seat or between their parents on the front bench seat and watch the telephone poles flash by and dream. Maybe it was unsafe, but Elizabeth had found memories of driving with her family quite comforting.

After about three hours they stopped for gas, a bathroom break, and a driver change. Boston was a little more than an hour away. As Elizabeth got out of the car, her cell phone rang. She noticed it was a Brooks Harbor number.

"Hello."

"Elizabeth, is that you? This is Pat calling, Pat Sullivan."

"Oh, hi, Pat, how's Quigley?" Elizabeth said, feeling a bad vibe.

"Well, not too good. That's why I am calling," Pat said.

"Is he sick?"

"No, he's lost!" Pat's voice quivered.

"Oh, no, how long has he been gone?"

"Since this morning," Pat said. "We waited to call because we thought he might come back, but we cannot find him anywhere, and soon it will be dark. I wasn't sure how Catherine would take the news, with her heart trouble and all."

"Yes, I know she will be quite upset. Let me talk it over with Marty," Elizabeth added. "I'll call you back. Maybe you could call the Blakey boys, and they could help you look around Catherine's house and my house. Quigley may be somewhere in between."

"That's a good idea. I just have no idea why he took off. I feel so bad." Pat sounded very upset. "We just have to find him."

"You'll find him. I'll call you back soon," Elizabeth replied.

Marty came out of the convenience store first, and Catherine was nowhere in sight. Elizabeth explained the situation to Marty. They agreed that they should go straight home instead of spending the night in Boston, and that meant they would have to tell Catherine why their plans had changed.

"We'll just have to take that risk," Marty said. "I hope we can keep her calm. You know how attached she is to Quigley."

"Here she comes," Elizabeth said. They had decided not to start the car until after the conversation. When all four women were back inside with Janet at the wheel and Catherine and Marty in the back seat, Marty looked at Catherine and spoke softly, indicating no panic.

"Catherine, we've decided to change plans and drive back to Brooks Harbor directly. Pat just called Elizabeth to tell her that Quigley has run away from their home. They've been unable to find him."

"Oh, no! How long has he been missing?" Catherine asked. "Have they checked my house and your house? Sometimes he runs off in the springtime, but he usually returns by supper. He just may not know which house to return to with me gone."

"I'm sure they'll find him soon, but we should probably head straight back," Elizabeth added.

"Oh, I think that's right. Will it be too long a drive for you all?" Catherine asked.

"We can keep switching off. We'll be fine," Janet said.

"I need to call Pat back and tell her we are on our way. Would you like to speak with her, Catherine?" Elizabeth said.

"Please, I would. I bet she's really upset right now," Catherine said.

Elizabeth pushed the callback button on her iPhone. Pat answered immediately, perhaps hoping for some news of Quigley's whereabouts.

"Hi Pat, it's me, Elizabeth. We have decided to drive straight back and should be able to get home by about ten tonight. Catherine suggests that we should have someone watching for Quigley at her house and at mine. Here, she wants to talk to you." Elizabeth passed the phone to the back seat.

"Hi Pat," Catherine said, "I just heard the news. I'm sure you are terribly worried about this and all. Don't worry. Quigley will come back. He sometimes runs off in the spring."

"But Catherine, it's my fault because I didn't put his leash on. He had been so good yesterday and seemed to be getting accustomed to us. I never should have done that. I am so sorry," Pat said.

"Pat, we'll find him, I'm sure of it," Catherine said. "Call us back if you hear anything."

Elizabeth took the phone and called her son Michael to let him know they would not be stopping for the night. When he didn't answer, she just left a brief message and asked him to call Libby too. Elizabeth knew her children would understand. They both had dogs.

Marty was impressed with Catherine's composure, but still she worried about the stress. Getting home would be the best thing. Janet asked if everyone would like to listen to more of the book, and they all agreed that would be a good distraction. No one really wanted to carry on a conversation at this time.

"Chapter 19," the female voice continued. "It is 1963. The Space Age they're calling it. A man has circled the earth in a rocketship. They've invented a pill so married women don't have to get pregnant...." Marty recalled medical school at that time and learning about the birth-control pill, which did give more freedom to women, but over time, as was predicted, it progressed to an increase in premarital sex. Later, use of the birth control pill instead of condoms exposed women to the dangers of HIV transmission, and it also turned out not to be a harmless panacea for symptoms of menopausal women. In her lifetime Marty had noted many stages of sexual activities, venereal diseases, and acknowledged side effects of these hormone pills. Marty turned her attention back to chapter 19.

Catherine couldn't focus on the story either. She couldn't believe Quigley had run away. How could Pat have been so careless as to not put the leash on? Catherine thought she had warned Pat and David. She never should have left Quigley. The trip certainly wouldn't be worth it if she never saw her precious dog again. For so many years he had been in her life, her closest companion, her confidant. She closed her eyes, trying to picture his small, white body and dark black eyes. Where could he have gone? Breathe, she said to herself, breathe deeply and try to be calm. Listen to the story and breathe. Quigley will be found, she prayed.

Out of the corner of her eye, Marty noticed Catherine taking in some deep breaths. Though relaxation might work, Marty still worried. Maybe talking would be better, but she would give Catherine a while at her own technique.

Janet looked in the rear-view mirror and watched the sun poke out underneath a dark cloudbank. Her body sensed the longer days. The digital clock on the dashboard read 6:45 p.m. Soon the western sky would be a long streak of orangey pink as the sun set. She adjusted the mirror to get a fix on Marty, whose eyes expressed concern. Catherine was quiet.

Elizabeth's stomach growled, and she wondered if anyone else was hungry. They should have purchased some food at the gas stop but got too engrossed in Quigley's disappearance. Everyone seemed to be listening to the southern tale. Miss Skeeter, one of the characters, was getting herself into quite a predicament, and Miss Hilly continued to annoy Elizabeth, who decided to wait a bit longer to request a stop.

A while later, Janet yawned and scratched the back of her head, a sure sign of road fatigue. "Janet," Marty said, "Why don't you let me drive the rest of the way?" Elizabeth turned off the recording.

"Well, I have to admit I am ready to switch" Janet said. "Maybe we should get something to eat. We could stop at the McDonald's just beyond Freeport," Janet said.

"Let's stretch our legs and get some fast food. What do you say?" said Marty. Catherine didn't really feel hungry, but she could definitely stretch her legs and visit the ladies' room.

As Catherine walked slowly off to the bathroom, Marty confided to Janet that she continued to be concerned. "I think Catherine is trying to be a good sport, but she's hiding a lot of tension. Will you sit in the back seat and keep an eye on her while I'm driving? We have about three hours to go."

"Sure, I can do that. Let's go get some food," Janet said.

Back on the highway Marty noted the slightly heavier traffic flowing south, returning from the Easter weekend. Once they got beyond Freeport, the northbound cars thinned out. It was now pitch dark except for the occasional headlights going south. The biggest threat on the night roadways in Maine was hitting a moose or a deer. One time Marty had come across three deer standing right in the middle of the highway. She remembered braking slowly, and fortunately all three animals ran into the median strip. If one of them had bolted back toward the breakdown lane, a significant collision would have occurred. Marty always drove a little slower in the dark.

Elizabeth started *The Help* again. At the point in the story when Miss Skeeter's family was just about to have dinner with her boyfriend's family, Elizabeth thought about her parents' first meeting with Cliff's parents. It was actually just three nights before the wedding. Cliff's mother was quite talkative, but his father was reserved, answering her father's questions with short one- or two-word answers. By the end of the wedding, however, the Vermont engineer and the Wall Street tycoon had established a cordial relationship. Actually, when Elizabeth thought about it, her parents had met Cliff's parents only two other times.

Catherine was quiet, trying hard to listen to the story but with little success. She just kept picturing her dog out in the dark. Luckily the temperature remained in the high fifties, and rain was not in the forecast. Despite trying to imagine him returning to Pat and David's house, she couldn't seem to convince herself that that would really happen. As she watched the headlights go by across the highway, tears filled her eyes, and she wiped them away in the darkness of the back seat. This was so silly, she told herself. Then she felt the need to talk with her daughter. She should have had Pat call Sarah to help them look. Why hadn't she thought of that?

"Elizabeth, may I use your cell phone to call Sarah? Maybe she can help find Quigley." Elizabeth had Sarah's number on her contact list and dialed it for her housemate.

"Here you go, Catherine. It's ringing." Elizabeth handed her the cell phone.

"Hello, hello, Sarah, is that you?" Catherine said.

"Oh, yes, Mom, it's me. Where are you?" Sarah asked.

"We are on our way home from New York and have about an hour to go." She continued. "Do you know about Quigley? Pat called to say he had run away." She took another quick breath.

"Yes, I know, Mom. Pat called me right away. We searched all afternoon, and Paul is over at your house now in case Quigley shows up there. We have David and the Blakey boys searching around Elizabeth's house. So far there has been no sign of him, but Mom, he'll come back, I'm sure," Sarah said.

"We'll be home soon, dear. Thanks for helping with the search." As Catherine handed the phone back to Elizabeth, she coughed and felt a strong tightening in her chest; it was different from her previous experience. She coughed again to try to relieve the sensation.

Marty turned around, taking her eyes off the road, trying to see Catherine in the back seat. "Catherine, are you okay?" Marty asked.

"I don't feel exactly right," Catherine replied. "It feels like something is pushing on my chest."

Marty pulled the car over, and Janet attempted to take Catherine's pulse. "Marty, her pulse is irregular and weak. Catherine, I wonder if we need to get you to a hospital," Janet said.

Marty replied, "We are very close to Sebasticook Valley Hospital, and they have ties with Eastern Maine Medical Center." She instructed Elizabeth to dial 911, as she calculated the distance to the Pittsfield exit. Marty had been to this hospital to interview the CEO about their relationship with the regional healthcare system, and she knew it would take only a few minutes to get there. Elizabeth handed the phone to Janet, who was experienced with medical emergencies.

"Yes, we have a potential heart-attack patient and will be pulling up at the Sebasticook Hospital in a few minutes. Could you alert them to our arrival? Yes, I am a nurse, and we have a physician driving the car. Yes, the patient has a history of atrial fibrillation and is now having chest pain. Thank you." Janet put her arm around Catherine. "We'll be there in just a minute. It's going to be okay," she said.

"Thank you, I am so lucky to have you all here." She grimaced from the pain.

"Save your strength, Catherine, and don't try to talk," Marty instructed.

A few minutes later, she pulled up to the entrance of the emergency room. Immediately two assistants rushed out with a gurney. They carefully transferred Catherine to the horizontal position, attaching a portable oxygen mask as they wheeled her into the ER. Janet accompanied Catherine while the others parked the car. This time Elizabeth elected to stay in the small waiting room, with Marty joining Janet and Catherine. The ER nurse attached wires for an electrocardiogram, and another nurse drew blood for testing. Very quickly they would know the results. Time was important to save valuable heart muscle from ischemic damage.

Marty noticed that the nurse had raised her eyebrows. "What do you think?" the nurse asked the physician's assistant.

"Definite ST elevations. Send the electronic tracing on to EMMC, stat!" the PA said.

Within minutes the cardiac team in Bangor ordered a LifeFlight helicopter to pick up Catherine in Pittsfield, anticipating a possible emergency cardiac-stent procedure. The blood test showed elevated troponin, indicating ongoing muscle damage.

Marty stood by Catherine, stroking her head, as Janet held her hand. The morphine seemed to be easing Catherine's pain. Elizabeth began to pace in the waiting room, not knowing the situation. Marty soon came out of the ER and called Sarah, who was terribly upset to hear this news and stated that she would start driving to Bangor immediately.

Time was of the essence, and luckily the weather was clear for the helicopter landing. Marty sat by the window, waiting. She thought about her medical-school training on caring for heart-attack victims. If they made it to the hospital — and many didn't — you gave morphine, oxygen, and nitroglycerin under the tongue. Back then, few people had the opportunity to live beyond their first heart attack. So many things had changed. Catherine was in a precarious spot at the moment, but if a stent were put in and if it worked, she could have several more good years of life.

"How is she doing?" Elizabeth asked.

"Her pain is a little better, but this is a very danger-ous time. The race is on to prevent as much heart-muscle damage as possible. The cardiologists are ready for her in Bangor. Now she just has to make it there. I think they said the helicopter takes twenty minutes from liftoff." Mar-ty looked out the window again. She was well aware of a new medical study showing that loss or grief increases the risk of heart attack by twenty-fold in those with cardiac disease, and mortality increases too. The helicopter pad was lit up, ready for their arrival. For Marty and all the Winter House women, it couldn't come quickly enough.

Soon Janet, Marty, and Elizabeth watched the Life-Flight helicopter take off, carrying Catherine away to Bangor. The transfer team had wasted no time getting their patient into the aircraft. As the flashing red lights disappeared into the night sky, the three women said a little prayer for their special friend Catherine and one for Quigley too.

Elizabeth's phone rang. "Hello, Elizabeth, this is Sarah. How's Mom doing?"

"They've just taken her off in the helicopter. They should be back to Bangor in about twenty minutes. Where are you?"

"I'm within about twenty minutes of the hospital. Thanks so much for all you've done. Will you come directly to Bangor?"

"We will come to Bangor and check in, and then Janet and I might return to Brooks Harbor. Marty wants to stay with you and Catherine."

"I could use the support," Sarah confessed. She was not yet ready to lose her mother, and neither were the new housemates.

When Marty arrived at the hospital, Catherine had already been taken to the cardiac-catheterization lab. She and Sarah could do nothing now but wait.

Elizabeth drove the last leg home to Brooks Harbor with Janet. Neither wanted to listen to *The Help*. Janet was afraid to snooze, as she wanted to make sure Elizabeth had companionship and stayed awake. There was occasional fog in the valleys.

"Did you know Brad well?" Janet asked, trying to take their minds off Catherine's crisis.

"Oh, we had a few dates during our freshman year, nothing serious. After I began dating Cliff, I never really saw Brad too much."

"He's very handsome, I'd say."

"Yes, that white hair is striking."

"It's his eyes and the way he looked at you that I noticed."

"You don't miss much, Janet." Elizabeth felt flushed. She, too, had been struck by his penetrating eyes. This had actually been the first time since her husband's death that she had allowed herself to think of another relationship: life beyond Cliff.

"Would you like to see him again?" Janet probed.

"I just might," Elizabeth confessed, but she didn't want to get her hopes up. She started wondering what her life would be like in a year, in five years, in ten. So much could happen in a split second, in a summer.

This time Elizabeth changed the subject. "What are you planning to do this summer?" With only ten days left of the Winter House arrangement, none of the women had asked about each other's summer plans.

Janet replied, "I've been thinking I need to go out west

on a road trip. It's time for me to visit with my son in Colorado. Peter leads a busy life, and we haven't seen each other for two years. That is just too long." With the demands of her own life and the thousands of miles between them, she'd let her family connections slip away.

"That sounds like an adventure." Elizabeth said. "Have you been out there before?"

"I haven't spent any significant time in the Rockies, except around Boulder, where Peter attended graduate school. However, I enjoyed the wide-open spaces and mountains, but still don't think I could give up our lakes or ocean."

"I do know what you mean. They're addicting," Elizabeth agreed.

Janet replied, "I suppose the mountain peaks and vast open spaces can hook you too. I may just give it another try."

Janet had lived in Brooks Harbor since she married John, whose church work kept him busy, especially during the summer when the congregation's size increased. She also had had her mother to watch over. And then there was her vegetable garden, which took tending. Hospice work kept her active too. Each summer John's children and grandchildren visited, but she was beginning to wonder if they might like to have the house to themselves on their vacations. They knew they would inherit it. Though they were always cordial and loving to Janet even after their father's death, she had once overhead John's children talking about eventually owning the place.

"I guess we are all in for some changes," Elizabeth said.

"Change can be good," Janet replied.

"I sure hope Catherine pulls through this and can get back to her precious Dendall Hollow. And boy, I hope we can find Quigley. That's our next big project."

As Elizabeth pulled into the driveway on Spruce Point, she noticed the old green pickup that belonged to the Blakey boys. Then she saw Jerry and Jimmy sitting inside the truck. The boys walked over to her car. "Hi, Miz Sloan," Jerry said, leaning on the door. "We're glad you're back. Mr. Sullivan told us to hang around here in case Quigley came back. But we ain't seen or heard nothing. Mr. Sullivan just left to check out by the old dump. He said he just had a feeling."

"Well, thanks for being here. We're just getting back from New York City. It's been a very long day," Elizabeth said. She wasn't sure if they had heard anything about Catherine.

"How's Miz Catherine?" Jerry asked. "We heard she's having some trouble." Word travels fast in a small town, Elizabeth thought. "We don't know yet, but we hope she'll be okay."

Jerry shook his head. "She sure loves that little dog. We gotta find him for her."

Jimmy stood next to his brother. "Maybe Quigley will show up tomorrow," he said softly.

"I hope so," Elizabeth said. "We'll leave out some food."

Jerry suggested that they lay out a coat or piece of clothing belonging to Catherine. "I heard once of a dog who was lost for a week, and he was eventually found lying on his master's coat that had been left out in the woods."

"Yeah, them dogs can smell from a long ways off," Jimmy added.

"That's a good idea, Jerry. We'll put Catherine's winter coat out on the porch near the food. He just has to come home," Elizabeth said. "Well, guess there isn't much more we can do tonight. Thanks for helping. Maybe we can spread the news to the neighboring towns tomorrow."

"I just hope the little guy is okay. We got coyotes in these woods, you know," Jerry said. Jimmy nodded.

"Well, I don't want to think about that," Elizabeth replied, as she and Janet climbed out of the car. The boys helped them bring their suitcases inside and then said good night.

After laying Catherine's coat outside along with a bowl of kibble, the two women went upstairs to bed. Janet took a long, hot bath to unwind from the exhausting trip. Many things were up in the air: Quigley's disappearance, Catherine's condition, and Janet's own future plans.

With barely enough energy to brush her teeth, Elizabeth collapsed into bed. Tomorrow had to be a better day.

Four hours after arriving at Eastern Maine Medical Center, Catherine was in the intensive-care unit, hooked up to sophisticated digital monitors displaying continuous electrocardiogram readings, blood pressure, and oxygen saturations. She appeared to be sleeping when the nurse allowed Sarah and Marty to approach the bedside.

"That was quite a stress on her system," the nurse said. "I think she'll sleep for a while, with her medications.

Sarah gently stroked her mother's hand — the steady hand of a woman who had always been there for her family, the strong hand of a woman who wanted to remain independent for as long as she could. She was ten days away from her eightieth birthday. Sarah prayed that her mother would make it. Emma and Ella loved their Nanny, and she hated to think of the little girls losing this special relationship. Sarah looked up at Marty, who was checking the monitors. "Things are going to be okay," Marty said to Sarah, who looked very worried. "Your mother's blood pressure is improving, and her heart rate has stabilized somewhat. The oxygen saturation is right on target." Marty reviewed the continuous cardiac-rhythm display. A few irregular beats remained, but on the whole she felt the EKG was much better. "I think your mother is a tough old gal. She's going to make her birthday party, I'll bet on it." Marty smiled at Sarah, a devoted daughter whose blue eyes resembled her mother's.

After a while Sarah fell asleep in the recliner chair. Marty, exhausted mentally and physically, could not sleep. She walked the halls of the hospital, which at night were empty. Marty recalled many all-nighters she had spent in hospitals during internship, residency, and private practice. Back then, physicians worked until the job was done. It was not shift work. She remembered many times when she had worked all day, all night, and then all day again. It was insane, but that was the way it was. You certainly knew your patients and were there for follow-up, but your decisions could be a bit foggy by the end of thirty-six hours on the job. It pleased Marty to know that she never regretted choosing to become a doctor. For her, the profession was the perfect combination of science and human connectivity.

Marty was quite sure that Catherine would make it, but the next twelve hours would be critical. For a while she sat in the hospital chapel, and even considered lying down on the pews. Eventually, she wandered back past the nurs-

ing station, where the charge nurse indicated that a recliner chair was available in an empty room at the end of the
hallway. Marty thanked her and went to find it. It wasn't
long before she fell asleep at last, completely exhausted.

By the next morning Catherine was awake. The doctor explained that he would like her to stay another day
for observation. During the procedure her heart had actually stopped beating, and they had to "put the paddles
to her." That's what he had said, and Catherine was glad
she couldn't remember that part. Dr. Gold also told her
that two of her vessels were 80 to 90 percent blocked, but
they were able to put two stents in place, greatly improving the blood flow. She would have to be on a few more
medications, watch her diet, and try to get more exercise.
Catherine was impressed that Dr. Gold had the time to
spend with her now. If only she had seen him right after
the atrial fibrillation episode; maybe he would have evalu-
ated her and diagnosed the blockage earlier. The problem
was that her scheduled appointment with him wasn't until
the end of April. Catherine had not thought anything of it,
as most consultation appointments took months to get.

He asked her about any acute stresses she might have
experienced. It was then that Catherine told him about
Quigley's disappearance. The doctor, a dog lover himself,
understood the troublesome situation. "I'm sure you'll find
him. Don't give up. I've heard of dogs that have been lost
for weeks and then reappear," he said.

"I sure hope he shows up soon," Catherine said. She
was eager to get home to help find Quigley, but resting
in the hospital for another day would probably do her
some good.

Sarah and Marty arrived to see Catherine just as Dr. Gold was leaving. He told them she could probably go home after another twenty-four hours. He just wanted to be sure things continued to improve. "That was a close call. It was lucky you were near Pittsfield; any longer and the damage might have been much more severe. She's got a real fighting spirit." He turned and went on to his next patient.

"Mom, you look great. What a difference from last night," Sarah said.

"Well, I sure feel a whole lot better. Have you heard anything about Quigley?"

"The whole town is mobilizing to find him. They're putting posters up at the post office, the kiosk, the market, and in the nearby towns. Janet called WERU, and an announcement will be aired several times today. The veterinarian's office sent out an email alert to all dog owners in the area. He's bound to be found," Sarah said, trying to comfort her mother.

"Oh, that should help. I just cannot imagine life without him," Catherine said.

"He'll be found, Mom. I just have that feeling," Sarah repeated.

"I sure hope you're right, dear." Catherine had always been a positive person. She had inherited that from her grandmother and mother, who used to quote Norman Vincent Peale and his *Power of Positive Thinking*. At a seminar more recently, Catherine had learned that several twentieth-century psychologists viewed Peale's techniques with disfavor; by not mastering the skills to deal with hard issues but instead being intent on fleeing and avoiding negative thoughts, those who followed Peale's teachings might well have experienced more mental distress. That insight might have influenced Catherine's opinion of Peale, but it hadn't made her look less to the brighter side of things.

"I bought you a *Bangor Daily News*," Marty said. "I thought that might keep you occupied for a while."

Sarah handed her mother a present. "And I found a book by Dr. Tom Palmer called *Cracked Marbles* in the gift shop. Didn't he take out my appendix?" Sarah asked.

"Yes, he did, and he removed my gallbladder before that. He was a marvelous surgeon. I've been meaning to borrow that book from the library, but it has always been checked out," her mother replied.

"Well, we're going off to Brooks Harbor. You've got things to occupy you now, and maybe you can even take a nap."

"You know I don't nap — well, usually I don't," Catherine replied. Maybe she should put that into her routine. Recently she had been found sleeping in her favorite kitchen chair.

"I'll be back this evening, Mom," Sarah said. She was happy to see her mother feeling better. What a miracle!

"Okey-dokey," Catherine said, as Marty and Sarah left. She raised the head of her bed with a push of the button and dove into the newspaper. First she skimmed the headlines. Then she flipped to the editorials and finally the obituaries and was happy to find she wasn't there. She smiled at her Uncle Cyrus's old joke. At one time she contemplated preparing her own obituary in case of an untimely demise but then figured it would be a good bonding exercise for her three children to accomplish together. After reading the first three death notices, she scanned the others to see if she knew anyone. Her eyes stopped cold at the name of Anson Grange. A veteran flag marked the short obituary, which noted his army service in the Korean War and his distinguished honor. She discovered that he had died the day the Winter House women left for New York City. No cause of death was mentioned, and there were no traditional phrases: "he was surrounded by his loving family" or "he loved the Red Sox." His three sons were listed. Two lived out of state, one in California and one in Massachusetts. The third son, whom Catherine remembered from her teaching years, had a wife, Maureen, and a son, Byron, who lived in Sedgwick, a town near Brooks Harbor. No funeral service was planned. Contributions could be made to the Korean War Veterans Association. Catherine sighed. May he rest in peace, she thought. He certainly suffered in life.

All the school kids were notified of the little lost dog. They knew Catherine from the library's reading program and were anxious to help search for him. There was no way of knowing in which direction Quigley went after leaving Pat and David's house. He could be anywhere after a day of wandering, and the town had many wooded areas. Everyone hoped that if enough people kept their eyes open for a small, white dog, Quigley would be spotted.

Pat and David continued to think of ways to find Quigley. A friend of theirs had recommended a psychic, Sadie Paige, who had helped to find her lost cat. The psychic volunteered to help in the search, having heard about Quigley on WERU. Though Pat and David were skeptical of her ability to communicate directly with Quigley, they promised to email a picture of the dog to make it easier for her to visualize him. "Oh, please tell

Quigley that Catherine will be home very soon," Pat said to the psychic, "and tell him she really needs him to come back."

"I'll see what I can do," Sadie replied, knowing that few folks believed in her abilities, but she had collected enough anecdotes of successful pet findings that knowledge of her mysterious talent was spreading.

Marty and Janet decided to hit some tennis balls. Both had been exhausted by the long drive, not to mention the added stress of Catherine's heart attack. Exercise relaxed them. Janet returned a solid backhand. After almost four months of playing tennis, thanks to Marty, Janet was enjoying the sport again. At sixty-eight she had thought her tennis days were over, but Marty had insisted she try it again, mostly for the social fun. In addition to getting to know a few new tennis buddies, Janet was stronger and healthier, feeling the effects of her rediscovered endorphins.

"Three more balls, then we should probably get going," Marty said. They did do some final stretches. Marty had learned recently that stretching after exercise was better for muscles than stretching beforehand.

"Will Catherine be coming back to Elizabeth's or do you think she will stay at Sarah's house for a while?" Janet asked.

"It sounds like Catherine wants to complete her time at the Winter House with us. She's still an independent soul and not yet ready to move into Sarah's place, but it may be in her future. You know me, I support her spirit of independence," Marty said.

"Yes, and we still have the surprise birthday party and our last lobster feast," Janet commented.

"Let's hope Quigley decides to return for those activities too," Marty said. "Should we go and pick up the groceries on Elizabeth's list?"

As they drove to the market, the announcement on WERU played again on the car radio: "We have a lost-dog alert. Quigley is a small, white dog with floppy ears and a fluffy tail. Lost yesterday in Brooks Harbor on Johnson Road. He has a red collar and identification tags. He likes cheese. He may be shy. If seen, please call WERU at 469-6601."

"With any luck, that announcement will help," Marty said.

Back at the Winter House the land phone rang. Home alone, Elizabeth quickly picked up the receiver. The only people who called this number, as a rule, were Catherine's friends and many marketers. The women had decided to give this local number for news of Quigley.

"Hello," Elizabeth said. "Hello," she repeated quickly.

"Oh, hello. Is this the owner of the lost dog?" the voice asked.

"Well, no — I mean, yes — we are looking for the dog, but the owner is unavailable at this time. Do you have any information?" Elizabeth questioned in a wishful tone.

"Yeah, well, we were hunting for fiddleheads down by the river bank this morning, and across the river we saw a little, white dog sniffing around. You know, out there on the back side of the Sedgwick dump," the man said.

Elizabeth did not know this location and asked him to describe it a little better so she could give the information to Marty or Pat. Oh, my gosh! she thought, maybe we'l find him even before Catherine gets home. The caller saic he had seen the poster in the post office and heard the an nouncement on the radio. "I sure hope you find the little guy," he said.

"Me too, thanks so much for calling," Elizabeth said.

Marty and Janet returned with the groceries, but before they placed the bags on the counter, Elizabeth began to tell them about the phone call.

"Someone saw Quigley down by the Sedgwick dump!" Elizabeth said excitedly.

"Really, that's quite a ways from here or from Pat's. He's either wandering aimlessly or heading somewhere," Marty said. "Janet and I can drive over there now. Why don't you call Jerry and Jimmy and see if they will meet us there. The more eyes we have, the better. I'll take my cell phone in case you receive any more calls." The two women quickly changed out of their tennis clothes and grabbed a leash and some doggie treats. "We're off!" They flew out the door.

"Don't forget your cell phone, Marty," Elizabeth said. Marty was not used to taking her phone everywhere, but she realized there were times it could be a great help. For a while there was poor coverage in this area and carrying a cell phone wasn't very useful. But with all the cell towers popping up on mountaintops, signals were more reliable.

"Don't let the ice cream melt," Janet said, as they raced out the door. Elizabeth laughed. She was left to put away the groceries, a job she actually enjoyed.

Janet, Marty, and the Blakey boys searched for several hours around the dump. They started down by the river's edge, where Quigley had been seen. They all called his name over and over again. Marty tried to whistle the way Catherine did, but she knew it did not sound the same.

"Quigley, Quigley," Janet called. "Please come here, Quig." She was beginning to think the dog wasn't around this area anymore and that their continued searching was futile.

"I guess we aren't going to find him here," Marty said. She thanked Jerry and Jimmy for helping and asked them if they wanted to come over for pizza and ice cream. Jimmy looked at Jerry.

"That would be great," Jerry said.

"Good, we'd love to have you," Marty said. Who knew if the boys had anything planned for their supper? She wondered how they were doing since their mother's death last month.

"Hi, Elizabeth," Marty said on her cell phone. "We didn't see any sign of the little guy, and we're calling it quits for the day. He's obviously wandered farther off. Maybe we'll get another phone call. Say, we've invited Jerry and Jimmy for supper. Janet and I bought some pre-made pizza dough today, and we can just add the topping." Should I get anything else?"

"Oh, I wish Quigley would stay put. Then maybe we could find him. No, I think I have everything to fix up the pizzas. Come on home," Elizabeth said. "Do you want me to call Catherine with an update? She called and I did tell her someone had seen him near the dump.' She really didn't want to tell Catherine there was no good news.

"We can wait awhile. I'll call her after supper," Marty said.

"Okay, see you soon."

That night there were no more sightings, and the only call came from Catherine. Marty tried to put a positive spin on the situation and sound confident that he would be found tomorrow.

The next day Sarah drove her mother back to the Winter House. Catherine was happy to be alive, to be out of the hospital, and to be returning to her special friends. She and her daughter had a long conversation in the car about Quigley, who was nine years old. Sarah pointed out the hard fact that owners usually outlive their dogs and that loss can be intense. "Mom," Sarah said, "in one sense, Dad was lucky. He didn't have to see his old Colonel die, but you did. And you thought you'd never get over Colonel's death, but eventually a new dog came into your life."

"I know, dear, you're right. Quigley and I bonded right away...I just hate to lose him, that's all. He's been with me nine years now, and I was hoping we'd have several more years together. I even figured you'd take him if I died first."

"Well, I'm not ready to lose you yet, and I still think we'll find him. Remember he was spotted yesterday, so we know he's still alive and no one has stolen him." Sarah was trying to comfort her mother, but it was clear that this loss would be hard.

For the next four days the women tried to go about their usual routine. Catherine didn't feel up to reading at the library. When Marty and Janet went off to yoga, she just wandered around the house, looking out at the water. Elizabeth had gone on some errands, needing more paint supplies. It was almost warm enough to begin painting outdoors. From the south window Catherine could see three yellow daffodils open to the sun as well as the remains of the purple crocuses. Tulips would arrive soon. Spring was definitely here, but Catherine felt no elation. Where coul Quigley be?

Sarah and Elizabeth met to plan Catherine's b eightieth birthday party for the following Friday. Even Quigley didn't return, they figured they had to have th celebration. All the townspeople knew about the party, an probably all of them knew about Quigley's disappearanc Pat Sullivan had gone ahead and organized the Happ Helpers, who all wanted to cook for the event. Lotti Lyr strom had volunteered to get the ukulele band ready an to line up a few more musicians. With Catherine abser from the library, the librarian had the children make a bi birthday card and sign their names. Billy Gray and his fa ther were delighted to help with hanging up the lights a the community center.

Sarah's brother Will had called to see how his mothe was doing. He had enjoyed being with her in New Yor City and was shocked to hear about her heart attack. Wi could not make the party, but his brother, Harold, planne to come from Portland.

"That's great. Your mother will be pleased," Elizabet said. "Do you really think we can keep this a surprise unt next Friday?"

"I don't know, but we can try. It all depends on whethe you women are good actors."

"At this point she's totally distracted with Quigley's al sence. I'm not sure she's thinking about her birthday."

"Well, the party preparations all seem to be falling int place. Now we just have to find her dog."

"Right," Elizabeth said.

After a week of being home, Catherine returned to Bar

gor to see Dr. Gold. Sarah drove her, as she wanted to hear the doctor's comments and to be sure her mother was up-front about her progress.

"Your blood work looks good, and your blood pressure is fine. The incision site is almost healed. I'm very pleased with things, Catherine," Dr. Gold said. Catherine's affect seemed a bit subdued in view of this good news, and only then did Dr. Gold remember their bedside conversation. "I'm guessing you haven't found your dog yet," he said softly.

"No, there's been no sighting in over a week," Catherine said, looking down.

"I'm sorry, but don't give up. He can still return. It's spring. Maybe he is just out feeling his oats, as they say." Dr. Gold tried to cheer her up. "In church last week a member of the congregation announced that their dog had been found after two weeks. So it happens," he added.

"I'll keep hoping," Catherine said. She knew she needed to pull out of this. It wasn't at all like her, and she hated to be acting blue. For her health, she needed to move on.

At yoga class Marty and Janet continued to work on headstands. "You're almost there," Beth said, encouraging Marty to press evenly on her forearms, keep her shoulders set, extend her toes up to the ceiling, and move her hips over her shoulders. It was a lot of instruction all at once, but Marty attempted to follow it, one step at a time.

"There, you've got it!" Beth said. "Now try to hold it for the count of ten." She stood right next to Marty to help steady her. Eventually, an inversion should last for several minutes, but if Marty could hold for ten seconds to start, that would be a major accomplishment for her. She was amazed that she felt little pressure on her head in this so-called headstand. Her fingers were webbed together, nestling the top of her head, and her forearms and shoulders provided a secure base. At the count of eleven, Marty felt her shoulders begin to tremble, and she decided to come out of the pose. Beth helped her slowly lower one leg and then the other.

"Great job, Marty. Congratulations! You have been working on that for quite a while, and today you did it," Beth said.

"That's amazing. It really isn't so bad, once you get balanced. But I know my shoulders will feel that tomorrow," Marty said. Although her wrists and forearms were fairly strong from tennis, she didn't use her shoulders much except in the "downward-facing dog" yoga position.

Janet, who had been slightly ahead of Marty in the preparation work, still wasn't quite sure she could do the final pose. Though Marty was a better athlete than Janet, this hesitation was probably just a small psychological barrier, she thought.

"Do you want to try it, Janet?" Beth asked. "You can use my body to assist in the ascent if you'd like."

"I just may need to do that," Janet said. Beth slowly gave Janet the instructions, this time more slowly. When Janet felt well positioned, Beth assisted her in raising her legs. Janet was almost ready to stretch her legs to the sky when Beth told her to come down a minute.

"Your base is not quite right," Beth said. "Pull your elbows in toward you a bit more, and really push down on your forearms and lift and set your shoulders." Janet followed these instructions. "Good, now let's try that again." Janet concentrated and, with help, she stretched her feet toward the ceiling. Beth held on gently to one leg to steady the swaying. "Now, try to bring your hips over your shoulders by moving them away from the wall. There, that's it!" Beth said with excitement. Janet couldn't hold the position long, not even getting to a count of seven. She had gotten upside down, however, and would try it again next time.

"Whoa, I can't believe I inverted," Janet exclaimed.

"Good job, you two," Beth said. "I think you are good for each other." Both women smiled.

After her doctor's appointment in Bangor, Catherine phoned Elizabeth to say that she and Sarah would stop in to visit Pat and David, who were continuing to feel bad about losing Quigley.

Elizabeth decided to join Marty and Janet for lunch after yoga. She had pretty much given up on receiving phone calls at home about the missing dog. Much as she hated to admit it to Catherine, Elizabeth had lost hope that Quigley would ever return. She worried about hungry coyotes.

When Elizabeth arrived at the market, Janet and Marty appeared to be deep in conversation. She chose some beef-barley soup and sat down.

"Oh, hi," Marty said, looking up at Elizabeth.

"No news, I assume," Janet said.

"No, I figure a watched pot never boils," Elizabeth replied. She didn't want to tell them she had given up on Quigley's return. "How was yoga?" she asked, to change the subject.

"Great," Marty said. "Janet and I finally turned upside down on our heads."

"Wow, that is impressive! You both have been working hard at that. I guess persistence pays off," Elizabeth said. As a Vermont teenager, she had tried to ski with her brothers, but she gave up too soon and always regretted it. Although her kids learned to ski with Cliff, she never joined them. Looking back, that was a big disappointment in her life — her lack of perseverance. "What will you two accomplish next?" Elizabeth asked.

"Ha, maybe we'll try a one-handed flip," Janet said.

"You're kidding," Elizabeth replied.

"Oh, yeah," Marty said, "She's kidding." They all laughed. The older couple sitting at the next table left, leaving the small café empty except for the three women.

"Marty, did you hear Suzanne say that her husband is leaving her?" Janet asked. At the end of yoga class, Suzanne, a local artist, had mentioned to a few of her friends that her husband wanted a divorce. Janet and Marty did not hang around to get the gruesome details; both knew personally how painful and messy divorce could be.

"Do I know Suzanne?" Elizabeth asked.

"You'd probably recognize her if you saw her. She's a talented artist and has lived here for quite a while," Marty said.

"I pity anyone who has to go through it. It isn't easy," Janet said. That was an understatement. Her divorce had been very hard on her. After twenty years of marriage, Brent had decided he was in love with his young legal assistant. It didn't seem to matter to him that they had Peter together, that they shared plenty of good times. His affair seemed to her like the perfect male midlife crisis. He traded in his Oldsmobile for a red Corvette convertible, attached himself to a younger woman, and moved his law practice to Virginia, leaving Janet in an old house with rotting sills. "Brent totally messed up my life and hardly looked back." Janet shook her head. "I hate to say this, but I think it would have been a lot easier if he had died." Janet saw the look on Elizabeth's face. "Oh, I'm sorry, Elizabeth, I shouldn't have said that." She touched her friend's arm.

"That's okay. I know what you mean. When your husband dies, you mourn his loss, you miss him, you're alone, but your opinion of yourself — your self-image — isn't challenged," Elizabeth said. Then she thought about the widow image, even the "*vedova*" image. It *was* challenging her.

"I went into such a tailspin," Janet continued. "I felt unlovable. I was a has-been wife, deserted for a beautiful and selfish..."

"Bitch," Marty interrupted. She'd been there too, and knew the pain, even though she had been married only a short time. After the end of her quick marriage, she was able to plunge right into medical school, a path that occupied her full attention for many years.

"You've got that right, Marty," Janet replied. "I can't help it. Anyone who breaks up a twenty-year marriage is a bitch in my book too." The divorce happened long ago, and still discussion of it made Janet's blood hot.

"But thank goodness, you found John," Elizabeth said, trying to simmer things down. "That seems like a silver lining." Elizabeth knew there were usually two sides to a story of divorce, but that never stopped the pain for the one deserted.

"You're right, Elizabeth. John and I had eleven wonderful years of marriage, and each of us knew by then that marriage must be a constant work in progress with no one taking anyone for granted," Janet said. "Maybe Brent and I had let things grow stale — you know, routine. It happens without our even realizing it."

"I agree with you," Elizabeth said. "Marriage is work,

and nobody tells you that when you're young and in love. Newlyweds probably wouldn't even listen."

Marty piped up: "I remember what an old doctor friend told me about his divorce after thirty years of marriage. He said, 'Just keep talking, talk about the good and the bad aspects of your marriage, because once the lines of communication close down, you'll just start to drift apart, suppress your feelings, and sometimes even with marriage counseling, it's too late to turn back the clock.'" Marty paused.

Elizabeth took a sip of her Diet Dr. Pepper. "My parents used to call it a bulge. My dad and mom were married sixty-three years, but they admitted that in the first thirty years, they went through bulges where they drifted apart a bit and didn't feel they were communicating well, or they were having just too many silly spats. They'd actively try to pull back to a closer relationship…. In fact, I remember one time when Cliff and I weren't doing too well, and I visited with my folks for some advice. They said we were having a bit of a bulge. Dad said, 'It's pretty normal, Betsy Ann, just go back and take more time with each other, maybe even ignore the children a bit. They'll do fine, but not so well if the marriage falls apart.' It was sound advice. Cliff and I had our rough times, but in general I look back on them as positive."

"Do you see yourself remarrying?" Marty asked Elizabeth, who knew by now that Marty could ask some pretty pointed questions.

"You know, I haven't really thought about that much and honestly, it's a bit daunting to think I'd have to train another man." All three women laughed. "I do want to tell you two that the Winter House arrangement for this year has been so helpful. The winter seems to have flown by," Elizabeth said.

None of the four women had yet raised the issue of next winter. In fact, it seemed that they had purposely not addressed that situation. May was right around the corner, and the deal they had made was to move in December 1 and out May 1.

"You're still young, Elizabeth. Remember seventy-two is the new fifty-two!" Marty said.

"Well, I think that's a bit of an exaggeration," Elizabeth replied.

"That Brad Thornton is a handsome guy." Pushing her housemate a bit, Marty added, "Is he available?"

"Actually, I didn't quite get his story. His daughter and granddaughter were walking in the Easter parade for breast cancer. After a comment he made about Cliff's death, I assume his wife might have died. But who knows?..., at least he knows where to find me, if he's interested." She blushed.

"Well, keep your eyes open. Things happen when you least expect them," Janet said. The three women paid for their lunches and went home.

A red number 2 was blinking on the answering machine when they walked into the house. Two new messages. Elizabeth pushed the playback button.

"Hello," said a taped voice, "we are calling about your car warranty. It is about to expire." Elizabeth hit the delete button. She was sick of those robo-messages from probably fraudulent companies.

The next message began to play: "Hello, this is Byron Grange over here in Sedgwick. Me and my girlfriend are pretty sure we found Quigley, your lost dog."

"Oh, my God!" Elizabeth said. All three women were still, trying to hear the complete message.

"He seems to be okay but a little skinny and timid. He didn't have no collar on. We've given him just a little food and water, and he's lying on a blanket in our kitchen. Lisa actually found him waiting outside the kennel door. He's been here many times before for his grooming. He acted happy to see her but was shivering when she picked him up, probably from fright, 'cause it really wasn't too cold out last night. We can bring him over any time if you'll give us a call. My number is 424-2012."

The three women hugged each other and actually jumped with joy. "Holy cow!" Marty said. "There really are miracles. Let's give him a call right away."

"When do you think Catherine and Sarah will be back?" Janet asked.

"It should be soon. They were going to visit Pat," Elizabeth said.

"Oh, I wish Catherine carried a cell phone. Wait, I think I have Sarah's cell-phone number," Elizabeth said. She dialed the number, but it went directly to messages. "Should I leave a message?" she whispered to Janet and Marty. They decided to forget it and just call this Byron boy. Maybe Catherine and Sarah would be home anytime now.

Elizabeth was too nervous to call. Marty did it. The number rang four times. "Hello, Feeling Good Kennels and Grooming," a young woman answered.

"Hello, we are calling about Quigley. Do you think you found him?"

"Well, actually he found us. This is Lisa," the woman said. "I'd recognize Quig anywhere, but he is kind of thin, though."

"We are just so happy. You have no idea," Marty said. Janet and Elizabeth were holding their ears close to the receiver.

"Is Miz Catherine around?" Lisa asked. "How long has he been missing?"

"It's been about nine or ten days, way too long for any dog," Marty said. "Can you bring him over soon?"

"Well, I have some more grooming jobs to do, but my boyfriend, Byron Grange, said he would drive him over. He wants to know your address. He knows Brooks Harbor pretty good. His grandfather lived there. Here I'll give him the phone."

Marty explained how to get to Spruce Point. The young man seemed to be familiar with the area and said he'd be there in twenty minutes or so.

"Look forward to seeing you real soon," Marty said. "Keep good hold of that little guy."

"Don't worry, he'll be on a leash," Byron said, and hung up.

Janet looked out the window to see if by any chance Sarah's car was arriving. No sign of it. The women couldn't sit still and just kept beaming at one another.

"It's a miracle, really. Nine days in the woods and two towns over. He had to cross two bridges. I just wonder why more people didn't spot the little guy," Elizabeth said.

"Maybe he chose to travel only at night. Who knows? We'll never know, unless Quigley cares to share his journey." Marty smiled. "It's so great!"

"Do you think this will be too much of a shock for Catherine?" Elizabeth asked.

"Oh, I think she can handle this dose of sheer happiness. Her heart will be overjoyed, but her perfusion is so much better with the stents. We might want her to be sitting down, though," Marty said. "I suppose she could faint."

"Who wants to tell her?" Janet said.

"Are you kidding? We are not going to have to tell her. She will read it all over our faces," Marty said, "especially as you move the kitchen chair toward her."

"You're right. This is exciting," Elizabeth exclaimed. "Do you think we should call Pat's house? They've felt so responsible for losing Quigley."

"Let's let Catherine call them once Quigley is home," Marty replied.

"Oh, I'd better pee before this spectacular event occurs," Elizabeth blurted out.

"Me too," said Marty. She dashed upstairs, and Elizabeth used the downstairs bathroom. While sitting on the toilet upstairs, Marty smiled at Elizabeth's use of the word "pee." She remembered the first time that she had written in a progress note in a medical chart, "The patient peed." The attending physician corrected her, suggesting that the word "void" was much more appropriate for an official medical record. Her mother had used the word "tinkle" for the process, and Marty had sworn she'd never ask anyone if they "had to go tinkle."

"Hey, they're here!" Janet called out. The three women gathered in the kitchen. Catherine and her daughter entered. Sarah saw the smiling faces first and knew immediately there was good news. Catherine hung up her coat in the mudroom and walked in behind Sarah.

There was silence for a split second as Catherine looked at her housemates, who seemed to be in suspended animation.

"What?" Catherine said. "What are you staring at me for?" she asked, and then she got it. "Someone found Quigley?" she said, just as Janet pushed the chair over toward Catherine, who had put her hands over her mouth.

"Yes! Yes!" Elizabeth cried out, "He's okay!"

"Oh, my gosh!" Catherine said. She sat down. "I cannot believe it. Dr. Gold told me not to give up, and all the way home I was praying for news." Sarah crouched next to her mother while the others surrounded Catherine, placing their hands on her shoulders. For a second, she was speechless, and then she cried. The women all rejoiced with tears of relief, joy, and friendship.

Missy peered out the window, looking down the driveway. Her feline instincts told her something was about to happen. She had been out of sorts too with Quigley's absence. When Catherine heard that Quigley had shown up at Lisa's grooming place, she was astonished at the distance he had traveled. Lisa had always been so kind and gentle with Quigley when he went to get his coat trimmed, and she always gave him a special chicken treat. Catherine had not known that Lisa's boyfriend was Byron Grange. What a coincidence, she thought, that Anson's grandson would now be bringing her such a priceless gift.

A maroon pickup truck pulled into the driveway, and a young man climbed out, lifting the small, white dog down onto the ground. He held the leash as Quigley strained to climb the back stairs. Catherine noticed that the handsome man resembled his grandfather in his youth. She opened the door to let them both in.

"Quigley, Quigley, I missed you so," Catherine said. He jumped up for a greeting, then turned around three times in a tight circle and stood up on his hind legs. She picked him up, and she noticed that he felt lighter. He licked her face, and it looked as though his front paws clung to her neck. His body wiggled in her arms. "You silly, silly doggie," Catherine said. "I hope you never do that again." Quigley licked her ears and nuzzled his black nose into her neck. The others all watched this joyful reunion.

"Thank you so much, Byron, for bringing Quigley back to me," Catherine said. Quigley had calmed down in her arms. "You have no idea what this means to me."

"He must have finally decided he wanted to be found, and maybe he got so hungry that he wanted some of Lisa's special dog treats. And really, I'm so glad I could do this for you, Miz Catherine." Byron and Catherine chatted a bit more, and she introduced him to her friends. His kind and gentle demeanor was evident.

Marty offered him a soda, but he said he had to get back to help Lisa with more grooming. Quigley hopped up on his favorite chair, obviously glad to be back. Catherine walked Byron out to his truck.

"I don't know if you know it, but I taught your father in high school many years ago," Catherine said. "And also I was sorry to read about the death of your grandfather last week."

Byron turned and looked down at his feet. "I've known about you for years," the young man said. "My father said you were his favorite teacher." He paused as though he had something else to say.

"What is it, Byron?"

"I want to apologize." Byron's face flushed.

"Apologize for what?" Catherine placed her hand on his arm.

Byron took a deep breath. "I was the one who found my grandfather. He was lying on the rug next to the kitchen table. Two empty bottles of booze sat on the table. He must

270

have been dead for a few days, 'cause he was real cold. It was awful."

"I'm so sorry," Catherine said. "He wasn't a happy man."

"No, he hardly wanted to see his family, and my grandmother died four years ago. Dad had just about given up on visiting him, but I stopped in every once in a while. He taught me how to hunt and fish," Byron said. "But he had gotten pretty grumpy...he used to say life wasn't worth livin' no more...and..." Byron stopped. Catherine said nothing, giving the young man time to put his thoughts into words. "And he'd started doing funny things, awful things...." He stopped again, letting out a deep sigh. "I found some awful scribbles and crunched-up pieces of paper. Many envelopes and notes were addressed to you. I don't know if he ever sent any of them."

Catherine heard the humiliation in his voice.

"Gramps wasn't right when he died. He had gotten really forgetful and foul-mouthed. The doctor had told my father that he thought Gramps was getting slowly demented ...probably from all the booze or from mini-strokes. The doc said he didn't think it was Alzheimer's." Byron paused again. "So I want to apologize to you if Gramps ever mailed any of those. They were really ugly, and it's not the way the Grange family feels about you or your lady friends."

"Your grandfather had a difficult life. I'm not sure he was ever quite right after the war, losing his leg and getting that concussion. But he must have loved you, Byron, to teach you hunting and fishing. Those are great skills to have around here," Catherine said. She didn't have to tell him that one of the letters had been sent. "Byron, dear, remember the good in your grandfather, and let time erase the harder side you saw." Catherine saw tears in his eyes and gave the young man a hug. "Thank you, Byron, for sharing this story; I know it was hard." Their eyes met. "And thank you again for bringing my dear little Quigley back."

He climbed into the truck. "Miz Catherine, it was a pleasure to finally meet you. You're a lovely lady, and Quigley is lucky to have you and your friends." He started his engine and was gone.

Catherine remained outside for a quiet moment. She thought of poor Anson Grange, dying in a drunken state, suffering with his demons until the end. What a shame. Then she thought of dear Quigley and his joyous return and the warmth of her relationships this winter. She also thought of her family, especially her daughter, Sarah, who was willing to honor her mother's independence and yet be there for her when needed. Catherine had survived the heart attack with assistance from so many people. She felt blessed.

Things settled down over the next several days. Pat and David stopped by to visit Quigley. Apart from Catherine, perhaps no one was happier to have heard of his return. As the April showers lessened, Marty and Janet began dreaming of playing more tennis outside. Both were also determined to continue working on their head and shoulder stands in yoga. Janet secretly practiced with her ukulele class for Catherine's surprise party. The whole town seemed to be gearing up for it.

One morning Janet asked Elizabeth if they should contact Jerry and Jimmy Blakey to schedule move-out day. "It is coming up fast, you know," Janet said.

Elizabeth laughed, "Are you in a hurry, Janet?"

"Well, no, not at all, really, but I thought May 1 was the arrangement."

"Well, it was, but that was before I knew you all. There really is no rigid date," Elizabeth replied. When she first got this idea, she had fears of it not working out and was afraid she might want to end it as soon as possible. She really never expected that they would enjoy themselves as much as they had. Now that the departure date loomed, Elizabeth wondered if she was ready to live alone again.

Janet said, "When the warm weather comes, I'm sure Marty will be ready to go back to her house on the bay." Actually, Janet and Marty had been talking about living together in the summer at Marty's place and giving Janet's stepchildren more time alone in the family house. But nothing had yet been decided. "Catherine's talking about digging in her garden again and rearranging some of the perennials. She's put in a big order for some new heritage plants. If you haven't seen her gardens, you must go over this summer when they are in full bloom. She does a remarkable job. I heard that her grandson asked if he might live with her this summer, before he starts medical school next fall. So she'll have company."

"That's good. I know how much she loves her flowers and her grandson. I'll definitely go see her gardens this summer." Elizabeth paused. "So I guess we should all sit down together and arrange for a convenient move-out date. We don't have to pull it off in one day."

Janet thought she noted a twinge of loneliness in Elizabeth's tone.

That afternoon Marty brought the mail in and distributed it into four piles on the side table. She had received two letters. Her brother and his wife were returning to

Cape Cod near the end of May and hoped to visit Maine for Memorial Day weekend. Steve and Camilla and the boys hoped to come up too, and they would, of course, help her open up the waterfront. The second letter was a brochure for a week-long tennis clinic at the Balsams Grand Resort Hotel in Dixville Notch, New Hampshire. She thought of Janet and considered asking her to go with her for a fun week of tennis. Many years ago Marty's parents had traveled there from Vermont. Her father had been ranked in New England and almost won the Vermont men's singles championships. He started tennis lessons for Marty at an early age, and for that she had been forever grateful.

Catherine's mail pile grew. Marty counted five colorful envelopes, probably get-well wishes or early birthday cards. Janet's yoga magazine arrived. Elizabeth's stack included an official-looking envelope from a New York City law firm plus a letter from the Belfast Art Festival Association. Marty knew Elizabeth had been waiting to hear the results of the art competition that she had entered.

"Elizabeth," Marty called out, "You've got mail." She laughed. That's what her computer used to say.

"I'll be right down," Elizabeth replied. "I'm doing some spring cleaning." It was almost time to put away the woolens and pull out the lighter sweaters, though not exactly shorts season yet.

Elizabeth's heart rate raced as she slit open the letter. My gosh, she thought, it felt like opening her college-acceptance letter or getting her first high-school report card. She unfolded the notification.

Dear Elizabeth,
The Belfast Art Festival Committee has completed

an extensive and thorough review of over two hundred splendid paintings submitted for this year's art festival contest. All of the pieces exemplify the extraordinary and varied artistic talent that we have here in Maine.

Your exquisite oil painting titled The Winter House *has been awarded the Blue Ribbon in Category I and will be proudly displayed as the first-place winner during our street festival in June and in the Belfast Free Library for the summer months.*

We extend our congratulations and thank you for your submission. We hope you will be able to join our Belfast Art Festival on opening day or anytime during that weekend, June 20-23.

> *Sincerely,*
> *Stephen Rigley, Chairman*
> *Belfast Art Festival*

Marty could tell from Elizabeth's face, before she said anything, that the news was good. Elizabeth grinned from ear to ear, like the pearly-white toothpaste ads. "A blue ribbon," she whispered. "I can't believe it."

"I can," Marty said frankly. "You have talent, and now the secret is out."

"Oh, my gosh! It really is what I have always wanted to do. There just didn't seem to be the time for me," Elizabeth confessed. She'd had a good life with Cliff and her four children, and she never really dwelled on it being a sacrifice. "I guess most women just do what they have to do," Elizabeth said. But now she was beginning to understand that there was a bigger world out there for her to explore. And if it had to be done on her own, Elizabeth had begun to think she could do that too.

Janet walked in from the kitchen, having overheard her friends' conversation. There weren't many secrets left in this house.

"Congratulations, Bags," Janet joked. She sort of liked the more informal name for Elizabeth.

"You're funny, Janet," Elizabeth said. "I am not exactly sure I am ready to reclaim that name for the outside world. However, if you think it suits me, you can use it here in our Winter House."

"Thank you, I'll be discreet," Janet said, "with our now renowned artist-in-residence." She and Elizabeth laughed.

Marty passed Janet the brochure for the Balsams tennis week. "Take a look at this," Marty said. "It might be a great adventure, and you could use some more work on your backhand." Marty demonstrated a steady backhand stroke.

"Very funny, Marty, you know I'm improving and may just beat you soon," Janet quipped. Having a little friendly competition in her life was refreshing.

That night at supper while planning their final week, they talked about the past five months. Everyone but Marty implied that the experience had been much better than they could have imagined. Marty just said it outright. It was hard for them to believe that last November the Winter House was just an idea.

"I guess we'd better tell Alice to change back to our old mailing addresses. You know she will insist that we all fill out the correct forms," Janet said. Everyone in the town loved Alice, the postmistress, though she was a stickler for protocol.

"I can call Jerry and Jimmy and see what their schedules look like. I think I heard at the library that they have jobs with All Seasons Farm, but I don't know if that work has begun yet," Catherine said.

"Great, I guess we all agree that anytime in the first week of May will be fine," Elizabeth said.

"When we know the move-out day, I'll call Billy Gray and order up those ten pounds of lobster that I won for the door prize back at the Christmas Fair," Catherine said. "I'm sure he has his traps in by now."

"I almost forgot about those lobsters," Janet said.

"That's a great idea. It will be our Last Supper," Elizabeth joked.

"I don't think they had lobster," Janet retorted. They laughed.

Marty, Elizabeth, and Janet planned their strategy for keeping Catherine in the dark about the surprise birthday party. "Say, Catherine, I know you said you don't want to do anything special for your birthday, but how about we all go out for dinner in Blue Hill on Friday night to celebrate Elizabeth's good news about winning the Belfast blue ribbon?" Marty said. "And maybe we could have a little cake, give you a few funny cards, and sing 'Happy Birthday'. We could make it an evening of two celebrations."

"Oh, I think that would be very nice," Catherine replied. "Sarah has planned a small family affair to celebrate my eightieth on Saturday. I think that will be enough fuss for me."

The next day Elizabeth's cell phone rang. She dug for it out of her purse. Maybe it would be Frank or Michael or Libby. Nell almost never called. It actually didn't ring too often, though she carried it in her purse for emergencies.

She noticed it was a local number, but there was no name indicated on her cell phone screen.

"Hello, Elizabeth?" the male voice asked. She responded. "This is Bob Chester."

"Oh, hi Bob, how are you?" Elizabeth asked.

"I'm just fine but a better question is 'how are you?' I mean, I received a list of the award winners yesterday from the Belfast Art Festival Committee. I was a judge last year, and they send notification of the award winners to past judges. Congratulations. I had a feeling they'd like your painting."

"Well, I couldn't have done it without your encouragement, Bob," she said. He really had been a great help. She might never have taken up oil painting if he hadn't challenged her comfort level.

"You were my star pupil this semester," Bob said. "I do hope you'll sign up for my seascape class this August. We have lots of fun, visiting beautiful but lesser-known scenic areas up and down the coastline. Have you ever tried to capture breaking waves on canvas?" he asked.

"Well, no, not really. Once I tried to paint a bucolic scene on Lake Champlain, but that was with watercolors," Elizabeth said. For an instant she wondered if Bob was interested only in her artistic talents.

"We use all different media — even pastels work." There was a pregnant pause. "Well, I hope you'll think about the class. I'd love to have you join us."

"I'll think about it. I'm not exactly sure what I am up to this summer," Elizabeth replied.

"Well, again, congratulations. Maybe I'll see you at the Belfast festival in June."

Elizabeth ended the conversation. "That would be

great, and thanks for calling." She hung up slowly, thinking about his offer.

Around five o'clock on Friday, April 27, the four women prepared to celebrate Elizabeth's honor. At least that's what Catherine thought. Marty, Janet, and Elizabeth knew better. Marty had told Catherine they had reservations at the Arborvine restaurant in Blue Hill. The prices were steep for Catherine's pocketbook, but she did enjoy the atmosphere and top-notch food.

"Are we all ready?" Elizabeth asked. She had just called Sarah to tell her they were on their way and would be there in about five minutes.

"Let me just feed Quigley," Catherine said, as he waited by his bowl. He didn't like being left alone, but certainly he wanted to be fed before they left. To fatten him up, Catherine had been supplementing his diet with chicken. Other than preferring to be with Catherine all the time now and being a little slimmer, Quigley seemed no worse for wear from his solitary escapade.

Janet had hidden her ukulele in the trunk and would pull it out as soon as they arrived at the community center. At some point Catherine would catch on. She would see all the cars when Elizabeth turned off the main road.

"What does it feel like to be on the verge of becoming an octogenarian?" Marty asked Catherine, as they left the driveway.

"I just feel I'm mighty lucky and hope I can appreciate every new day that I have," Catherine answered.

The conversations in the car had distracted Catherine for a while, but she wondered about Elizabeth's right turn onto Harbor Lane. At first she thought Elizabeth might be picking something up at the market, but when they passed by the store, she grew suspicious. As they rounded the corner, she saw cars parked everywhere and a crowd gathered on the steps of the center. A big "Happy 80th Birthday, Catherine!" sign hung over the door. Emma and Ella were in front, jumping up and down. When Elizabeth stopped the car, the little girls ran over and yelled in the window, "Surprise, surprise, Nanny!" Sarah and her husband walked over and opened the car door. Catherine had been surprised. There was no doubt about it. The Winter House women had pulled off a good one, and Sarah had played her part well too. Catherine could not believe the number of townsfolk there.

As she walked up the steps into the community center, everyone cheered and followed her inside. Small white and red lights hung all around the old gymnasium, giving it a very festive feeling. The Star of Bethlehem over the stage had been replaced by an enormous bunch of colorful balloons filled with helium. In the kitchen Catherine recognized the Happy Helpers, hustling around the stoves and setting up the food tables. More chairs were added as the crowd grew. Each table had a floral arrangement of red and white carnations on red-and-white check tablecloths, making the room resemble a Fourth of July celebration.

"You really fooled me," Catherine said to Sarah, who was pleased with the turnout. Her mother was truly loved in the Brooks Harbor community, and the successful recovery from her heart attack, as well as the happy ending to Quigley's adventure, drew people out to celebrate with her. One by one, folks came over to wish her the best.

Catherine knew most of them by name. Many she had

taught or tutored. Even after retiring, she had remained active in community projects and served on town committees and local boards.

Harold, Catherine's son from Portland, arrived a little late and went straight up to greet his mother. "Sorry I'm late, Mom," he said. "Happy Birthday!"

"Oh, Harold, it is great to see you. I guess you were in on this too. I bet Will and Justin knew about it when I saw them in New York," said Catherine.

"Mom, they've been planning it for months," Harold replied. "Guess they fooled you."

Pat Sullivan rang a bell, calling the crowd to order. Reverend Perry said the grace before the meal. When everyone sat down, high-school students served the specially prepared lasagna, green salad, and homemade bread. Almost every one of these students knew Catherine from their elementary after-school reading program.

Catherine sat with her family, while Marty, Elizabeth, and Janet sat together and remembered the Christmas party, when they were new housemates. In some ways it seemed like just the other day; in other ways the winter had been a time of growth for each of them and as a group.

For entertainment Lotti Lynstrom directed the ukulele band to play in honor of Catherine. Five women and two men strummed a few familiar tunes and ended with a difficult piece, "Jailer Man." Janet struggled with the rhythm and abandoned the words halfway through, knowing she needed more practice.

Ronnie Anderson and his mother, Valerie, gave a beautiful performance of Bach's Flute and Cello Duet in D minor. As the sound filled the large room, the audience was quiet. Just twelve years old, Ronnie captivated the townspeople. After their performance he and his mother brought Catherine a small gift.

Sue, the librarian, asked Catherine to come to the podium. Harold assisted his mother up a few stairs that had no railing. Then Sue invited any children in the audience who had ever been in Ms. Catherine's after-school reading group to come up. Though a few of the kids seemed shy, others rushed up the stairs to stand beside Catherine.

The librarian turned to Catherine and spoke: "The children of the library reading room want to thank you and have made you a big birthday card." Sue sent a few of the older boys behind the stage curtain. They returned with a three-foot-by-four-foot card. On the front, a big red "80" stood out, with a small drawing of a cake holding close to eighty candles. When Catherine opened the card, with the help of the children, she saw many signatures, stick figures, smiley faces, squiggles, and small handprints, covering both pages.

"Oh, thank you so much," Catherine said. As they left the stage, almost every child wanted a hug, and Catherine graciously doled them out. Emma and Ella stood by proudly. Not every child was lucky enough to have a great-grandmother this great.

Finally, Pat Sullivan came on stage. She and Catherine embraced.

"Catherine, your friends of Brooks Harbor want to give you a special gift. We all know how much you love to travel, and you have been talking about taking a cruise down the Danube River someday. We think it's time for that dream to come true." Catherine looked shocked. "We have collected enough money to send you and a companion on a Viking River Cruise down the Danube for a week this summer. "

Catherine was speechless. True, it had been her dream, and she had enjoyed several trips out of Maine after her husband's death, but she never thought she could afford the flight to Europe and the boat trip. Her hands were over her mouth. As Harold put his arm around his mother, Sarah joined him on stage. When Catherine regained her composure, she held the microphone and spoke from her heart.

"I cannot thank you all enough. I am lucky to have lived in Brooks Harbor all my life, and I do believe it is without a doubt the greatest place in the universe to live. Oh, you all know we have our problems — just a few." Some folks in the audience chuckled. She continued, "But we have something special. We have community, and we look after each other. I need to thank you for all your get-well cards, and, by the way, my heart is doing fine, so my doctor tells me. I also want to thank you for helping to search for Quigley. That little rascal finally showed up, but not until he caused me some heartache." She laughed. Then she looked at Pat. "I especially want to thank you all for your generous contributions to help me live my dream to see the Danube. I'll send postcards." Everyone laughed. "And I especially want to thank Marty Austin, Janet Gott, and Elizabeth Sloan for giving me one of the best winters I have had in Brooks Harbor for many years." Catherine put both hands over her heart.

With that, the Happy Helpers rolled a gigantic, four-tiered chocolate cake into the center of the room, and Valerie started everyone off on a rousing rendition of "Happy Birthday" as the cake was cut. With plenty to go around, some folks returned for seconds.

The cleanup happened quickly, with many helping hands. "Well, that was some party," Catherine said to no one in particular as the last few folks went home. Jimmy and Jerry, who helped put away the tables and chairs, said they could come over on Tuesday after work and help move the women back to their homes. The boys figured it wouldn't take too long, and it was still light until about seven-thirty. Billy Gray took the order for lobsters for Monday night. He said he'd try to bring four two-pounders and promised they would be fresh out of the ocean. Billy also promised to go over to Dendall Hollow, Catherine's house, and turn on the water. He had drained the pipes for the winter.

Harold told his mother he would be staying at Sarah's house for the night and understood the family would get together there for a family birthday dinner. Catherine thought that would be just fine but admitted she wanted to spend most of these last few days with her friends at the Winter House. Her children seemed to understand.

Saturday morning Janet and Marty competed as a doubles team in an indoor tennis tournament in Ellsworth. To their complete surprise, they managed to reach the finals after winning a very close semifinal match that went to three sets, finishing with a tiebreaker. Neither Marty nor Janet had much energy remaining for the finals, and though both made a noble effort, they had little chance against a pair of forty-year-olds. They graciously accepted a case of tennis balls for the runner-up prize. Just before the pair left the facility, one of the winners spoke with them: "Thanks so much for playing. I just want to say I hope I'm still playing tennis in thirty years. You both are great role models," the young woman said. That made Marty and Janet beam as they walked toward the car.

Elizabeth had decided to complete her springcleaning

by getting rid of most of her city wardrobe — clothes and shoes that she would never use again. Oh, she would keep a few black outfits to visit New York and Rome, but her lifestyle was changing, and her wardrobe needed to as well. In one box she placed all but two pairs of spiked heels. She wasn't even sure that women in Maine owned any of these toe-killer torture chambers. She would give them to the Tree of Life thrift shop, and they could throw them away if the shoes just gathered dust on the shelves. Maybe some young girls would like them. At any rate, she was done with uncomfortable shoes. As for her mink stole, which she had inherited from her mother-in-law, it would most likely only take up room in her crowded closet. Her mind flashed back to the last time she had worn it. She and Cliff had attended the inauguration ball for the mayor of New York some fifteen years ago, and she recalled lots of the women there wearing fur pieces of some kind or other. That night Cliff was so handsome in his tuxedo. But that was then, and this is now, she thought. I will move on. It occurred to her that maybe her sister would like the mink for cool evenings in Florida. Elizabeth laughed at that suggestion, or maybe she should just list it on eBay.

In her bedroom Catherine opened the cards she had received. The variety was amazing. Some pet lovers gave cards of congratulations for Quigley's return. The get-well cards called for her to bounce back quickly. Many made wisecracks about hospital stays and the skimpy patients' gowns. The birthday cards ranged from sweet to sassy, some portraying the active, white-haired granny skateboarding or taking implausibly flexible yoga positions, while others pointed out that "age is all in your mind." Many jokes jabbed at memory — or lack of it — and aging. One frank card read,

"Old age is not for sissies." Catherine was thankful that at eighty, she still remembered people's names and her schedule for the day. Her mother had begun to get confused in her mid-seventies and was dead by seventy-nine. She had now made it beyond that milestone, and she had a feeling that Dr. Gold had given her a few more years.

On Sunday the Winter House women chose to attend a local church service together. Though Catherine attended fairly routinely, the four hadn't gone together since Christmas Eve. Back then they were acquaintances; now they were friends. The church wasn't even half full, a post-Easter-Sunday phenomenon. Reverend Perry acknowledged Catherine's speedy recovery as well as Quigley's safe return. He also mentioned the passing of Anson Grange, who had been a member of the church in his youth. Catherine could not miss the irony that they had been mentioned together in almost the same breath.

Reverend Perry said, "For today's reading I have chosen a passage from the New Testament: 1 John 4-7,12. 'Friends, let us love one another, for love comes from God. Everyone who loves, has been born of God, and knows God. Whoever does not love, does not know God, for God is Love…. if we love one another, God is in us, and his love is perfected in us.'" He shuffled his pages. "And now a teaching of the Buddha from 'Give Up Anger,' reprinted in *God Makes the Rivers to Flow*. Buddha said, 'Conquer anger through gentleness, unkindness through kindness, greed through generosity, and falsehood by truth…. Use your body for doing good, not for harm. Train it to follow the dharma. Use your tongue for doing good, not for harm. Train it to speak kindly. Use your mind for doing good, not for harm. Train your mind in love. The wise are disciplined in body, speech, and mind.' "

Marty thought to herself: my sentiments exactly. At some point she rebelled against the organized church. Though she tried not to judge, it seemed to her that many so-called Christians these days were spreading hatred and interpreting the Bible in their own narrow framework. Marty wondered if Jesus would have approved of them using his name. Jesus preached loving your enemies, not defying them or threatening them with hell. At the gathering after the service, Marty thanked Rev. Perry for his sermon on forgiveness and love. Janet seconded Marty's appreciation, saying she particularly liked the message from the Buddha.

Later, after a lunch of vegetarian chili and a brief rest, the four decided to take a walk along the beach. The low tide provided safe walking space as long as they avoided the slippery seaweed and the muddy sections. Because the timing was right, Marty offered to pick mussels and prepare them in a spicy linguini dish for supper. "Sounds good to me," Janet said.

As the women walked along the Reach coastline, the sun reflected brightly off the water, throwing little diamonds into their eyes. Catherine noticed that the glare didn't bother her as much, but she did wear sunglasses. Exploring the rocky crevasses, Quigley found and munched on old, dried crab legs left by the seagulls. Janet spotted a seal raising its head out of the water as a pair of loons floated by. Soon the loons would leave their winter quarters by the sea and return inland to their summer lakes. Catherine also noticed the birch leaves, which were now the size of mouse ears; her Uncle Cyrus had claimed that indicated fiddleheads were ready to harvest.

It was a perfect Maine spring day with a blue sky full of small cumulus clouds, a gentle sea breeze, and fresh, clear air. It wouldn't be long before snowbirds would return from the South, summer folk would retreat to their second homes away from the crowded cities, and tourists would come to see a place they had heard about and "always wanted to visit." The year-rounders observed this cycle, this up and down of the peninsula's population that brought to Maine two distinct phases, like the tides, like breathing. The exhale: a cleansing snowy winter, a clearing time, a calming time, an inward darker time with fewer external demands on most folks, and less traffic, for sure. And the inhale: a summer bringing new fragrances and a flood of activity, sometimes more than a person could handle — the festivals, the concerts, the parades, the boat races, the barbecues, and the houseguests. Many winter activities ceased for the summer interlude, but winter would come again.

Now the four women were embarking on the summer season. Each had her own independent life. Each had begun to think about the change that was almost upon them. It was as though the Winter House had taken on a life of its own, and for that life, the future was uncharted.

That evening, after a delicious meal, they all played Bananagrams well into the night. Once again Catherine and Elizabeth, the crossword-puzzle experts, shone. They allowed Marty to use medical terms in Greek and Latin, which gave her a little help. Janet enjoyed the geometry of the word game and managed to win twice. She preferred the informality of this game, a quicker and less complex version of Scrabble.

"Well, it's been a splendid day," said Catherine, "but it is way past my bedtime." She had changed to slightly later hours since moving into the Winter House, perhaps because she had company and didn't just crawl into bed with a book. Marty offered to join her in taking Quigley out for his nighttime walk. Outside they noticed the Big Dipper, almost directly overhead, and the full moon rising to the east.

"Isn't that beautiful?" Catherine said. "A lovely night."

"Sure is," Marty replied. After a while they went back inside.

The others made their way to bed as well. It had been a great day, and tomorrow they would begin to pack up and have their last night.

As Janet soaked in her routine hot bath, she thought about the coming summer. Peter had responded to her email: "Mom, I'd love to have you come visit me in Colorado. Would you be up for some gentle hikes?" He hadn't seen her in two years and had no idea what physical shape she was in. Janet chuckled. He just might be surprised to know that his mother took yoga weekly, could do a shoulder stand for two minutes, and came in runner-up in a tennis tournament. Not bad for a seventy-five-year-old. Who knows what humans are capable of if they have the will to change? Janet thought about these changes and her personal growth during this winter. She had made three special friendships. Though she didn't know what lay around the next corner, her second husband, a gentle soul, had convinced her to have faith in herself, her fellow human beings, and God. Janet, who continued to work on her own definition of God, liked what Reverend Perry had read: "God is Love."

As Catherine reached to turn out the light, Quigley jumped up on her bed, circled around twice, and flopped down next to her. This warm connection between man and beast — she wasn't a man and Quigley wasn't a beast — was still very special. How lucky Catherine felt to have him near again.

When Marty checked her email, as she usually did just before bed, she found a message from her brother, Tom. It seemed that Camilla, Tom's daughter-in-law, had found a lump in her breast, and her local doctor thought it was suspicious. She had an appointment with a cancer specialist at Brigham and Women's Hospital the next week. Tom and his wife were flying back from Tucson early to help their son with the little boys, Harrison and Connor. Her brother added that Camilla had not wanted to alarm Marty until they knew more. Marty decided she would drive down to Boston after she got settled back into her house, as she wanted to be there to give her family support and comfort. She knew well that cancer is a scary diagnosis for anyone, but she had seen amazing advances in treatment over the last forty years.

In the morning Marty was already downstairs with her coffee when Catherine and Quigley came into the kitchen. "You're up early," Catherine said. "How did you beat me?"

"I had a hard time sleeping last night," Marty said.

"Anxious about moving out?" Catherine asked.

"No, it's not that. I got a message from my brother that my nephew's wife, Camilla, might have breast cancer. She found a lump," Marty said.

"Oh, I'm sorry to hear that, Marty," Catherine said. "Isn't she young for breast cancer?"

"She is younger than the average age of sixty," Marty said, having checked the recent statistics online when she couldn't sleep. "Camilla's mother had breast cancer, and that increases her daughter's risk. I just hope she caught it early," Marty added, knowing that the survival rate for those with early detection by mammograms was now almost ninety per cent.

"Well, I'm sure it's going to be okay, Marty," Catherine said, trying to ease her friend's mind. "You know my friend Pat? Well, she was diagnosed with breast cancer more than fifteen years ago, had radiation and chemotherapy, and she's done just fine. You'd never know she had a problem. I remember when Dr. Horne told Pat she didn't have to come back for checkups anymore. Pat was sort of sad because she really liked her once-a-year visits with him, but she realized he had to spend his time with new patients." Catherine, too, had loved Dr. Horne, who had been so kind to her husband during his cancer treatments.

Marty understood the bond that could develop between doctor and patient. She never forgot many of her patients, even after all these years. She still received occasional notes from some. "I'm sure she'll be fine too, but it's the not-knowing that's hard," Marty added. Catherine topped off Marty's coffee and added another splash of cream. "Don't know what I'm going to do without you two as company with my morning coffee. Who's going to top off my cup?" Marty quipped.

Quigley was ready for his walk down the driveway.

"Looks like another beautiful Maine morning. Should we go get the paper?" Catherine asked.

"Sounds like a good idea." Sometimes they walked down to the mailbox with their coffee cups. Today was one of those days. They looked out at the water, shimmering with the reflection of the eastern sun. A bald eagle soared above, riding the gentle air currents.

"I'm going to miss our morning coffees too," said Catherine. In the past she usually had kept her opinions and emotions close to her chest, but in the last five months, some of her companions' openness seemed to have rubbed off.

"Oh, I'll stop by. We don't live too far from each other, really," Marty said.

"I hope you will," Catherine said, but she knew it wouldn't be the same. Catherine also knew that Quigley and Missy were going to be yearning for each other. She had noticed how they sometimes cuddled together on the couch in the afternoon. In the beginning she never would have predicted that these two animals would warm up to one another. But why not? Relationships change.

That afternoon Billy Gray dropped off four live lobsters, which were big and active, coming straight out of the chilly waters. He started to remind Elizabeth not to boil them in too much water but just to steam them. Then he recalled that Catherine, a true-blue native, was in this group of women. She had eaten lobsters all her life and knew just how to cook them — not too much water and not too long.

"Miz Catherine, I turned the water on at your house," Billy said. "Everything looked okay. The water looked just a little rusty, but it cleared pretty good. Just let it run awhile before you drink it for the first few days. Oh, and I noticed a crack in the window by the kitchen door. I can come by and fix that for you, if you'd like. I think a branch fell on it this winter."

"Thanks, Billy, that would be great. I'm sure there will be some maintenance work to do this summer," Catherine said. She wasn't sure she was ready to return to the solo responsibility of a house. Funny, that had never bothered her before. But she was still eager to dig her hands in the soil and prepare her summer gardens.

Marty and Janet drove to the Blue Hill grocery store. A week before, Marty had asked if the store manager would save some cardboard boxes for her. She had collected more stuff than she had moved in with, and a few extra boxes would be necessary. Janet took a few for herself and for Catherine. In the stationery section both Marty and Janet got the idea of finding a card for Elizabeth, who had been so gracious in opening her home to three near-strangers. Most of the cards were about someone leaving and wishing them well. However, Elizabeth wasn't leaving; they were. Janet found one that said simply, "We'll miss you," and that was the right sentiment. Another card had three stylish women on the front, the inside saying, "Thanks from the bottom of our hearts."

"These will have to do," Janet said. "I know she'll get the message."

That afternoon Elizabeth noticed snowflakes beginning to fall. "You've got to be kidding," she said out loud. She had heard on the radio that the temperature would drop, bringing a chance of snow, but after their wonderful, warm walk along the shore yesterday, it seemed unthinkable. When Marty and Janet came inside with their boxes and a few white flecks of snow on their heads and shoulders, Elizabeth laughed. "This is crazy," she said.

Catherine came into the kitchen. "Oh, we usually get a late snow," she said. "I remember my kids building a snowman on Mother's Day.

As Janet brushed off the snow, she remarked that her husband John was once outside mowing their lawn on his riding mower, and it started to snow. "It was a very funny sight," she said.

"It won't last," Marty said. "It's just a final April Fool's joke. I bet it will be all gone tomorrow for our move-out day." There was a silence.

"Anyone want to help me set the table?" Catherine asked.

"I will," said Janet. "Just let me put these few boxes upstairs."

The snow kept falling throughout the evening. As the women enjoyed their lobster dinner and conversation, Catherine told them that she had invited her daughter to go with her this summer on the Danube River excursion. "I'm just so thrilled," she said. "It's a dream come true. I have always wanted to take a trip with her, but our schedules never quite fit. Sarah's excited too. Now that she's a vice-president of the bank, she is pretty sure she can get the time off."

"That's great," said Elizabeth. She had traveled some with Nell, mostly to European art galleries. "I should plan a trip with Libby, now that her children are in college." Elizabeth knew that getting to know a daughter as a friend and travel companion was a gift to oneself.

"Have I told you that I'm planning to drive out West to see Peter this summer? I've always wanted to hike in the Rockies, and we have lots of catching up to do. I realize phone calls and even Skype are not enough," Janet said.

"I agree with that," Elizabeth said. "I've decided to go see Alcee graduate in June."

"Alcee will be happy to see you, I'm sure," Marty said. "I'll be going to Boston fairly soon to be with Camilla, Steve, and the boys. They're just like family to me and if it's cancer, they'll need extra hands." Marty changed the subject, asking Elizabeth if she planned to attend the Middlebury reunion. She suspected that Brad Thornton would like that, but she didn't say it.

"I'm considering it," Elizabeth replied.

After supper they decided to finish listening to the recording of *The Help*. Life had been somewhat busy since their road trip home from New York, and Sue, the librarian, had called to say the tape was overdue and in high demand. This was about their last chance, so with snow falling outside, it just seemed right to settle into the living room. Marty lit a fire for atmosphere and a little warmth. Janet made some decaffeinated hazelnut coffee, and each had a small serving of mint-chocolate-chip ice cream with a tiny spoonful of Cool Whip. "Why not?" Janet said. "It's a celebratory night," She lifted her coffee cup and toasted: "To us."

The other three held their cups high: "To us!" and they all laughed heartily.

Without interruption, except for a quick bathroom visit halfway through, the women listened to the end of the saga by Kathryn Stockett. The skillful author had painted a vivid portrait of southern living in the sixties, but in the end *The Help* was all about relationships, women's relationships.

As the book ended, the women heard rain on the roof. April showers would quickly wash away the last snow, and the first day of May would be lush and green.

MAY

*T*uesday brought sunshine and temperatures in the forties, with a prediction of a high of sixty-five degrees. Marty checked the weather forecast on her computer. She smiled at the old saying "If you don't like the weather in Maine, just wait a minute." Freezing one day, warm the next. It certainly wasn't boring.

Before she went downstairs, she stripped off her bed sheets to wash before leaving. Then she would just put them back on her own bed to start the new season.

That morning the women went grocery shopping together. They thought it would be fun to shop for each of their own kitchens. Elizabeth didn't really need anything, maybe some more half-and-half, but she wanted to go along for the ride. In the car Janet and Catherine encouraged each other to try more creative cooking for themselves. For each, it had been a great luxury to not have to think about dinner preparation for the past five months.

"We know you can do it," Marty said. "Maybe you two should sign up for Vincent Montaine's cooking classes this summer." Elizabeth laughed.

"I don't think so," Janet replied. "I'll probably be eating a whole lot more macaroni and cheese, or better yet, Weight Watchers Diet meals, and I may even stop at the Simmering Pot for a great bowl of soup. But don't worry about me, I'll be just fine," she added jovially. Elizabeth had loved having folks to cook for, especially such appreciative ones. Marty hadn't minded taking turns with her, and both appreciated the complete joy of avoiding the dirty dishes.

After picking out ground coffee, cream, grapefruit juice, English muffins, rye bread, milk, peanut butter, grape jelly, margarine, a dozen eggs, bacon, yogurt, and a few bananas, apples, and red grapes, Marty planned her first dinner with a small piece of Atlantic salmon, Brussels sprouts, and a sweet potato. She skipped the ice-cream aisle.

Catherine bought a can of Snow's clam chowder, a quart of skim milk, and some crackers, along with coffee and breakfast food for the next morning. Janet picked up cottage cheese, sardines, and a bag of baby spinach for dinner, along with Grape-Nuts, milk, coffee, and orange juice for the next day.

Elizabeth had never seen Janet's house or Marty's. She'd driven by Catherine's little cape many times but had never been inside it. As they stopped at each of the houses, the foursome went inside to drop off the food. It was an opportunity to picture where their housemates would be located. After living away from their homes for five months, the women felt a little different in their old spaces. Catherine had never noticed how small her kitchen was, and the living room wasn't much bigger. Nevertheless, her familiarity with each square inch was comforting.

Janet's place, up on the hill just past Catherine's, provided a view of the church steeple and the distant ocean. Marty thought she could even see Great Spruce Island, and Janet pointed out several other islands.

When they drove around to Marty's home, past the lighthouse, they watched a few lobster boats heading out for an afternoon pickup. The minute Elizabeth entered Marty's living room, she exclaimed, "Wow, Marty, this view is amazing. You have such a broad view of the water. You must just love this."

"I do. On summer days I enjoy watching all the sailboats cruise up and down the Reach," Marty said.

"No wonder you get up early; the morning sun must flood in here," Janet commented. She hadn't been here before either. She liked the feeling of the place; it was so Marty.

Jimmy and Jerry arrived a little after three. Marty, Janet, and Catherine had each packed up their boxes and suitcases and tried to organize their stuff for easy transportation. Just before the boys arrived, the three women had chosen straws to see who would depart first, second, and last. Though it was obviously a coincidence, they would be leaving in the same order as they had arrived.

The boys carried out Catherine's red recliner first, then the three plants, which, with her loving care, had all survived, and the small television that she really hadn't used much. She realized she had spent a lot more time in conversation than she had anticipated. As the boys loaded their truck with the last of Catherine's suitcases and boxes, she turned to the three women who were there to see her off.

What could she say that would capture her feelings for them? The Winter House experiment had certainly been a success, and companionship had far outweighed any small inconveniences or frustrations. In fact, as Catherine had said at her birthday party, it really had been one of her best winters in a long time. How could she put this into words? Perhaps she didn't need to. She gave a big hug to Janet, then Marty, and finally she turned to Elizabeth. "Thank you so much for having this idea of the Winter House and for including me." The two women hugged.

"It's truly been a pleasure getting to know you, Catherine," Elizabeth said. "And I know we'll be seeing each other around town. I'll be over to look at your famous gardens, and once we all figure out our summer activities, I hope we can have some lunches or dinners all together, if your busy schedule will allow." Elizabeth had learned much from Catherine, from her community involvement and her can-do spirit.

"I'd like that a lot, I really would," Catherine added. The boys had the truck running and were waiting to follow her car. "Well, I guess I'd better get a move on. Jerry and Jimmy have a few more trips to make."

"See you soon," Marty said. She wasn't about to say good-bye.

"Take good care of yourself and Quigley," Janet said. "Maybe we can walk together. I'm just up the hill." Janet had been up the hill for years, and they hadn't ever walked together. Maybe it would be different now.

Catherine turned toward Marty and promised she would sign up for a Lifeline emergency-alert button. This obviously pleased the house physician. Then, just as

Catherine opened the car door, Quigley jumped over into the passenger seat. He loved car rides. She climbed in after him, rolled down the window, and waved, driving her Buick down the long driveway, the boys following.

The three friends waved back. "She's a wonderful woman," Janet said.

"I agree with that," Elizabeth replied.

"Not sure they make them like that anymore," Marty added, and the three went back inside. Elizabeth suggested some tea while they waited for the boys to return.

To expedite her departure, Marty carefully carried the mahogany dragon lamp downstairs. She loaded it into her Subaru along with the computer, yoga mat, tennis bag, and cross-country skis, leaving the boxes, suitcases, and bookcase for Jerry and Jimmy. It amazed Marty how little paperwork she had to keep after converting to computer files. The Internet was an instant resource for medical knowledge, giving young physicians the latest research right at their fingertips. Nowadays medical textbooks were outdated even before they were printed. Marty occasionally contemplated throwing her old books away, but sentimentality prevented her from doing it.

When Jerry and Jimmy returned, ready for the second load, they passed on a message to Elizabeth: "Miz Catherine says she's sorry, but she left her winter coat hanging in the front closet and Quigley's bag of dog food in the pantry. She asked if we could take it to her on our way to Miz Austin's house."

"I'll get the coat," Marty said. "Mine may be there too." Indeed, she found not only Catherine's heavy winter coat but also her own down jacket and sturdy boots. With such warm weather no one had thought about winter clothing.

Janet offered to find the dog food and suggested that the three remaining women do what she called a "grandmother check." When she was small, her mother used the term to describe an inventory taken whenever the family departed from somewhere, like a motel or a relative's house. Janet wondered what distant relative had started the first grandmother check. So the three women roamed around the house together, checking each of the bedrooms they had occupied as well as common spaces such as the laundry room, front closet, living room, and mudroom. Janet had left a raincoat hanging on the back of the mudroom door and some ukulele music books on the living-room bookshelves. Elizabeth found Marty's half-full bottle of rum in the liquor closet. "Guess we didn't drink many Dark'N'Stormies this winter," Elizabeth quipped. "You better take this with you." Both Marty and Elizabeth realized that having two of their housemates as nondrinkers had actually helped them cut down on alcohol consumption, and that was probably a good thing.

The boys waited patiently as Marty put the coats, boots, and dog food into her car, along with Missy in her cage. At the last minute she ran back inside and dropped off the two thank-you cards in Elizabeth's bedroom. She had almost forgotten. Then she found Elizabeth and Janet outside.

"I'm not good with good-byes," Marty said to them, "and I figure we'll keep in touch regularly. Let's not wait too long to have a dinner together." She gave Elizabeth a hug. "It's been great," she said. Janet and Marty had made plans to go to tennis camp and would see each other at yoga sessions, which would continue during the summer months.

Marty climbed into her car. "I guess I'm off. See you soon," she said, putting her car into reverse. This time the boys led the way out to Virgil's Point. The longer days gave them plenty of time to complete this moving process.

Elizabeth and Janet decided to stroll down to the shore. Elizabeth loved to check in with the sea. Something about living on the coastline — the tides, their consistency and yet their daily variability — had always comforted her. At the Winter House Janet had also enjoyed the opportunity to be right next to the water, a significant change from living up on the hill. But Janet still loved the long vistas from the hilltop and was looking forward to her trip to the Rockies and their spectacular peaks.

"When will you head out West?" Elizabeth asked.

"I'm not exactly sure," Janet replied. She hadn't raised the idea to Marty yet, but was hoping to invite her along on the trip. Janet would still go with or without Marty, but it would be more enjoyable with her. They had spent quite a lot of time together this winter, sharing many activities and developing a deep respect for one another. Janet definitely felt safe with Marty. "I'm going to take the summer off from my hospice work. There are others to step in, thank goodness," Janet added.

"Thanks to your training courses," Elizabeth added. "I really admire all you've done for the community, Janet." Elizabeth had begun to think of what she could do in the town. So far, her choices since Cliff's death had been focused on stabilizing her own life. The Winter House women had all shown her the enriching value of community work.

Janet added, "My commitment to hospice was a successful survival technique for me." They walked along. Janet knew that turning one's energies outward is one way to tip the scale of self-absorption and self-pity. But her talk with Catherine had shown her that an inner journey to grapple with personal demons is equally necessary. It had taken her a very long time to disclose these demons, and she now vowed to consider addressing them with counseling and support groups. "And this winter having you all here for support and sharing has been just wonderful."

Elizabeth wasn't exactly sure what to say. Janet had certainly been quiet when she first moved in. Of course, they were almost complete strangers back then. It took an adventuresome spirit and some guts to jump into such an unusual arrangement, and maybe that was why they all mixed well, each having these traits in common. Everyone had wanted it to work out; everyone had known they could bail out if things got rough. But all those worries evaporated rather quickly as the Winter House women grew to know one another. "I'd say you have your head on pretty straight," Elizabeth said, giving Janet a little nudge.

"I'm getting there," Janet replied, with a smile. They walked a little farther. Then Janet bent over and picked up a perfectly intact sand dollar lying on the beach. She knew the legend of the sand dollar with the five angels inside and cherished its intricate beauty. Janet reached out her hand to Elizabeth. "Please accept this gift of gratitude for giving us all a wonderful winter home."

Elizabeth accepted the sand dollar, smiled, and said, "Thank you."

On the way back to the house, they spotted Jerry and Jimmy coming up the driveway for their final load. Janet felt bad that she hadn't brought anything downstairs. She would pay them well.

"Would you boys care for a soda?" Elizabeth asked.

"That would be great, Miz Sloan," Jerry said, and Jimmy nodded. Both remembered the extra-heavy suitcase and rocking chair that they had dragged upstairs and figured a little hydration first would be a good idea.

"How's work going at All Seasons Farm?" Elizabeth asked. She was glad to know they had employment for the summer.

"It's starting good," Jerry replied.

"We have to get up mighty early, though," Jimmy added.

"I look forward to eating some of those fresh vegetables you'll be planting," Elizabeth said.

"Me too," Janet added. "Well, guess we better finish this moving job." She was getting anxious to complete the task. It was a hard day.

The boys made several trips up and down the stairs. Janet carefully carried her ukulele and guitar downstairs. When Jerry commented on the handsome guitar, Janet asked him if he played.

"No, but I always wanted to try it," he said.

Janet didn't think she would be playing the guitar anymore, finding the ukulele so much easier and more portable. "Jerry, I would love to give this to you, if you think you'd like to play it." The young man was surprised and unsure whether it would be appropriate to accept such an offer. "Really, I insist. It's just going to sit in my closet at home."

Jerry would have loved to offer to move her for free in exchange for the guitar, but he needed the money. He just stood there, not knowing what to say.

"Here, take it, and if you find you're not using it, you can give it back." She handed it to Jerry, who thanked her and placed it carefully in the front seat of the truck.

"I guess we're about ready, then," Jerry said. Jimmy

was sitting in the passenger seat, listening to the radio.

"I'll be right with you," Janet said. She walked over to Elizabeth, who was standing by the porch. "You take care now, Elizabeth. It's been a pleasure, and have a great time in Italy. Please give Alcee my best. Who knows maybe sometime I'll get to Rome too." Janet laughed, and Elizabeth extended her arms for a hug.

"You take care too, Janet. The pleasure's been all mine," Elizabeth said, giving an extra-tight squeeze.

Elizabeth watched the old truck and Corolla drive away. Janet gave a final beep-beep on her horn, and away they went. Slowly Elizabeth climbed the stairs to the porch. She faced the water. The sun peeked out from below a layer of clouds. It was going to be a beautiful sunset. She inhaled deeply, breathing the fresh sea air — a spring fragrance that settled her soul. A lone seagull cried in the distance. Inside, the house was still.

Epilogue

CATHERINE

That summer Catherine dug into her perennial gardens, making them more beautiful than ever before. She learned to take catnaps in the afternoon while her grandson Justin was out lobstering with Billy Gray or visiting his new girlfriend, who worked at the Brooks Harbor Yacht Club. Justin's parents planned to visit for a week to get away from the heat of New Jersey, and on the July Fourth weekend she would attend the parade in town and go to the annual Historical Society barbecue. Her son Harold and his family always came up from Portland for the Fourth. That's when the summer activities picked up.

In August Catherine and Sarah would leave for an eight-day Danube River trip. She was thrilled to be going with her daughter to experience this European cruise. The tickets had arrived. She read the detailed itinerary and realized she had better walk more with Quigley to get herself in shape for the extensive sightseeing. They would fly to Budapest, explore the capital, and then board the small cruise ship and go on to Vienna. Catherine looked forward to viewing the Austrian countryside as the boat sailed on the Danube. Their cruise would end in Nuremburg, Germany. In her high-school classes Catherine had taught students about the famous Nuremburg Trials. After talking with Sue, the librarian, she signed out William F. Buckley's historical novel *Nuremberg: The Reckoning*. Catherine was halfway through it.

Dr. Gold, her cardiologist, cleared her for travel and encouraged her to continue her exercise program. He was pleased that she had lost five pounds. "Now, Catherine," he said, "Have a great time, but don't eat too much wiener schnitzel."

MARTY AND JANET

Marty spent a few days at her home and then drove to Boston to be with Camilla, Steve, and the boys. Tom and Susan arrived a day or so later, just before the biopsy. They all spent a lot of time on the Internet, researching the latest treatments. Marty knew that breast-cancer surgery had changed significantly since she began her practice, and the disfiguring radical mastectomy was now rarely used. Before she returned to Maine, she felt comfortable with the oncology team's treatment plan. Marty had a good feeling about Camilla's outcome.

Janet spent the first week of May going through her garage and attic. Both areas had been neglected since John's death. In the garage he had collected all sorts of fishing gear and ropes. No less than three broken-down snowblowers sat in a corner. In the attic old boxes of John's files and religion books gathered dust. She hadn't had the strength to throw them away. She still had some of her nursing books from the fifties. It was ridiculous. One box of mementos had become a nest for the mice that enjoyed free range of the attic over the winter. Janet felt ready for a new beginning. Perhaps she would investigate a medical mission trip to Nicaragua in the fall.

As Marty drove into Brooks Harbor on her return from Boston, she stopped to see Janet to discuss the plans for the Balsams tennis clinic in August. The two had been in frequent contact since they had left the Winter House, and Marty had decided to accept Janet's invitation to drive out West in June to visit Peter. Both were thrilled to be taking another road trip. The experience of spending five months under the same roof had been too positive for them to live in separate houses again. So, after they returned from Colorado, Janet and Marty planned to spend the summer together in Marty's house on Virgil's Point, leaving Janet's house atop Dendall Hill to the stepchildren, who would then feel free to use the Brooks Harbor vacation spot more often and invite their own friends for summer visits. Marty and Janet figured it was a win/win arrangement.

ELIZABETH

In May Eve came to Maine for a sisters' weekend. She and Elizabeth talked for hours and reconnected, as Elizabeth explained all the reasons why Brooks Harbor was the best place now for Eve's "little sister." Each agreed it was a shame that distance often impeded adult-sibling relationships.

Elizabeth's June calendar was filling up. She had decided to attend the Middlebury reunion after all and had informed the director of alumni relations that she would be happy to accept their recognition for her and Cliff's outstanding alumni support. Not only had Sandy, her sophomore roommate, called to encourage Elizabeth to go, but Brad Thornton had also called to inquire about her plans for their fiftieth class reunion.

Right after the reunion, she would fly to Italy to see Alcee graduate. Then she, Nell, and Alcee would spend a week vacationing at Monterosso al Mare, a favorite getaway spot of Nell's. Immediately after that, Elizabeth would return to Maine in time for the Belfast Art Festival at the end of June. Then Michael and Mason wanted to visit for two weeks in July, enjoying a few concerts at Kneisel Hall. Elizabeth recalled that she would need to look out for Alden and attend his student cello performances near the end of July. And during the first two weeks of August, she would participate in Bob Chester's seascape class, as she seriously wanted to keep up her painting skills. Finally, Libby and her family would come to enjoy late August at Spruce Point. Summer would be busy.

Elizabeth found herself truly missing having a dog around the house, especially one like Quigley. Although she stopped in at the Ark Animal Shelter once, just to see if any dogs won her heart, she decided that it would be risky to make such a commitment in the summer and that she should wait until fall.

One evening, after her sister left, Elizabeth sat alone on the porch. Her summer activities were going to center around her family and herself. She now knew there had to be more to carry her through the entire year. Having watched Catherine, Marty, and Janet joyfully and selfless-ly volunteer in this community, Elizabeth again contem-plated what she might do to give back to the place she now called home.

Dr. Joan MacCracken, a retired pediatrician who specialized in pediatric endocrinology, practiced in Bangor, Maine for twenty-three years. Since childhood, she has enjoyed telling and writing stories. Her first book, *The Sun, the Rain and the Insulin: Growing Up with Diabetes*, published in 1996, described a special family camp, Camp Kee-to-Kin, which operated for thirteen years. In 2005 she adapted a Nicaraguan folktale, creating the book *Trisba and Sula*, which was awarded Best Bilingual Children's Book of 2006 by *Skipping Stones* magazine. MacCracken also edited and published *Cracked Marbles*, a collection of Maine stories by the late Dr. Tom Palmer of Bangor. For the past six years she has continued her passion for writing by producing her small town's quarterly newspaper, *The Brooksville Breeze*.

Her community involvement with the At Home Downeast project stimulated her to think about the folks who prefer to remain in their homes, "aging in place." She has two children and three grandchildren, and, along with her husband and their dog, lives on the Maine coast.